HIKING THE NORTH CASCADES

FRED T. DARVILL, JR.

SIERRA CLUB BOOKS/SAN FRANCISCO

Library of Congress Cataloging in Publication Data

Darvill, Fred T., 1927–
    Hiking the North Cascades.

    Bibliography: p. 360
    Includes index.
    1. Hiking—Cascade Range—Guide-books. 2. Hiking—Washington (State)—Guide-books. 3. Cascade Range—Description and travel—Guide-books. I. Title.
GV199.42.C37D37   917.97'5   81-14451
ISBN 0-87156-297-9   AACR2

Illustrations by Marjorie Domenowske
Book design by Nancy Warner
Printed in the United States of America
10 9 8 7 6 5 4 3 2 1

This book is dedicated to those mountain-lovers and conservationists whose dreams of preserving the splendor of the North Cascades, and unceasing efforts toward that end, resulted in the establishment of the North Cascades National Park, the Ross Lake and Lake Chelan National Recreation Areas, and the Glacier Peak, Pasayten, and Alpine Lakes Wilderness Areas. Generations to come will be grateful for their foresight, wisdom, involvement, and concern.

This book is also dedicated to the many people, living and dead, who have walked the footpaths of the North Cascades with me over the past 25 years. All are fondly remembered, most particularly Lois Brooks Webster, a lady of quality, whose influence on my life did not terminate at the time of her death in 1969.

TABLE OF CONTENTS

ACKNOWLEDGMENTS

The author is indebted to the following people and organizations for providing data, photographs, and expertise. Drafts of each section of this book were reviewed by authorities in that field. Most suggestions were incorporated into the publication; the author takes responsibility for the final product.

Organizations: Bellingham Historical Museum; North Cascades National Park; Mt. Baker–Snoqualmie National Forest; Wenatchee National Forest; Okanogan National Forest.

Individuals: History: Dr. A.D. Martinson (Pacific Lutheran University, Tacoma, WA); Fred Beckey; Eunice Waterbury Darvill; Glee Davis; Dolly Connally.

Natural History: Dr. James Monroe (Skagit Valley College, Mt. Vernon, WA); Terry Wahl (on birds); Dr. Arthur Kruckeberg (University of Washington, Seattle); Dr. R.S. Babcock (Western Washington University, Bellingham, WA, on geology); Victoria Stevens (on mountain goats).

Dr. Winston Jones (on whitewater boating); J.W. Miller (on the "greening" of Cascade Pass); Byron Fish, Ray Kresek and Simeon Beeson (on lookouts).

Ginny Darvill, my wife, for encouragement, support, editorial assistance, companionship on trails, and most of all for her willingness to accept the loss of consortium during the many months that this book was in preparation.

PREFACE

Many northwesterners feel a deep personal involvement with the Cascade Mountains, born of wet boots squishing in soggy forest duff, of lenticular cloud caps streaming from icy summit domes, of the solipsist experience of warming themselves over the first tiny rockbound campfire ever lighted in a hidden hanging valley, of acceptance into a magical plant and animal environment. Dawn in a high Cascade pass is as dreamlike as waking up on a Nepalese col, face to face with the great peaks of the Himalayas. People have spent lifetimes exploring the Cascades, worlds within worlds, and yet there are still areas that have never known a bootprint or a backpacker's high mountain tent, lonely vantage points from which to grasp the powerful statement of the mountains.

The author began his love affair with the North Cascades in 1957 when he spent the Labor Day holiday in the Mazama Park area and first visited the Park Butte Lookout. During those three days, he contracted a virulent case of "mountain fever." There is no known cure, but the condition may be controlled with frequent visits to the high country.

Eleven years later, in the White House, he witnessed the signing of the bill creating the North Cascades National Park complex.

The author believes in the continuing need to protect the North Cascades while developing their recreational potential. He is pleased to share his knowledge and enjoyment of Washington's wilderness alps.

Glacier Peak and Image Lake

PART ONE

ABOUT THE
NORTH CASCADES

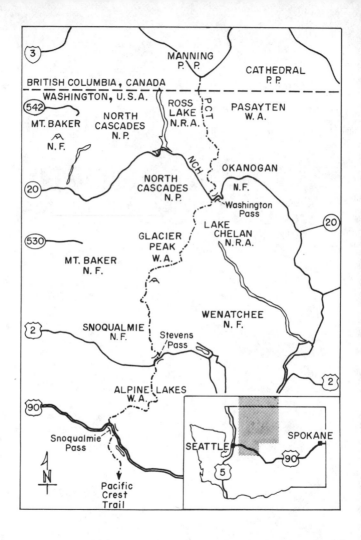

1

GENERAL
INFORMATION

The North Cascades, often called the Wilderness Alps, separate the wet northwestern and the arid northeastern sections of the State of Washington. Their northern and southern boundaries are ill-defined; for the purposes of this book, they will extend from Stevens Pass (U.S. 2) north to British Columbia HW #3. The range is accessible from Seattle on the south to Vancouver, B.C. on the north, a distance of perhaps 120 miles as the crow flies.

Closely resembling the Swiss Alps, they are a wilderness range of extraordinary beauty. The marked differences in precipitation and altitude have created a wide variation in terrain within the range. Specialized animal and plant communities are found in each of the many life zones. The range offers splendor and solitude for the stroller, backpacker, and climber. The naturalist has excellent opportunities to observe wildlife. The equestrian, cross-country skier, snowshoer, fisherman, photographer, and boater will find challenges and delight in the hills and valleys of Washington's sierra.

Here is a summary of terms applied to federal lands that are dedicated to recreational use:

National Parks are spacious land and water areas of nationwide interest established as inviolable sanctuaries for the preservation of scenery, wildlife, and wilderness in its natural condition.

National Forests are federally owned forest lands administered by the U.S. Forest Service under the "Multiple Use" policy. Multiple use theoretically means the balancing of resource extraction (logging, mining, grazing), watershed protection, conservation of wildlife, and recreation.

A Wilderness Area, generally under federal ownership, is a tract of land which, by act of Congress, is to be indefinitely preserved in its wild state. Minor modifications of the environment (such as trails) are generally acceptable. Roads and entry by mechanized equipment are excluded. All commercial development is banned, as is resource extraction. Mining on patented claims can not be prevented, but it is regulated by the government. Prospecting for minerals may continue until 1983 under present law. Hunting, fishing and other recreational uses are allowed.

The National Recreation Area might be best described as a cross between a National Park and National Forest. Resource extraction is usually prohibited. Hunting is permitted. More intensive recreational development, even if it substantially alters the natural scenery, is also allowed. Briefly, they are playgrounds of national significance.

In the North Cascades National Park, nothing is to be defaced or changed. Wildlife may not be disturbed; flowers may not be picked; rocks may not be removed. Mechanical equipment on trails is prohibited. Dogs and other pets are allowed only in areas accessible by road, and even there they must be continuously confined on a leash. Hunting is prohibited, but fishing is allowed.

Hunting is allowed elsewhere in the North Cascades, subject to the laws of the State of Washington. Certain animals, such as marmots and pikas, are protected throughout the year.

In the National Recreation Areas, dogs (and other pets) are allowed on the trails if leashed and under control at all times. In other areas covered in this book, pets may accompany their owners, subject only to outdoor courtesy.

Within reasonable limits, specimen collecting is permitted outside of the National Park, but it should be recalled that a picked wildflower does not reproduce, and that a removed rock will not be seen by subsequent visitors. The accumulation of thoughtless acts can cause substantial destruction in areas of fragile beauty.

There are innumerable campgrounds in the North Cascades. Camping areas available to backpackers vary from the designated campsites within the North Cascades National Park complex to the "camp wherever you like when you are ready" policy within the National Forests.

The National Park Service requires permits for overnight camping anywhere within the Park and the National Recreation Areas. Permits are required for overnight camping in the Pasayten and Glacier Peak Wilderness Areas. Permits are not required elsewhere in the North Cascades. Information about campgrounds can be obtained from the land management agencies in the North Cascades, listed under Resources at the end of this book.

WEATHER AND SAFETY

The North Cascades are some of the most elegant and splendid mountains on the face of the earth, when they can be seen. Mountain aficionados who know the weather patterns here say, "If you can't see the mountains, it's raining; if you can see the mountains, take photographs of them immediately since it's going to rain very soon."

In an average year, the range is reasonably cloud-free one day out of every six.

Weather patterns are quite different east and west of the Cascade crest. Many days when storm clouds hug the peaks on the west, eastern weather is overcast but rain-free. Occasionally there is a dramatic difference, with bright warm sunshine on the east and a wall of wet rain clouds meeting the traveler at the mountain passes. The difference is due to the prevailing storm winds which sweep in from the southwest off the Pacific Ocean. As the clouds are pushed up over the peaks, they cool and release their moisture. Most of the moisture is lost before the crest is reached; less is therefore available for the land beyond the crest.

Mt. Baker receives an average annual snowfall of 516 inches and a yearly precipitation of about 110 inches; Diablo Dam, near the Cascade crest, receives about 72 inches of precipitation. Stehekin, in the Eastern foothills, has an annual snowfall of 109 inches and annual precipitation of about 34 inches.

The west side lowlands have a six-month rainy season stretching from roughly November 1 to April 30; in the high country, this is the snow season. May and June are spring months; July and August summer; September and October fall.

West of the crest, the best weather, year in and year out, is during the last two weeks of July. June is often wetter than May. Intermittent storms increase in frequency after Labor Day. The height of the alpine flower bloom is August 1st; the peak of the fall color is October 1st. Snow begins again about October 1st. Snow closes the high country about November 1st, although this can vary from October 15th to November

15th. Snow can occur any day in the year above 5,000'. The hills are usually skiable by Thanksgiving; deep snow persists well into June. The average high trail is 90% snow-free in a normal year by July 15th and 100% snow-free by September 1st.

In the eastern foothills, winter is generally cold, with the first snow falling about December 1st and melting off sometime in March. Spring comes relatively early; daytime temperatures are pleasant by late April or early May. Summer weather there can be oppressively hot, with temperatures in the high 90's relatively common in late July and early August. September is the most delightful month, since daytime temperatures are pleasant, and all trails are snow-free. Autumn color adds zest to wilderness walking. There are fewer people on the trails, and there is less competition for popular campsites after Labor Day. October is comfortable in the valleys, but cold at higher elevations.

The hills east of the crest are generally snow-free in late June. Afternoon thunderstorms are not uncommon in midsummer. The first indication of bad weather in the North Cascades is often the development of a wind from out of the southwest. Storms may continue for several days, even in July and August.

A cloud cap may form over the summits of Mt. Baker and Glacier Peak, and less frequently over other summits. This lenticular-shaped, persistent cloud, which is not blown away by the wind, is often advance warning of deteriorating weather. Air is cooled as it is forced up and over the cold summit of the mountain by a prevailing, southwest wind. The water in the air changes from invisible vapor to visible cloud. When the air descends on the other side of the peak, warming occurs and the cloud disappears. Accordingly, a summit may be cloud-capped for several hours when there are few, if any, other clouds in the sky. Rain often follows within a few hours after the tops of the major peaks are

Cloud Cap Formation

obscured by these strange, stationary miasmas. When cloud-capped, the summits have an unusual scenic beauty. However, it is unpleasant and dangerous to be in a cloud cap when climbing a peak, since wind velocity can be substantial, and the lack of visibility is hazardous.

Temperatures can change dramatically in the high country within a few hours; one can start in a T-shirt in the heat and five hours later be in drenching rain, or even snow. It is important to be prepared for these sudden changes in temperature and precipitation.

Hypothermia ("exposure" is a misnomer) has been appropriately termed the "Killer of the Unprepared." Loss of body heat can occur rapidly high in the North Cascades, even at temperatures well above freezing.

The danger of hypothermia is greatest with a combination

of physical exhaustion and wet clothing; failure to eat may be a contributory cause.

To prevent hypothermia: (1) Carry effective waterproof outer garments, and use them immediately if it starts raining; (2) Be aware of the wind chill factor; (3) Bivouac before exhaustion occurs, and construct the most effective practical shelter; (4) Carry extra food; eat frequently, particularly starches and sugars; (5) Keep as warm as possible by huddling together, near a fire if possible; (6) Wear wool clothing if adverse weather is probable (wool is the best known material for retaining heat when wet); (7) Maintain fluid intake to prevent dehydration; drink warm liquids if possible.

The initial symptoms of hypothermia are marked shivering, a fast pulse, rapid breathing, and paleness. As body temperature falls further, the shivering stops, pulse and respiration slow, and the body begins to feel cold to the touch. Further body temperature drop is manifested by confusion and defective thinking.

If heat loss continues, consciousness is lost; the heartbeat becomes irregular; body functions deteriorate. Death occurs when the core temperature falls to about 80°F.

The treatment of choice is to provide heat as rapidly as possible without burning the patient. Minor hypothermia will respond to replacing wet with dry clothing, use of additional insulation, administration of warm fluids, and consumption of candy and sugar. More severe hypothermia requires the addition of heat from external sources such as contact with one or two non-hypothermic companions in an insulated cocoon: improvise, using sleeping bags, clothing, tarps, etc.

Until mid-July on the east side, and until late August on the west side of the Cascade crest, portions of almost all the high trails will be obliterated by snow. Early-season hikers should carry an ice axe routinely, and should know how to kick steps in fairly steep snow slopes and how to do a self-arrest if a step pulls out. Every year, there are significant

Self-arrest with Ice Axe

injuries as a result of uncontrolled slides down steep snow slopes.

Glaciers are also hazardous! An unroped fall into a crevasse is usually lethal.

Unless very experienced, stay off of glacial ice and steep snow. Dying is so permanent! Most mountain deaths are the result of carelessness or ignorance.

HIKING

Equipment

There are a great number of day hikes which can be made in the North Cascades. A small rucksack or day pack should be carried. In the rucksack should be a first aid kit, water bottle, food, insect repellant, and extra clothes.

Other useful items or emergency gear which should be in the pack of the mountain walker include a map and compass, waterproof matches and a firestarter, sunglasses, pocket knife, flashlight, and whistle.

Water is almost always available west of the crest, but the east side can be dry, particularly in the late summer and early fall. Carry water if in doubt, particularly if the weather is hot.

For overnight backpackers, a light, waterproof alpine tent is essential in the North Cascades because of the unpredictable weather. Down sleeping bags are recommended, but they must be enclosed in a waterproof container. Fiberfill sleeping bags are heavier and not as warm as down, but they insulate better than down when wet. A durable and effective waterproof pack cover is also recommended. As fires are inappropriate or prohibited in many areas, a lightweight camp stove is essential. Raingear and extra clothing for warmth are also mandatory. Good boots, well broken in, are another important item.

Overnight campers should protect food supplies from bears. Many campsites are equipped with bear cables or bars strung between trees or posts; a few camps have stringers connecting the cable with the ground. Campers should carry about 40 feet of nylon cord. At night, all food supplies should be placed in the pack or other suitable container, and strung over the bear cable. If there is no cable, hang your food on a tree limb at least 10 feet above the ground, and five feet from the trunk of the tree (see diagram). Supplies left in camp during the day, if no one is present or if people are napping, should be similarly protected. Other suggestions for avoiding problems with bears: (1) Never leave uneaten food in the camp area or, even more important, within a tent; (2) Place garbage in plastic to decrease odors, and be sure the garbage

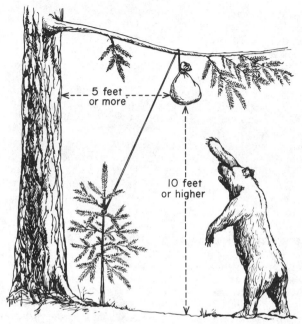

5 feet
or more

10 feet
or higher

A Bear-proof Stash

is packed out of the camp area; (3) Do not feed any wild animals, most particularly bears.

The black bear is far less dangerous than the grizzly; there are probably no grizzlies in the North Cascades. Although many campers have lost food to bears, there has been no serious injury from bear attacks in the Cascade Range. Do recall that it is unwise to get between a mother bear and her cubs; the mother may attack if she feels her cubs are threatened.

The bear-proofing method will usually prevent rodent damage, as will storing foods in metal or glass containers. Grey jays and Clark's nutcrackers can also ravage a camper's food supply; in a few areas, raccoons and skunks can also be a problem.

For those preferring to enter the area on horseback, there are packers available at Stehekin, Winthrop, and Merritt; the Forest Service provides a list of packers that serve the North Cascades. They will also supply a list of resorts in the area.

Photography

The North Cascades offers superb opportunities for quality mountain photography. However, camera enthusiasts in the North Cascades follow the only semi-facetious rule that if you can see it, photograph it immediately because you may not be able to see it later for the rain. Scenes with snow and ice in brilliant sunshine require one-half to 1½ f-stops downward compared to standard exposure (i.e., f16 rather than f11). In the woods, photography is best done on hazy or foggy days when the light is more uniform. Unsettled weather often produces the best photographs. Photographs into the sun can be very effective in the mountains, but require a much shorter exposure time and some good luck to avoid artifacts from the starburst effect of the sun.

A wide-angle lens is occasionally helpful for recording broad panoramas. For example, the view of Mt. Baker and the Black Buttes from the tarns a half mile east of the Park Butte lookout requires a wide-angle lens to photograph the mountain and its reflection in the water. Quality animal and bird photography generally requires a 135 mm. telephoto.

This lens is probably the largest that can be used without a tripod, and most backpackers do not have the space for a tripod nor the time to set one up for on-the-spot animal pictures.

Climbing

Mountaineering opportunities abound throughout the North Cascade range. Peaks of every degree of difficulty offer challenges to the mountaineer. An ardent climber could probably climb throughout his lifetime and not do all the routes on all the mountains in the North Cascades. Some summits can be reached simply by a vigorous uphill walk; others involve great technical difficulty and require great skill. Routes up a single peak can vary from simple to highly difficult.

Most climbs in the North Cascades involve an approach through a lowland valley, preferably by trail, less pleasantly by bushwhacking. There is generally a traverse across subalpine meadows. From timberline, the ascent to near the summit generally involves crossing snow or glacier. Save for the volcanic snow cones, the final route to the summit usually involves a scramble, generally on rock. Most of the rock in the North Cascades is not solid; hand- and footholds must be tested and re-tested, to avoid serious falls. The ice axe is an absolutely essential tool; the ability to do a self-arrest using the axe is mandatory. Crampons are necessary if any significant amount of ice must be traversed. A quality climbing rope must be carried. Climbing parties should invariably "rope up" if crossing glaciers. The ice and rock of the summit areas are hazardous to the inexperienced; those without climbing experience and proper equipment should stay on the trails.

Climbing parties should register at an appropriate Park or Forest Service office before climbing, and should sign out when they have descended.

Those planning climbs near the areas where camping is restricted (Cascade Pass, for example) should discuss potential high camps with a ranger prior to leaving the Golden West Lodge in Stehekin, or the Marblemount ranger station. High camps on ice, snow and bare rock for practical purposes have no environmental impact and are allowed by the Park Service, even in areas otherwise closed to overnight camping.

Climbers should have experienced companions. Solitary climbing may be uniquely satisfying, but it is quite hazardous. Particularly in view of the unpredictable weather, a minimum climbing party should be three people and desirably four to six. All the climbers should have had the equivalent of a basic climbing course and, if crossing glaciers, should be experienced in crevasse rescue techniques.

Fishing

Fishing is one of the pleasures of travel in the Pacific Northwest wilderness. Almost all of the lakes and streams in the North Cascades contain trout.

Fishing at the head of Lake Chelan generally requires a boat since the best lake fishing is at the mouth of the Stehekin River. However, it is possible to fish with some success from the docks around Stehekin, or from places on the lakeshore where there is a fairly sharp dropoff into deep water.

Ross Lake trout fishing has been legendary for many years, and it can still be quite productive. The usual technique is to troll a series of spoons followed by a hook baited

orms or salmon eggs. Still fishing on Ross does not
s effective. The best locations are at the mouths of the
streams. Boats can be rented from the Ross Lake
t.

shing in Diablo Lake is generally not as good as on
, but the lake is more accessible. Boats can be rented
the Diablo Lake Resort, and there is a launching area
private boats at the Colonial Creek Campground just off
North Cascades Highway at Thunder Arm.

For stream fishing, worms, salmon eggs, and flies are the
commonly used lures. The Stehekin River in the fall may
yield large trout, often taken on mosquito flies. The thick
brush which lines most rivers, particularly on the west side,
is an impediment to fly fishing. Hip boots or waders are
therefore suggested for use by the avid fisherman.

Most of the high lakes have been stocked with trout. Indeed, two or three contain exotic species, such as the Arctic
grayling and the Sierra golden trout. Flies generally are the
most effective lure. Trout under six inches in length should
be returned to the water with as little damage to their mouth
as possible and with a minimum exposure to air. A
Washington license is required; temporary licenses for non-
residents can be obtained at most sporting goods stores.

Fishing gear for backpackers has become relatively
miniaturized. A flyrod, reel, leaders, and flies usually can be
fit into most backpacks without great difficulty. Supplement-
ing a spartan backpackers' diet with fried trout is delightful!

As with fishing almost everywhere, the farther one gets
from a road, the more likely it is that quality fishing will be
found.

Other fish in the rivers draining the western slopes of the
North Cascades are the anadromous game fish, which in-
lude the steelhead and the various varieties of salmon (king,
ver, humpback, chum, and sockeye). The steelhead is a
eagoing rainbow trout; both steelhead and salmon return to

spawn in the small streams in which they were hatched. A substantial fishery, both commercial and sport, exists for both types of fish. There has been controversy over the past several years about what percentage of the catch should be reserved for the Indian tribes, and what percentage may be taken by non-Indians. Pollution, overfishing, loss of spawning areas, and dams have reduced the fish runs to a fraction of their former magnitude. Nonetheless, the Skagit and its tributaries still contain substantial numbers of these fish. Dead salmon carcasses are a major food supply for the eagles that winter along the upper Skagit.

Hunting

Hunting is allowed everywhere in the North Cascades, except in the North Cascades National Park. The most common animal hunted is the deer. Bear are also pursued. There are limited seasons on mountain goats and cougar. Some people hunt grouse. Certain animals such as the marmot and pika, and certain birds such as the eagle, are protected year round.

A hunting license is required. Dates of the fall hunting seasons are set each year by the State of Washington.

In the early fall, there is a Cascade "high hunt" in certain areas of the mountains. Hunters during these times usually establish horse-packed base camps and use the pack animals to remove their kill. Hikers should try to stay in the National Park if at all possible, particularly during the first weekend of the high hunting season. Some hunters shoot at noises and ask questions afterward! Unfortunately, the high hunt starts in September, which is prime backpacking time. The regular deer season begins in mid-October and lasts through the first week of November.

Hikers should use caution in all areas of the North Cascades, except the National Park, during the fall hunting seasons. Stay on the trails if possible; avoid "bushwhacking" through brushy areas. Wear high-visibility clothing, such as international orange, and make substantial noise (sing, talk, whistle, carry a tinkling bell).

In Winter

There are opportunities for cross-country skiing and snowshoe exploration away from the developed downhill ski facilities at Heather Meadows (Mt. Baker), Stevens Pass, Snoqualmie Pass, and at Loup-Loup between Twisp and Okanogan. For the very experienced and well equipped, the summits still beckon, even in the dead of winter. Only the main cross-mountain highways are plowed, limiting access to many back-country areas between December and April.

Those interested in winter mountaineering and wilderness travel should consult the several references listed in the bibliography for information about routes, techniques, and winter survival skills. Hypothermia and avalanches are substantial hazards to those who challenge the North Cascades in the winter.

On the Rivers

North Cascade area rivers offer a wide range of whitewater experiences, including major rapids, breathtaking scenery, and riverside camping. All the rivers are fairly cold, even late into the summer. As a result, hypothermia due to prolonged emersion in these rivers can be a life-threatening problem. Also, trees from the surrounding forest often fall into the rivers: dangerous obstructions develop unpredictably. Tree limbs, submerged logs, and log jams increase the danger for boaters, even though the whitewater itself may be relatively mild. Consequently, the first time down the river for the season, take extreme care. Scout ahead, and obtain advance information if available from other boaters.

South Cascade Glacier (Photo by Austin Post—USGS) This is one of the largest glaciers in the North Cascades.

2

THE LANDSCAPE

GEOLOGY

North Cascade geology is most complex!

Extensive volcanic flows covered central Washington in the past to great depths. Lavas covered the areas now occupied by the Cascade Range. Over the past five to six million years, the range has been elevated more than 10,000 feet, reaching its maximum height in the region of the current U. S.–Canadian border. Because of its greater elevation, this northern part of the range was more aggressively eroded by both ice and water than the southern portion. As a result, most of the volcanic material has been removed from the North Cascades, exposing the underlying complex rocks. (To the south, these older igneous and metamorphic formations are still beneath the lava cover.) The exposed rocks are of two varieties: recrystalized or metamorphic rocks (schists and gneisses) modified by high temperature and pressure, and associated igneous intrusions (granites) which cooled slowly under pressure and are therefore coarsely crystalline. Both of these rock groups are present as the steepest and tallest peaks of the range. Examples include: many summits between Snoqualmie and Stevens Pass, eroded from the Snoqualmie batholith; Sloan, Del Campo, and Gothic Peaks of the Monte Cristo group, etched in granodiorite; Snowking and Mt. Buckindy, sculpted in granite; Dome Peak, also formed of intrusive granite; and the orange granitic peaks of the Liberty Bell–Early Winter Spire area, sculpted from the Golden Horn batholith.

The highest of all the nonvolcanic summits in the North Cascades, Bonanza Peak, is composed of granitic gneiss.

The oldest rock in the North Cascades is the Yellow Aster Complex, approximately two billion years old. This material was moved up along faults from very deep in the earth, and eventually exposed by erosion. It can be seen today as patches on Winchester Mountain, rock blocks in the Yellow Aster Meadows, and at the Park Butte lookout area.

Mt. Shuksan was moved at least 15 miles upward and westward in an incredible geologic convulsion called the Shuksan thrust; the entire mountain rests on a totally different kind of base rock called the Chilliwack formation. A thrust of similar magnitude moved Jack Mountain six miles where it, too, sits on a different type of base rock.

In the Twin Sisters area between Mt. Baker and Puget Sound is the largest single deposit of olivine (peridotite) in the western hemisphere. Newly exposed olivine is a homogenous igneous mineral, light green in color; weathered rock is orange, accounting for the rusty color of the peaks. Many geologists believe that this rock is an exposed sample of the mantle (the part of the earth that underlies the crust).

The current theory of volcanic formation is that a large plate of rock from the Pacific Ocean floor is continuously being forced beneath a similar rock mass lying under the continental crust. Physical and chemical reactions occurring where the two plates converge cause the already hot rocks in this area to liquefy. This molten rock, called magma, moves up toward the surface along areas of weakness in the earth's crust. Eventually, subsurface rocks are displaced or assimilated to form an underground reservoir called a magma chamber. Heavier components of the molten rocks settle downward, and lighter components, including volatile materials such as superheated steam, rise. When a major weakness in the earth's crust is encountered, or when the volatile pressures exceed the gravitational and cohesive forces of the overlying rock, an opening is blasted to the surface and an eruption occurs.

Explosive eruptions produce clouds of gas and volcanic ash. Relatively quiet eruptions produce lava flows.

Both Mt. Baker and Glacier Peak are composite (or strato) volcanoes: they are composed of both lava flows and fragmental material (i.e., ash), reflecting alternating explosive and quiet eruptions.

An eruption from Glacier Peak 12,000 years ago (or perhaps nine eruptions closely spaced in time) laid down a layer of dacite pumice up to 12 feet thick as far as 12 miles downwind from the crater, and deposited lesser amounts of dust and ash over thousands of square miles of what is now Washington, Oregon, Idaho, Montana and Alberta. After the major pumice eruption, a glowing avalanche devastated the Whitechuck Valley.

Since that time, Glacier Peak appears to have been inactive. Glacier Peak, however, is not considered "dead" by the USGS, in view of evidence of an eruptive history somewhat similar to that of Mt. Mazama, the Oregon peak that blew its top away, forming Crater Lake in the process.

There is evidence of persistent eruptive activity of Mt. Baker over the past several thousand years. At least one flow of hot gas and fragmental material extended down the Baker River Valley almost to the Lake Tyee junction. The youngest lava flow from Mt. Baker issued from the cinder cone located in the Sulfur Creek Valley. The remnants of the cone can be seen today half a mile from the end of the Schrieber's Meadow Road; for well over a half mile the road is cut through red cinders deposited downwind from the eruption. The lava flow poured down the original Sulfur Creek Valley, splitting the stream into what are now Sulfur and Rocky Creeks. The exact age of this eruption is unknown, but it must be older than the several-hundred-year-old trees now growing on the site, and younger than the last major advance of the Easton Glacier.

Mt. Baker has sported steam plumes since it was first seen by the white man. There is fairly reliable data documenting some six eruptions between 1843 and 1884.

In 1975, volcanic activity within the summit crater increased nearly one-hundredfold. A 160' × 230', shallow, acidic lake formed in the summit crater, and there was substantial melting of the crater ice pack. When most active, the summit steam vents have spewed clouds over 2000' above the crater rim. The amount of sulphur-containing gas released by the volcano increased greatly.

Having dealt with the fire, let us now consider the ice. The North Cascade glaciers today, extensive as they are, are only tiny remnants of the alpine ice that once covered a much greater area, and extended to much lower elevations. During the most recent period of maximal glaciation, about 14,500 years ago, the ice sheet was a mile deep in the Bellingham area and extended a bit to the south of Olympia. The evidence includes the characteristic U-shape of North Cascade valleys; the cirques with nearly vertical headwalls at the upper ends of the valleys from which the glaciers originated; rocks deposited on the valley floor that clearly originated many miles up the valley; and the embankments of glacial moraines along the sides and floors of the valleys.

When the glaciers melted, the small, lovely, jewel-like lakes were left nestled high among the peaks.

A number of the many active glaciers still present in the

North Cascades can be seen from the North Cascades Highway. Ice is visible on the Picket Range to the west and on Jack Mountain to the northeast from Ross Lake. There is also an active crevassed glacier on Colonial Peak, best seen from the Diablo Lake overlook.

LIFE ZONES

The original concept of life zones reflected the relative latitude of a given area. The names identified these equator-to-pole locations (Lower and Upper Sonoran, Canadian, Hudsonian, Arctic). Later it was realized that life zones change in a similar way with increasing elevation. In the North Cascades, the amount of precipitation also exerts a significant effect. The types of trees and plants and, to a lesser extent, animal species in a given location vary according to life zone.

Because precipitation is less east of the Cascade crest, life zone boundaries on the east side of the range are more sharply demarcated than on the wetter west side.

On the east side, five life zones are encountered between desert and mountaintop:

The steppe zone, below 1000' elevation, is treeless, with bunchgrass and sagebrush predominant.

The yellow pine forest zone occupies the foothills between 1000' and 3000'. This zone is distinguished by its dominant tree, the ponderosa pine.

The grand and Douglas fir (Canadian) zone extends from about 3000' to 4500'; western larch and lodgepole pine are the other two common trees in this life zone.

The subalpine fir (Hudsonian) zone ranges from 4500' to 6500'. Common trees are the mountain hemlock, whitebark pine, Englemann spruce, and Lyall's larch. In this zone are the splendid alpine meadows. At the upper limits of the zone,

Life Zones of the North Cascades

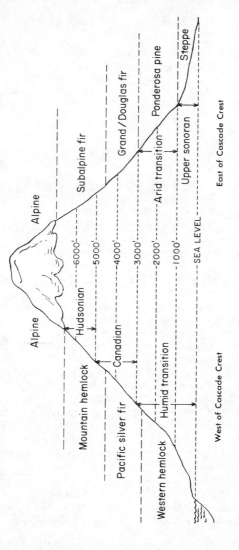

the trees become brushy shrubs (krummholz) as a result of the struggle to survive the extremes of temperature and violent winds common at these elevations.

The alpine zone includes all the terrain above timberline, about 6500'. Specialized flowers—moss campion, Lyall lupine, and the golden fleabane—survive and reproduce above the tree line, as do shrubs such as luetkea.

On the west side, there are only four life zones. The western hemlock, or humid transition, zone extends from sea level to about 2800'. Other trees found here include the Douglas fir, western red cedar and alder. The Pacific silver fir (Canadian) zone extends from about 2900' to 4400'. Alaska yellow cedar and western white pine are also found here. The mountain hemlock (Hudsonian) zone is from roughly 4500' to 6100'; subalpine fir and whitebark pine are other common trees. The alpine (Arctic) zone extends from about 6200' to the snow-covered summits.

PLANTS

Observing the many and varied plants and trees along the trail is one of the greatest pleasures to be enjoyed in the North Cascades. Most wilderness travelers are aware that blooms should not be picked: flowers can be taken home in memory or on film. Alpine trees also are fragile, and must not be cut for firewood.

Three plants which often form the ground cover in forested areas are the trillium, bunchberry or ground dogwood, and queenscup bead lily.

A number of species of saprophytic plants can be found in the deep forest of the North Cascades. These curious plants, which are devoid of chlorophyl, do not require light and can live in deep shade. Three species of the coral root, all members of the orchid family, flower in late spring. Pinesap and Indian-pipe have a similar appearance; they are yellow-white with heads suggesting the bowl of a pipe. Indian pipe is found in low-level forests only and consequently is not often seen, since it dies if the tall trees fall or are cut. The tallest member of this group is the red and white barber pole or candy stick. Pine drops is a white or pink plant with urn-shaped flowers.

The pinkish-red, chest-high flowers of the fireweed are ubiquitous in open areas in the North Cascades. The plant is found in areas of blow-down, clearcutting, and man-made or natural fire burns.

Perhaps the most beautiful flower in the North Cascades is the calypso orchid, otherwise known as the lady slipper or fairy slipper. These small flowers, around four inches high, are elegant both in their lavender color and in their structure. There are several spurs superiorly and an open sac-like lower petal with white, yellowish or darker reddish spots. Each plant has a broad, parallel veined leaf and a single, fragile stem topped by its splendid flower. Excessive flower picking has led to its virtual elimination from many areas where it had been common. It now occurs sporadically from the lowlands to perhaps 2500' in elevation. The plant flowers in mid-spring. These blooms must not be picked under any circumstances.

Mountain heathers usually are about nine inches high, with broad green leaves and bright cheery white or red flowers. Both are found in the high alpine meadow areas, generally on granitic soils that do not support much in the way of other wild flowers. A far scarcer yellow heather, with similar leaves and a few greenish-yellow closed bell flowers, grows at higher altitudes than the red and white varieties.

Heathers are fragile plants and should not be walked upon or used as sites for alpine tents.

Several varieties of Indian paintbrush are found in the North Cascades. Flowers may vary from a pale pink to a deep scarlet; less colorful blooms are ivory or yellow-white.

This plant grows from seashore to timberline. It is distinguished by its hairy leaves and clumped blossoms at the top of the plant, which also have small hairy projections from the bracts. Leaves are narrow and pointed at the tips.

The mountain daisy grows in a number of western states and is common in the high Cascade meadows. The plant, about a foot high, usually has only one flower head which is yellow in the center with a number of surrounding violet petals.

Yellow-flowered glacier lilies are wide-ranging in the Pacific Northwest. Most commonly found in the mountain meadows, the glacier lily blooms immediately after the snow melts, or sometimes sprouts and blooms right through the last one to two inches of melting snow. As the first high-meadow wildflower to bloom, it has a special place in the hearts of Northwest backpackers and climbers. The saying, "Any day you see a blooming glacier lily can not be a bad day" says much about the flower.

Less common is the white-blossomed avalanche lily.

The Columbia tiger-lily is one of the most beautiful and easily observed wildflowers of the North Cascades. It is a tall, impressive plant with large and attractive leaves and multiple orange flowers, usually six to eight on a stalk.

The columbine is tall, with brightly colored flowers with red spurs and yellow blades.

Two varieties of monkeyflower—red and yellow—are found only in moist or wet areas. Both varieties flower in mid-summer.

The broad-leafed lupine is probably the most common flower in the high mountain meadows of the North Cascades. At prime blooming time, around early August, acres of blue ripple in the summer winds. Occasionally when the air is still, a subtle fragrance suggestive of the odor of sweet-peas is noticeable. The lupine dies back to the ground in the fall, but springs up again after the snow melts. Less commonly seen, since it grows generally above timberline, is the small alpine lupine. Blue blossoms are borne on the ends of the spreading branches of this ground-hugging wild flower.

Other plants found in lower-elevation forest are the aster, beargrass, wild bleeding heart, wild currant, false lily-of-the-valley, foxglove, ox-eye daisy, pipsissewa, white rhododendron, Oregon grape, skunk cabbage, and pioneer and evergreen violets.

Alpine wildflower species include the western anemone, bellflower, cinquefoil, cow parsnip, elephant head, golden fleabane, moss campion, Jacob's ladder, marsh marigold, penstemon, stonecrop, spring beauty (also found in the lower woods), the edible thistle, the dwarf fireweed or red willow-herb, spreading phlox, and luetkea (partridge-foot; Alaska spirea).

The common trees of the lower elevations of the North Cascades include the Douglas fir, ponderosa pine, western hemlock, western red cedar, alder, vine maple, and dog-wood. At middle elevations are the mountain hemlock, Alaska cedar, and the aspen. Trees of the alpine meadows, each with a rather definite niche, include subalpine fir, Engelmann spruce, whitebark pine, and alpine larch. There is overlap between zones. Occasionally seen are the bigleaf maple, birch, black cottonwood, willow, Pacific yew, the noble, grand, and Pacific silver firs, western larch, and the lodgepole and western white pine.

The most familiar and common tree in the North Cascades is the Douglas fir. This tree reaches the height of 200' or more only west of the Cascade crest in Oregon and Washington.

The western red cedar, a commercially valuable tree, grows between sea level and 3500' in elevation in the moist parts of the North Cascades. A closely related tree, the Alaska cedar, is usually found between 2500' feet and 6500' feet in elevation in the North Cascades. It does best in moist areas, and it may be the longest-lived tree in the North Cascades.

The ponderosa pine is uncommon west of the Cascade crest; east of the crest at lower elevations it forms a vast forest, covering the foothills of the Cascades. Ponderosas are often seen growing close to small streams in otherwise treeless sagebrush country.

Hikers in the upper valleys in the fall will be impressed by the brilliant fall color of the vine maple and Douglas maple. The leaves of vine maple begin to turn red or yellow as early as midsummer. When it grows in clearings, or in avalanche chutes, vine maple can form a bushy, multi-stemmed tree that is 20′ to 30′ tall.

Small groves of aspen are found tucked away in the high valleys of the North Cascades. Their leaves turn yellow, golden, and occasionally even reddish in the fall, making the mountain landscape splendid.

A common and spectacular tree in the lower valleys is the Pacific dogwood, the most beautiful flowering tree in these mountains. It is able to survive and bloom in the forest understory. In most areas, the dogwood bloom peaks around Memorial Day.

There are four alders in the North Cascades. Red alder is the largest and most plentiful; the sitka or slide alder is found in avalanche paths. White alder occurs almost exclusively east of the Cascades, and thinleaf alder grows along water courses east of the Cascades.

Sooner or later, the cross-country hiker in the North Cascades will tangle with slide alder, with its intertwined, slanted, tough, springy trunks which generally incline downhill in the direction of winter avalanches. Because of their elasticity and direction of growth, these trees are able to survive avalanches which would uproot most other trees in the path. This 10′ to 15′ high shrubby tree characteristically pioneers fresh gravelly sites at the foot of retreating glaciers. Sitka alders form almost impenetrable clumps at mid-elevation of the steeper slopes of the range.

The western hemlock, which grows from sea level to

3500' in elevation, is the climax tree of the west side forest. Because of its prolific seed crops and remarkable shade tolerance, it ultimately will dominate, assuming that no disaster such as fire, blowdown, or logging occurs. After perhaps a thousand years, the forest, if undisturbed, will be primarily pure western hemlock with perhaps an occasional red cedar. In dense climax forests, the canopy is so thick that little light penetrates and, therefore, the forest undergrowth is very sparse.

Mountain hemlock is found from about 3500' to 6000'. It survives best in mountains with heavy snowfall.

The most unusual tree in the North Cascades is the alpine, or Lyall's larch, commonly known as a tamarack. This member of the pine family grows in small open stands and is rarely found below a mile in elevation. This tree is one of the very few deciduous conifers. Larch is found roughly from Wenatchee in the south into Manning and Cathedral Parks in the north.

One of the crowning magnificent sights in the North Cascades occurs in the last week of September and the first week of October (in an average year), when the larch turns a golden yellow before it drops its needles. When backlit by the sun, the trees glow. Anyone who has walked in a golden larch forest in the fall will never forget the experience.

The subalpine fir, a majestic and distinctive high-country tree, grows in clusters, shaped like splendid gothic cathedral spires, at hundreds of locations across the subalpine meadows of the North Cascades. It is the most widespread true fir in North America.

The Englemann spruce is usually found in moist locations between 3000' and 7000' east of the Cascade crest. Old-growth trees can be three feet thick and up to 140 feet tall.

Whitebark pine is another common tree of the high country, more common on the east side of the Cascade crest than the west. At low altitude, it can be slender and straight. At higher elevations, it develops a stout, short trunk and a large spreading crown.

Near the upper range of timberline, trees become dwarfed and stunted and assume atypical bushy forms; this phenomenon is called krummholz (from the German meaning crooked wood).

Fungi are common at lower elevations in the North Cascades. A variety of mushrooms grow in the valleys and foothills, particularly on the west side. Common in the area is the fly amanita, with its brilliant red-orange cap speckled with cream-white warty particles. They are found most commonly in the fall on the forest floor beneath the conifers. These fungi are enjoyable to look at, a pleasure to photograph, and gastronomically disastrous! When eaten, they produce nausea, diarrhea, an intoxicated madness, and in severe cases, convulsions and coma. Fortunately, the taste is repugnant so it is seldom ingested.

Another form of fungus commonly seen in the North Cascades is the bracket type. These woody or leathery relatives of the mushroom have no stalk: the cap is attached on one side to the wood on which it feeds.

High-country hikers who cross snowfields may be startled from time to time by red snow beneath their feet. The coloration is due to a high concentration of microscopic algae. There are more than a hundred species of snow algae. Because the dark red pigments of the algae absorb solar energy, the cells melt their way into the snow, increasing the melting rate of snowfields.

When the North Cascades National Park was established in October, 1968, the new park administration inherited from the U.S. Forest Service problems of severe overuse in a number of the popular subalpine meadows and passes.

Cascade Pass, in particular, suffered from concentrated use. Sunny summer weekends in the late 1960s found as many as 50 parties camping in the vicinity of the pass, digging out the heather to level their tent sites and hacking at the ancient mountain hemlocks and subalpine firs for their campfires.

The pass was closed to camping and fires at the start of the 1970 season. Later that summer research biologists Margaret and Joseph Miller undertook a long-range program of revegetating the worn-out campsites and trails of Cascade Pass. After ten years they concluded that Cascade Pass could best be revegetated by propagating, at a lower elevation, plant material from the pass area. In a large greenhouse at the Skagit District Ranger Station in Marblemount, native plants are grown and later brought up for replanting at Cascade Pass.

Many other areas have received rehabilitation efforts. All the popular subalpine passes were closed to camping in the early 70's, but more than decreased recreational impact was needed to restore these damaged areas. Jute netting was brought to several locations and laid on worn-down campsites to retard erosion and discourage illegal camping. Revegetation through transplanting has been carried out at Park Creek Pass, Lake Juanita, Copper and Egg Lakes on Copper Ridge, and Boundary Camp below Hannegan Pass.

Many of the old closed campgrounds in the lowland valleys have been successfully replanted with young trees and shrubs from adjoining areas. In these lower elevations revegetation is more rapid than in the harsh subalpine climate.

The revegetation program of the North Cascades National Park, both in the subalpine zone and in the lower closed canopy forest, depends on the cooperation of the visitor. Several years of work can be wiped out by one thoughtless camper who erects his tent or builds a fire in a revegetation plot. All visitors to the North Cascades should understand the significance of the presence of jute netting, and cooperate with the efforts to restore the high meadow country to its pristine state.

ANIMALS

As snow melts in the spring, many mammals migrate up into the high country where they spend the summer and early fall. The animals return to the valley floors when early winter storms begin to fill the high meadows with the 15 to 25 feet of snow that usually accumulates by spring.

The animals most likely to be seen by the hiker include the deer, black bear, golden-mantled ground squirrel, raccoon, chipmunk, pika, marmot, and porcupine. Animals less likely to be seen include the cougar, mountain goat, and coyote. Rattlesnakes are not uncommon at lower elevations on the east side of the range.

Black-tailed deer are more common on the west side of the crest; mule deer predominate on the east side of the range. Black-tailed deer have Y-branched antlers, and an all-black-on-top tail. Typical mule deer have a dark horseshoe patch on the forehead, larger and wider-spreading antlers than the black-tail deer, and a tail that is mostly white with a black tip. They migrate upward to the lush high meadows in the summer, returning to the lowland valleys in the winter.

The American black bear is relatively common in the North Cascades. The animal is seldom seen in the winter, since bears sleep most of the time from December until March. The bear's fur can be cinnamon or dark brown in color, as well as black. It can be distinguished from the brown bear by the shape of the head seen in profile: the upper line of the black bear's muzzle arches slightly upward.

Bears tend to be more active at night, but in undisturbed wilderness they also range widely by day. The bear is omnivorous, eating everything including berries, roots, grass, insects, rodents, honey, yellow jacket nests, skunk cabbage, dead animals, young deer, salmon, and if given the opportunity, garbage and campers' food supplies.

It must be stressed that these animals are at all times very dangerous and unpredictable. They should never be offered food in the wild, however friendly they appear to be. The black bear is very powerful and can inflict severe injuries.

The Cascade golden-mantled ground squirrel, roughly ten inches long, resembles a large chipmunk. Its behavior is also quite chipmunk-ish; but the ground squirrel is less arboreal than the chipmunk, and is a true hibernator. These squirrels frequently visit campsites and picnic areas.

Animals of similar appearance and habits include the Douglas squirrel, or chickaree, and the northern flying squirrel; the latter is nocturnal.

The common North American raccoon can be found in the wilderness heart of the North Cascades, and is apparently equally comfortable in the Seattle metropolitan area. Raccoons may be observed at any season in the North Cascades.

Chipmunks, the smallest of the Pacific Northwest squirrels, are charming, active, and frequently seen in the North Cascades. Two species of chipmunk are common in the North Cascades: the larger, darker and less active Townsend's chipmunk prefers the dense Douglas fir and hemlock forests of the west side lowlands and the higher hemlock forests of the Cascade Mountains. The smaller, lighter, yellow pine chipmunk is a denizen of the ponderosa pine zone of the more arid east side mountains and foothills. Yellow pine chipmunks are curious, vociferous animals, not adverse to stealing food from campsites.

The two characteristic mammals of the high country are the pika, affectionately known as the coney, and the marmot. Pikas are fluffy little egg-shaped animals with small rounded ears, who live in communities beneath the loose rocks of talus slopes.

The hoary marmot, or whistler, also inhabits talus slopes. Marmots weigh about ten pounds and are a bit over two feet long. They have greyish, thick, coarse fur, compact bodies, short legs, small ears, and fairly bushy tails. The marmot often will sit on a rock or outcropping near his hole or den and survey his domain; when disturbed, he emits a high-pitched, shrill whistle which rises in pitch as whatever is disturbing him comes closer. When danger threatens, he disappears underground rapidly, only to reappear shortly thereafter, as he is very curious. Both marmots and coneys are protected animals even outside of the park boundaries, with a substantial fine for killing them.

The porcupine is often seen within the forested areas of the North Cascades.

The cougar, also known as the puma or mountain lion, ranges from southeastern Alaska to Patagonia. Still unprotected in some states, the cougar is now protected in the Pacific Northwest where it is considered a game animal with season and kill limits. The mountain lion is secretive and elusive. The cougar population of the state is presently estimated at 1500 animals. Some years ago, five cougars were seen at one time on the Bridge Creek bridge.

Cougars very rarely attack man; campers in the North Cascades are more likely to be struck by lightning than to be assaulted by a mountain lion.

Mountain goats are the true monarchs of the mountains. These splendid animals are found only in northwestern North America. They are the lone American representative of old-world antelopes; their closest relative is the chamois, found in the Eurasian mountains.

The North Cascades goat is a stocky, bearded animal. It tends to be found on or near massive rock outcrops where escape routes are available. It grazes on a variety of grasses and herbs there, but can also be found in the lush alpine meadows in the summer if it feels safe from predators.

These animals spend most of their lives in the high country. During the winter they may descend to areas that are protected by a coniferous canopy. Although temporary feeding groups of twenty to forty females and kids do occur in the summer and fall on optimal range, it is more common to see only one to three goats at a time.

These animals are almost never visible from roads or well-traveled areas. Binoculars are recommended for goat viewing since most sightings are a substantial distance away. Goats are most likely to be seen in the Black Buttes near Mt. Baker, Mt. Pugh, Crater Mountain, Mount Johannesburg near Cascade Pass, Copper Ridge, Hannegan Peak, and the high peaks around Lake Chelan.

The coyote is not uncommon in the North Cascades. Other relatively common animals in the North Cascades are the beaver, weasel, rat, mouse, mole, and shrew. An occasional moose, wolverine, lynx, marten, or fisher may also be encountered. There is a substantial elk herd in the Twin Sisters–Dock Butte area.

All animals within the national park are protected. Injuring or killing any animal within the park boundaries is a federal offense.

Rattlesnakes are often found at lower elevations in the eastern foothills of the North Cascades; they rarely venture above 3000′. All rattlesnakes are venomous and therefore dangerous; however, almost all snakes will go out of their way to avoid a human. Use caution in snake country, particularly at night. Wear high boots and long pants. The treatment for a bite with evidence of poisoning consists of rest and reassurance, immobilization of the bitten area, use of a constricting band above the bite, incision of the fang marks and suction (if the bite is located in a body area without major blood vessels or tendons, if the incision is done within five minutes of the bite, and if a hospital is over 20 minutes away), and immediate transportation to the nearest hospital. Antivenin is of unquestioned value in the hospital; use in the wilderness is controversial.

INSECTS

After God created the North Cascades, He saw that they were perfect. Since perfection by divine decree can not be allowed in this world, it was then necessary to create the mosquito, the horsefly, and the yellow jacket!

Insects are one of the major drawbacks of the North Cascades. With the exception of the yellow jacket, the rule in these mountains is that if an insect lands on you, slap it immediately. Yellow jackets unfortunately may sting even though killed; it's best just to take a deep breath and blow them off. Avoid leaving food attractive to yellow jackets near areas of human activity. Other common annoying insects are the ''no-see-ums'', or biting gnats, horseflies, deer-flies, and the ubiquitous mosquito.

Yellow jackets, hornets, and paper wasps are known for their potent sting and for their paper nests. By autumn, the nest may be as large as a pumpkin and contains 2,000 or 3,000 short-tempered inhabitants. There is no defense for the unfortunate person who blunders into a yellow jacket nest; the response under those circumstances is immediate, rapid flight from the area.

There is no good remedy for the yellow jacket sting. Discomfort lasts from twelve hours to several days. Serious allergic reactions to stings can occur and multiple stings can produce severe illness requiring hospitalization. Removal of the stinger (if visible), cold applications, and over-the-counter pain medicine (such as aspirin) are the treatments of choice. Antihistamines may help somewhat.

The high-mountain snow mosquitoes of the western United States are ice-age left-behinds. These mosquitoes lay their eggs once a year in pools formed from melting snow. Isolated at high elevations, they are the principal mosquito species of the coniferous forests of western North America. Most commercial insect repellants are generally effective for mosquitoes.

Biting midges, including "no-see-ums", sand fleas, and gnats, are small mosquito-like insects that breed in aquatic and semi-aquatic environments. Since they are small, the adult insects are not easily seen, and they may be able to penetrate screens that are effective barriers for mosquitoes and larger biting insects.

Black flies also attack man. Deer- and horseflies are stout-bodied, powerful, and frequently large insects most commonly found around lakes, bogs, streams, and ponds.

Commonly used insect repellants are ineffectual against the biting flies. The flies are active during daylight only; in general, the hotter the weather, the more prevalent the flies.

Bumblebees are common in the North Cascades. Fortunately they are not aggressive. They do have the capacity to sting, as do other bees, and some caution is therefore appropriate.

The western spruce budworm is the most destructive forest defoliator in western North America. In the North Cascades, this insect attacks principally Douglas fir and the true firs. When major outbreaks develop, measures to control the infestation may be attempted in national and commercial forests.

Another defoliator is the tussock moth. The Douglas fir tussock moth attacks Douglas fir, grand fir, and subalpine fir. Outbreaks develop explosively and after about three years usually subside abruptly.

Ticks exist in the lower portions of the North Cascade range, on both sides of the crest. The Rocky Mountain wood tick, common throughout western North America, transmits Rocky Mountain spotted fever, Colorado tick fever, and other illnesses to man.

Ticks position themselves on brush and transfer from the brush to the body of the host passing by. Clothing as well as skin should be checked; ticks should be removed prior to attachment. If a tick embeds itself in the skin, it should be removed as soon as possible. Removal is not simple. The body of the tick should not be crushed during removal. The best method of removal is for a professional to surgically remove the head of the tick, using local anesthesia. The mixture of 0.6% pyrethrins in methyl benzoate and camphorated phenol—a pharmacist can compound this—reportedly greatly reduces the force required to detach embedded ticks; application for at least twenty minutes before detachment, and the use of a slow and steadily increasing pulling force, is recommended.

The Rocky Mountain wood tick also transmits tick paralysis. Tick paralysis is characterized by a flaccid ascending weakness that can cause death by respiratory failure. It takes five to nine days after attachment for the toxin to be produced in sufficient quantities to cause paralysis. Removal of the tick before the paralysis has proceeded too far leads to rapid and complete recovery. Any unexpected weakness during or following hikes should lead to a search for a feeding tick.

BIRDS

The bird watcher will find traveling in the North Cascades a rewarding experience. The crest of the Cascades forms a racial barrier. Many birds on the eastern slopes belong to the Rocky Mountain races; those on the west to the Pacific Coast races.

Traveling the North Cascades from west to east, a bird watcher can see rich and varied bird life. Band-tailed pigeons feed on red elderberries. Common mergansers nest along rivers in spring and summer. Trail's and western flycatchers swoop out from perches. Various warblers glean the treetops; brown creepers, the tree trunks; black-capped and chestnut-backed chickadees and golden-crowned kinglets, the branches. Robins, Swainson's thrush, song sparrows, and redeyed vireos vie in song. Warbling vireos and yellow, black-throated, gray, and Wilson's warblers nest within this area. Barred owls inhabit the alder and bigleaf maple groves along the Skagit River from Hamilton to Thunder Creek.

As the hiker ascends the thickly timbered western slopes, he may see pine siskins and cedar waxwings. The tiny winter wren gives forth his bubbling song from the forest floor. The belted kingfisher and spotted sandpiper share the stream. A small lake may harbor coots, tree swallows, Vaux's swift, the common loon, and Barrow's goldeneye duck. Solitary vireos and Audubon and Townsend's warblers are summer residents in this region, as are evening grosbeaks.

At the upper limits of forest, the red crossbill, a seed cone feeder, may be seen occasionally. In the alpine fir copses of the open meadows, the Townsend solitaire and the hermit thrush sing from the treetops. Townsend warblers, Oregon juncos, Lincoln and fox sparrows flit through the thickets, and olive-sided flycatchers call their "quick, three beers" from dead treetops. Gray-hooded MacGillivray's warblers slink through the dwarf willows and alders in gullies. Horned larks feed on the grassy ridges, and will fly high with tinkling notes of song. In the lower, tarn-dotted basins, water pipits walk and bob from boulders. In fall migration times, hawks and passerines may be seen in numbers as the birds pass over mountain ridges and meadows.

The camper who sleeps under the open sky may see and hear nighthawks, the great horned owl, the pygmy owl, the spotted owl, and the screech owl. Cooper's hawk is the common accipiter of the coniferous forest. Sharp-shinned hawks, marsh hawks, kestrels, and black swifts scan the land from above, seeking prey.

As one descends into the drier life zones on the eastern slopes, new birds are encountered. In the semi-arid yellow pine forest are the ruby-crowned kinglet, mountain bluebird, Cassin's finch, red crossbill, pine grosbeak, yellow-bellied sapsucker, dusky flycatcher, Williamson's sapsucker, evening grosbeak, warbling vireo, goshawk, mountain chickadee and the house wren. Calliope hummingbirds may also be seen.

On Lake Chelan are found the mallard, great blue heron, western grebe, common goldeneye, western bluebird, brown-headed cowbird, American goldfinch, house finch, and the western tanager.

Grouse, ptarmigan, rosy finch, Canada goose, rufous hummingbird, water ouzel (dipper), eagle, harlequin duck, Clark's nutcracker, grey jay, Stellar's jay, pileated woodpecker, varied thrush, and the common raven are frequently found in the North Cascades.

The fortunate hiker will see a harlequin duck bobbing on the rapids of a mountain stream. This uncommon and shy duck spends the summer on swift western rivers. The two most likely locations to spot this aquatic bird are on Thunder Creek, and on the Stehekin River. It is distinctively marked with a combination of red, blue, white, and black plumage.

The rufous hummingbird male has a brilliant, fiery red and orange throat. These birds migrate fantastic distances, appearing in the foothills in the spring, summering in the meadows, and departing in the fall for Mexico and Central America. They are found from sea level to the highest peaks in the range. They are attracted to red colors and may closely approach a person wearing red clothing. They are a flying marvel.

Perhaps the most unusual bird in the North Cascade mountains is the water ouzel or "dipper," a grey-blue bird slightly smaller than the robin. The dipper is usually seen on an exposed rock in the middle of the turbulent stream; every few moments it dips or curtsies, a movement characteristic and unmistakable, and occasionally it disappears into the rushing water of the rapids. It can move effectively under water. Often its lilting song is audible over the sound of the rapids.

Canada geese usually nest in the spring and early summer at the upper end of Lake Chelan.

The golden eagle is found in the timberline regions of the Cascades. An expanse of open country, with an abundance of prey and a rocky ledge or cliff on which to nest, is their necessary habitat.

The blue grouse, or wood grouse, is one of the best known game birds in the North Cascades. It is found from sea level to timberline, migrating with the seasons. In the spring, the resonant noise of a grouse thrumming is one of the lovely sounds of the mountains. An alarmed bird will burst upward with a loud whirring noise, startling the approaching walker.

The spruce grouse, blue-gray in color with white patches, is relatively uncommon. The blue and ruffed grouse have a similar appearance, with the latter being a bit plumper and having somewhat more variegated markings.

The white-tailed ptarmigan is one of the most handsome birds in the Cascade Mountains. Mottled brown in summer and pure white in winter, this alpine grouse remains in the high country all year. The birds are very approachable. They often react to danger by becoming motionless until the danger passes, which may be one of the reasons why they are easily approached. Ptarmigan are scarce and should never be harmed.

The grey-crowned rosy finch lives in the high country much of the year, descending to lower elevations in midwinter. It nests in cavities of high cliffs above 7000'.

The Pacific varied thrush, commonly known as the snow or mountain robin, is an often-seen permanent resident throughout the dense forests of western Washington. In summer, it can be found from tidewater to timberline. The male is much like a robin except that the underparts are a rusty brown rather than a bright red. The adult female is a duller color. During he nesting season in the spring, the varied thrush sings vigorously. Its song is best described as a trill, with a mysterious far-away quality making it unique. The sound has been described as a prolonged note of a few seconds duration, repeated at short intervals.

The raucous call of the common raven is frequently heard by hikers in the North Cascades.

The Clark's nutcracker and the gray jay are members of the crow family and are roughly one foot in length. Both are found near camps and picnic areas. The Clark's nutcracker has a long pointed bill and a uniformly gray head; by contrast, the gray jay has a substantially shorter bill and contrasting black and white head markings.

The Clark's nutcracker has a drawn-out gutteral cry; the gray jay has a more varied cry, and is able to produce a considerable variety of notes.

Woodpeckers in the North Cascades include the common flicker, Lewis woodpecker, hairy woodpecker, downy woodpecker, northern three-toed woodpecker, and the yellow-bellied sap-sucker. The most dramatic bird in this group, and indeed the largest woodpecker in America, is the seventeen-inch-long, red-crested pileated woodpecker. The neck and face are white; the rest of the body is black. The blows of its bill produce a sound so loud that it has been frequently mistaken for the noise made by a hammer or axe in the hands of a vigorous logger.

The Steller's jay, sometimes known as the mountain jay, is a common resident in the forests of Western Washington, most often found in the western hemlock or humid transition zone. It is conspicuously crested, with the crest and upper body a blackish gray, and the tail and lower body a purplish blue.

Big Four Mountain and Inn (Photo by J.A. Juleen, 1934; provided by the Verlot Ranger Station.)

3

HISTORY

The Indians, at the time the first white man reached the North Cascades area, largely avoided the mountains. The coast Indians and the interior aborigines lived in substantially different environments and evolved dissimilar life styles and customs. However, trails to facilitate trading had been developed over the centuries between the two groups; wild hemp, for making fishing nets, was exchanged for the Higua shell, which served as a medium of exchange for the inland Indians. Most historians concur that the most used of the primitive transmountain routes was over Cascade Pass, but Indian Pass, Snoqualmie Pass, and perhaps the route of the current North Cascades Highway were also traveled.

Stehekin is a corruption of an original Indian word meaning, "the way through." Today little remains of the presence of the Indians in the mountains; a few pictographs can still be seen across from Stehekin when the lake is drawn down in the spring.

In 1792, Captain George Vancouver, during his exploration of Puget Sound, named Mt. Baker after his Third

Lieutenant Joseph Baker, who first saw the mountain while on watch. The Indians knew the peak as Koma Kulshan ("great white watcher").

Probably the first white man to traverse the North Cascades was Alexander Ross, a member of John J. Astor's Pacific Fur Company. In 1814, he crossed from the east to the west side of the range. Beset by problems with his Indian guides, he returned to the trading post at Okanogan without achieving his goal of reaching Puget Sound.

In 1856, Congress authorized a boundary commission to survey the 49th Parallel from the ocean to the Rocky Mountains. The task was formidable. Even today, much of the boundary is very difficult to reach. Astronomical observations were used to determine the boundary line.

One of the topographers, Henry Custer, became fascinated with the North Cascades, and attempted to describe the magnificence of the mountains as well as perform the more prosaic aspects of his assignment.

Custer first entered the area of today's park by traveling up the headwaters of Ensawkwatch Creek. He was among the first to describe the discomforts of breaking trail through a lowland Cascade Valley. Custer climbed Middle Peak, elevation 7,464 feet, and wrote, "The view from here was fine and extensive to all directions of the compass. I leave it to a better pen to describe the sublimity of true mountain scenery in the Cascade Mountains. . . . It must be seen, it cannot be described. Nowhere do the mountain masses and peaks present such strange, fantastic, dauntless and startling outlines as here. Whoever wishes to see nature in all its primitive glory and grandeur, and its almost ferocious wildness, must go and visit these mountain regions."

Metal and cairn survey markers were placed by both the American and British survey teams. Eventually, a swath 20 feet wide (10 feet on either side of the line) was cut through the timber along the border. This denuded area still exists. Aluminum-bronze markers, set in concrete, now mark each mile of the border; numbering begins in the west and progresses eastward.

In 1882, a U.S. Army expedition under the command of Lt. Henry Pierce crossed War Creek Pass and descended into the Stehekin Valley. Pierce confirmed the grandeur of the mountains as viewed from Boulder Butte. He descended into the Stehekin Valley, which he described as a "dense jungle," and proceeded up the valley on a "most imperfect trail." Pierce's party crossed Cascade Pass in late August and eventually descended to reach a logging camp near the present Sedro Woolley. Pierce's published account of this mountain transit gained public attention and first publicized the North Cascades to the rest of the world.

MINING

The lure of gold next drew people to these mountains. Although North Cascades mines have produced little of value, for some years mining was one of the most active industries in the North Cascades, and it resulted in a thorough exploration of the mountain wilderness and contributed to the settlement and development of the surrounding areas.

In the Skagit district, miners reached Ruby Creek in 1872. The creek was named from the finding of a garnet in the riverbed. Ruby Creek was the site of the first gold rush in the North Cascades when gold dust was found in 1878 along Ruby and Canyon Creeks.

The classic story of mining in the North Cascades began July 4, 1889, when Joseph L. Pearsall discovered the broad, glistening streak that was to become the 1776 lode on the side of Wilmans Peak. He convinced himself that it was a deposit of galena (lead sulfide), "as rich as Monte Cristo." The pass from which the deposit was first seen was later named Pearsall Pass.

After the ore proved to contain gold and silver, others became involved, including John Wilmans. Many claims were staked in the Monte Cristo and Goat Lake areas. By 1891 there were three small mining camps and a post office. National mining interests became involved; construction work began on the railway from Everett to Monte Cristo. The first engine of the Everett and Monte Cristo Railroad steamed into the mining camp August 25, 1893; the project had cost $1,800,000.

The mining camp was developing rapidly, and by 1893 there were a thousand people in the area. Tramways to the mines were completed in 1894. At its greatest development, between 1894 and 1897, Monte Cristo had 4 hotels, 4 restaurants, 6 saloons, 2 churches, a school, a hospital with one doctor, 3 barbershops, a drugstore, 2 butcher shops, a real estate office, a clothing store, one newspaper, and the usual mining camp brothels.

The economy was precarious; in 1893 a recession hurt financing. Floods in December 1896 damaged the railroad; the coup de grace was the flood of November 1897, which washed out much of the railroad. Rockefeller decided against further investment. The railroad was rebuilt in 1900 and the mines reopened, but the ore was still not rich enough. The population dwindled to 150 people by 1901. Monte Cristo was abandoned after a landslide and tunnel cave-in in 1906 and a depression in 1907. Most of the area has now returned to the control of the North Cascade jungle.

To be profitable, a mine must be near a railroad or waterway, and its ore must be of high grade in order to pay the freight. In the North Cascades, the story was always the same. With rare exceptions, North Cascade ore was not of high quality, nor easy of access. The remote veins usually hugged the glaciers. The odds were too one-sided for even the hardy turn-of-the-century prospectors. All of the patented claims in the National Park area have either been acquired by the Park Service or are in the condemnation process.

The Howe Sound Mining Company continued until about 20 years ago its substantial copper mining activity at Holden near Lake Chelan. Accumulated tailings from the mining are still a major problem to the environment of the Holden area and Railroad Creek.

The North Cascade Range offered little opportunity to homesteaders. The first real settlers came to sell goods to the prospectors, not to farm.

One of the most interesting and enigmatic North Cascade historical personages was Mighty Joe Morovits. (His name, slightly misspelled, appears on topographic maps as Morovitz Creek.) This immensely powerful and stubborn man lived alone in the area between Mt. Baker and Mt. Shuksan for 27 years. After homesteading in 1891, he prospected the mountains, blazed trails, possibly made first ascents of many of the peaks, staked claims, and kept looking for gold at the end of the Rainbow (Creek). It was common for him to pack 100 pounds on his back over the 32-mile trek from the Skagit River to his homestead. He is credited with moving a massive mortar weighing over one ton from Concrete to his 4th of July Mine on Swift Creek. He accomplished this by winching it from tree to tree over his own crude trail; the task required 2 years.

In the early 1900's he started providing mountaineering guide service to the Seattle Mountaineers. His record of first ascents on Mt. Baker is impressive: first ascent of the dangerous northeast ice face in 1892; establishment of the Morovits route via the ridge between Park and Boulder Glaciers in 1894; first ascent of Sherman Peak, the south, secondary summit of Mt. Baker, in 1907. In recognition of his feats on Koma Kulshan, many of us call the splendid meadows just south of Mt. Baker the upper and lower Morovits Meadows.

Joe disappeared from the mountains in 1918. His ultimate fate is unknown.

LOOKOUTS

Forest fires have always been a part of North Cascades history. Henry Custer observed that the Indians sometimes set fires in order to clear underbrush from their trails and to improve hunting. Most fires in the old days were caused by lightning strikes during summer thunderstorms. Man-caused fires, secondary to logging operations or from careless use of recreational fires, are now a substantial problem. The largest forest fire in recorded history in the North Cascades was the Big Beaver fire of 1926, which burned 40,000 acres, including the current east side of Ross Lake. Desolation Mountain was named because of its appearance following this major conflagration.

Most of the trails in the North Cascades were not constructed for recreational use. Miners made the first footpaths. Later, the Forest Service constructed trails, primarily to facilitate fire control: these trails allowed more rapid access to roadless areas than was possible by cross-country bushwhacking. The trails also served as access routes to the fire lookouts.

The first fire lookout in the Mt. Baker National Forest was a tent station on Gold Hill across from Darrington, erected in 1915. It was abandoned after only one season, in favor of nearby Jumbo Mountain (5880'), where a tent lookout was established on the summit. The Sourdough Mountain Lookout was constructed by Glee Davis, using hand-split cedar, in 1917. The current, more standard 14' × 14' lookout was built by the CCC in 1933. Active construction of lookouts continued through the 1930's; forty-three lookout stations were built in the Mt. Baker National Forest during that time. Most were constructed in the early 1930's, including Crater, Desolation, Park Butte, and Hidden Lake.

At first, Army heliographs were used to send messages. This device transmitted Morse code with a mirror and shutter mounted on a tripod. Communication was by telephone for a number of years after that. Telephone maintenance problems were formidable, and currently the lookouts use two-way radio for communication.

Before the logging roads pushed close to the summits, some of the lookouts were remote, requiring two vigorous days of hiking to reach them. Those manning the lookouts were generally unusual people (occasionally, married couples), self-sufficient and able to tolerate prolonged solitude.

As aircraft became more reliable, aerial fire patrol flights were thought to be cheaper and more efficient. Gradually, the lookouts were phased out. The buildings were declared no longer useful, and many were burned.

Currently active lookouts in the North Cascades include Copper, Sourdough, Desolation, Goat, Granite Mountain, Lookout Mountain (Twisp), Dillard Point, North Point, North Twenty Mile Peak, First Butte, and Mt. Leecher.

Lookout houses which are not manned save at times of great fire hazard remain at Winchester, Green Mountain, Sauk, Monument 83, Lookout Mountain (Cascade River), Miners' Ridge, and Slate Peak.

The remaining lookouts fortunately are beginning to be regarded by the public, and hopefully by the land management agencies, as historical structures, since many are now over half a century old.

Outdoor organizations or groups have "adopted" some of the lookout shelters and maintain them for the use of their members and the public. The Everett Mountaineers maintain the lookouts on Pilchuck and Three Fingers. The Skagit Alpine Club of Mt. Vernon leases and maintains the lookout at Park Butte. The Friends of the Lois Webster Memorial Shelter, also headquartered at Mt. Vernon, maintain the Hidden Lake Lookout. It is hoped that further senseless destruction of these buildings will cease; the cabins have a function both for historical interest and as shelters in inclement weather.

A number of the early rangers in the North Cascades will be long remembered. These include Tommy Thompson, who served on the Skagit between 1907 and 1943, and C. C. McGuire, who was in the area between 1908 and 1918, and again from 1925 to 1939. McGuire in later years wrote his memoirs of his early days on the western slope of the mountains, thus preserving history that otherwise would have been irrevocably lost. The most important historical figure in the Pasayten area was topographer Lage Wernstedt, who, during 1925 and 1926, singlehandedly mapped almost all of the present Winthrop Ranger District. During the course of his work, Wernstedt took over a thousand photographs. Many are still on file at the Winthrop Ranger Station. Some are a part of the Northwest Collection maintained at the University of Washington library. Wernstedt named many of the topographic features of the northeast Cascades. The Picket Range was named by Wernstedt because "its serrated peaks resembled a picket fence." In addition, he made the first ascents of over a hundred peaks.

MOUNTAINEERING HISTORY

The first successful ascent of Mt. Baker occurred in August 1868, when E. T. Coleman returned (after two unsuccessful attempts in 1866) with companions Stratton, Tennant, and Ogilvey. They ascended the ridge at the head of Wallace/Thunder Creek, gaining some 3000', to the subalpine meadow area west of the Black Buttes, which they named Lincoln and Colfax Peaks. The party feasted on marmots that evening. After roping up, the party progressed to the saddle between the main peak and the Black Buttes. The ascent from the saddle to the summit was accomplished in two hours on August 17, 1868, and the summit was named Grant Peak after General Grant. The crater appeared to be ice- and snow-free at that time, suggesting that the level of volcanic activity was substantially greater in the mid-1800s than it is today.

The Mazamas (Spanish for mountain goats), still a very active mountaineering group, were organized in the Mt. Hood and Portland area of Oregon in 1894. In 1899, forty club members arrived at Stehekin by boat and proceeded up the valley. Hiking up through Horseshoe Basin, the enthusiastic climbers scaled a peak which they named Sahale, an Indian term for "higher." The mountain still bears that name.

Later, the same organization constructed a cabin in Mazama Park, immediately beneath the south slopes of Mt. Baker. Mazama members named a substantial portion of the place names surrounding Mt. Baker as they explored, often using the Mazama cabin as a base camp.

Other first ascents in the North Cascades were:

Glacier Peak — 1898 by T. G. Gerdine and four others (USGS)

Boston — 1938 by Cox, Bressler, Clough and Meyers

Twin Sisters — 1891 by Hegg, Harris and Edson

Goode — 1936 by Bauer, Dickert, Hossack, Mac-Gowan and Halwax

Liberty Bell — 1946 by Beckey, Welsh and O'Neil

Mt. Challenger — 1936 by Dickert, Hossack and MacGowan

Bonanza — 1937 by Leuthold, Ijames, and James

Sloan — 1921 by Bedal and Skaar

Any discussion of the history of climbing in the North Cascades must include Fred Beckey, without doubt the most persistent and aggressive aficionado of the sport in the history of the range. Author of all the authoritative climbing guides to the area, and a legend in his time, Beckey has climbed hundreds of North Cascade peaks. Many of the routes have been first ascents.

CONSERVATION HISTORY

In the beginning, Western Washington had only three colors: the blue of the sea, the green of the forest, and the white of the ice- and snow-capped peaks. Loggers have changed that! From 1860 until about 1883, loggers started harvesting the timber at the seashore and worked inland, selecting timber at will. After 1883, most of the land had been claimed, and the logger either had to own the land or to pay private or governmental third parties for the privilege of cutting the timber. By 1888, there were sixteen logging camps employing 400 men and producing 800 million board feet of timber a year, operating along the Skagit alone. Gradually, the seemingly inexhaustible stands of first-growth timber were harvested. Reforestation was not even considered for many decades. Ultimately, little timber was left in private hands, and what remained was under the jurisdiction of major corporations. Loggers more and more looked toward the timber on the federally owned lands within the National Forest. Clear cuts spread at a rapid rate and in locations that led to the development of major conflicts, which continue today, with other users of Forest Service land. Between 1950 and 1963, some 332,000 acres of National Forest timberland located in the north and central Cascades were logged under Forest Service management. Loggers and timber companies have provided the major opposition to the establishment of parks and wilderness within the North Cascades.

Sheep and cattle grazing is still allowed in the Okanogan National Forest and in the Pasayten Wilderness Area, in spite of the adverse effects of grazing on the delicate ecosystems of the higher elevations.

In 1897 President Cleveland established a Washington Forest Reserve, which included the present North Cascades. In 1908, the Wenatchee, Chelan, and Snoqualmie National Forests were carved out of a portion of the Washington Forest Reserve.

The Mt. Baker Club of Bellingham was established in 1910 to secure inclusion of the mountain and the surrounding area within the national park system. To publicize Mt. Baker and the North Cascades, the club sponsored the three Mt. Baker Marathons in 1911, 1912, and 1913, in which hearty buckos from the logging camps raced from Bellingham to the 10,778' summit and back to Bellingham. These races attracted international attention, and the publicity they generated led to the filing of National Park legislation in Congress.

Starting point for the marathons was the Chamber of Commerce building in downtown Bellingham. Runners could choose either of two routes: one was through the village of Deming, approaching the mountain from the west via a 16-mile-long trail; the other route, via Glacier, was more rugged but four miles shorter. Both trails met at the "saddle," a low point between the Black Buttes to the west and the main peak to the east. Those going to Glacier rode a special logging train provided by the Bellingham Bay and British Columbia Railroad. Those going via the Deming route rode hopped-up cars over winding wagon roads up the Middle Fork of the Nooksack River to the road end at Heisler's ranchhouse. The first person to return to Glacier pre-empted the train for a wild dash back to Bellingham. Those on the

Deming route had cars and drivers waiting for them at Heisler's barn.

Only those who have climbed Mt. Baker or a similar peak can really comprehend how arduous and dangerous a task it is to run up an icy, steep, cold, dormant volcano.

Fortunately, no one was killed during any of the races. In addition to skill and incredible endurance, luck played a part in the outcome of all three races. The fastest time from Bellingham to mountaintop and back to Bellingham was 9 hours and 48 minutes, established by Harvey Haggard in 1912.

Realizing that a death was inevitable if the races continued, the Bellingham city fathers abandoned the mountain marathons, but not before one of the most incredible chapters in the history of the North Cascades had been indelibly placed in the record books.

In 1924 the balance of the Washington Forest Reserve was renamed the Mt. Baker National Forest. In the early 1970s the Mt. Baker and Snoqualmie Forests were merged, presumably in the interest of economy. Forest headquarters were transferred from Bellingham to Seattle at that time.

The grand argument to create a national park within the "Wilderness Alps" of the North Cascades lasted in various degrees of heat for 62 years. A national park was first proposed by the Mazama Club of Portland in 1906. In 1937 the Department of Interior investigated the area and reported that it was "unquestionably of national park caliber."

The final successful effort to establish a national park began about 1956 with the organization of the North Cascades Conservation Council. Then Washington congressman Thomas Pelly was persuaded to file in Congress an initial bill for creation of the park. Four or five additional years of hard work was required to generate sufficient political clout to persuade the Secretaries of Interior and Agriculture to appoint a joint study team to evaluate the area. After holding public hearings and extensive field studies, the team produced a substantial book containing their findings and recommendations, "The North Cascade Study Report." After this report was published, the Senate interior committee held further hearings on the proposal. Bills were filed in the Senate by Henry Jackson and in the House by Lloyd Meeds. The final bill to create the park and recreational areas was a compromise between the conflicting interests of those desirous of preserving the area for its recreational and esthetic values and those concerned with extracting resources, particularly timber, from the mountains. The North Cascades National Park Bill was signed by President Lyndon Johnson on October 2, 1968. Martin Litton, Brock Evans, Pat Goldsworthy, and this author were privileged to watch President Johnson sign the bill in the White House; many others, perhaps more worthy of recognition, exulted in the victory from afar. Space limitations unfortunately prohibit listing names of other major contributors to the creation of the park.

Changes instituted by the Park Service have been the closure of the alpine passes (Cascade, Park Creek, Easy and Whatcom) to camping and an effort to re-establish the alpine flora of these areas. Trails have been reopened (Desolation Lookout: Goode Ridge and McGregor Mountain). Over half of the private land in Stehekin has been acquired by the Park Service.

At the time of this writing, all three national forest administrations are in the course of studying and promulgating a long-range plan for management of those portions of the North Cascades under their jurisdiction. Input from concerned recreationalists and environmentalists is crucially important in this process. Readers should contact the forest supervisor to be put on the mailing list for information and should feel free to contribute suggestions to the forest administrators as the planning proceeds.

Wild areas are increasingly scarce. It is essential that

everyone entering the North Cascades leave them unspoiled for future generations. What was standard practice in the past is no longer acceptable, since the subalpine meadows are too fragile to tolerate intensive use, particularly by the inconsiderate and destructive. Therefore, walk softly in the wilderness! Stay on the trail if at all possible at all times; do not shortcut switchbacks. Doing so creates substantial erosion. If you brought it in, carry it out, unless you can burn it. Camp in designated campsites or in places previously used for camping. Use fire pits already in existence; do not build new ones. Use only dead wood. Carry a chemical or gasoline stove for cooking. If there are no obvious campsites, camp on sedge grass rather than heather, wildflowers, or other fragile flora. Do not cut tree limbs, pick wildflowers, or otherwise change the natural scene. Disturb the natural world that you are in to the smallest degree possible. Develop a deep awareness of the permanent impact of your presence in any alpine environment and act accordingly, recognizing that simply by being there, you are causing some changes to occur. The dictum of ten years ago, "Take only photos; leave only tracks," has been changed to "Take only photos; leave nothing."

Essential to the preservation of an environment suitable for truly enjoying life is a program to prevent overpopulation. It has been well said that "every cause is a lost cause until population control is achieved." A list of organizations supporting the concept that overpopulation must be prevented if life is to retain quality and meaning is included in the Resource section.

Unceasing vigilance still is necessary to protect the recreation areas established in the North Cascades, and to minimize environmentally unsound activities in the remaining splendid areas of the range still being administered by the Forest Service under the "multiple use" concept. This battle never ends! Now and in the future, all of us who love the hills and the wild places of this earth must join the fray. Magnificent, serene areas will not be left inviolate if corporations can profit from their destruction, as the attempt of Kennecott Copper to exploit Miners Ridge in the Glacier Peak Wilderness confirms.

Since only disciplined political activity is effective in influencing the decisions of politicians and land managers, those who love wild lands and wilderness must take an active part in preserving them. A number of local and national conservation organizations active in the cause of preservation in the North Cascades and nationally are listed under Resources.

PART TWO
TRAILS

Climbing Party on Mt. Baker, 1908 (Photo by Asahel Curtis, provided by the Whatcom Museum of History and Arts, Bellingham, WA.)

4

TRAIL INFORMATION

Of the approximately 300 trails in the North Cascades, the author has selected 93 which he feels most appropriately reflect the essence of hiking in the area. The author prefers high trails with vistas to lengthy lowland deep-woods walks, and this bias is reflected in the trail selection. Other considerations have included selecting representative trails in 18 subsections of the North Cascades. Several trails are described primarily because they can be explored in the early spring or late fall. The likelihood of solitude and a wilderness experience was also considered.

Trails requiring substantial uphill hiking with little scenery are generally omitted. Walking four hours up, spending half an hour in a beautiful location, and walking three hours down does not seem the most splendid form of hiking; however, many of the North Cascade footpaths require this type of commitment if done as a day hike.

Changes have occurred in a number of the trails in the past five to fifteen years. Many are due to the change in land management from Forest Service to Park Service. Some changes are due to acts of God, such as logging roads being washed out. The date when the author last walked the trail is in parentheses at the end of each trail description. The longer the time from that date to the present, the more important it is for the hiker to check with the land management agency involved to determine if there have been changes in that trail.

Astute readers will find errors. Updating and other responses will be appreciated so that corrections can be included in future editions of this publication. Please write to the author in care of Sierra Club Books.

ACCESS BY ROAD

Six west-side and four east-side roads provide access to the North Cascades National Park and associated recreational areas, as do the two "water roads" of Lake Chelan and Ross Lake.

Limited access to the area can be had through Canada. Forking off from the Trans-Canada Highway a short distance west of Hope, a gravel road reaches the north end of Ross Lake. Trails and fire roads from Canadian Provincial Highway 3 pass through Manning Provincial Park to reach the Cascade Crest and other trails. Cathedral Park is reached via the Ashnola road, which branches off British Columbia Highway 3 two miles west of Keremeos.

Stevens Pass Highway (U.S. 2), open all year, provides access to the Pacific Crest Trail at the pass, and to the Curry Gap section of the Crest Trail via Smith Brook Road just east of the summit. A number of other scenic trails are reached from the east section of U.S. 2 via state highways 207 and 209. These latter roads depart from Cole's Corner and Leavenworth respectively to reach Lake Wenatchee and Trinity.

U.S. 97 is the main eastern approach road. The eastern end of the Pasayten Wilderness is best reached via Tonasket and Loomis. State routes 153 and 20 lead to Twisp and Winthrop, gateways to the Twisp and Chewack valleys. West of Winthrop is Mazama, gateway to both Harts Pass and the eastern portion of the North Cascades Highway.

A road which deserves mention is the 23-mile road beginning at Stehekin Landing and ending at Cottonwood Camp. This road has aptly been described as ''beginning at the lakeshore and dead-ending at Paradise.'' The road, currently paved for the first four miles, follows the lakeshore for a bit over a mile and then enters wooded country at the northwest end of the lake. At about three miles, the Stehekin school, a National Historic Landmark, is passed on the right. The short side road leading to impressive Rainbow Falls is 0.1 mile further. A little beyond the 4-mile mark, the road forks, with the left fork leading to the Stehekin airport and to a number of residences on the southwest side of the river. The main road continues upriver at this point to reach the High Bridge Guard Station and shelter, the National Park boundary, and many trailheads at a little past the 10-mile mark. From this point on, there are numerous established campsites along the road, some with shelters. Fishing is good in the Stehekin River from almost its source to the mouth in season (July through October). Beyond High Bridge, the quality of the road deteriorates. In addition to High Bridge, forest camps are located at Dolly Varden, Bridge Creek, Shady Creek, and Cottonwood Camp. The Bridge Creek, Park Creek and Flat Creek trailheads are passed en route.

The Stehekin road is currently served by a shuttlebus

system during the spring, summer, and early fall. Check with the Park Service for the current schedule. Early in the season the road may not be passable.

Western road access, from the south northward, begins with the southern portion of the Mountain Loop Highway. The western terminus of this highway is at Granite Falls, where State 92 connects to State 9 and ultimately to Interstate 5. Good stream fishing is available at many areas along the highway in the south fork of the Stillaguamish River. The last few miles of the road, particularly after the turnoff from Barlow Pass to Monte Cristo, offer spectacular mountain vistas. (This turnoff ends at Monte Cristo about 30 miles east of Granite Falls. Monte Cristo, a commercial ghost town, is of historical interest.) From Barlow Pass, the Mountain Loop highway continues north through pleasant country. Side roads to the east allow one to reach trailheads on the Sauk and White Chuck rivers. The Mountain Loop highway terminates about a mile northeast of Darrington.

Darrington can be reached from Interstate 5 by taking the Arlington exit and driving east on State 530 approximately 30 miles. Fine fly fishing can be had in the north fork of the Stillaguamish along this road. From Darrington, it is possible to connect with the Mountain Loop Highway as mentioned above; there is also a good connecting road from Darrington to Rockport paralleling, in general, the Sauk river and offering opportunities for trout fishing in the summer and steelhead fishing in the winter. About midway between Darrington and Rockport, the access road up the Suiattle Valley is intersected. A number of forest camps, good fishing, and access to trailheads, as well as enjoyable scenery, are available on the Suiattle road.

The Mt. Baker Highway (State 542) is a high-grade, all-season road which terminates at the Mt. Baker ski area. A secondary road extends 3 miles further to Artist's Point. Tire chains are often required during the winter on this road. It does, however, offer access to the high country even when the snow is piled 25 feet deep at the Heather Meadows ski facility.

Probably the most spectacular access route to the park and associated recreational areas is the North Cascades Highway, (State Highway 20) completed in September, 1972. This route leaves Interstate 5 at Burlington and runs east through Sedro Woolley and Hamilton. Six miles east of Hamilton, and at Concrete, spur roads provide access to Baker Lake and to the scenic country of the south side of both Mt. Baker and Mt. Shuksan.

A joint Park Service–Forest Service visitor center is located a few feet off the highway at Concrete.

The North Cascades Highway continues north through Rockport (where there is a connection with Darrington) to Marblemount. At this point, the Cascade Pass Mine to Market Road crosses the Skagit River and continues approximately 18 miles to the Cascade Pass trailhead.

From Marblemount, State 20 (west) continues northeast through the Seattle City Light town of Newhalem. The Goddell Creek campground is located to the east of the road just before entering the City Light village. The road then enters the scenic Skagit River gorge which it follows to near Diablo village, one mile off the main road. Note the major avalanche tracks that have necessitated road reconstruction. Near Diablo, the highway crosses Gorge Lake (the former Skagit River). The turnoff to Diablo Dam is 1.3 miles further. The road then contours above Diablo Lake, passes Thunder Lake, and shortly thereafter crosses Thunder Arm, an extension of Diablo Lake. Fine camping is offered at this location in the Colonial Creek campground, maintained by the National Park Service.

The road continues eastward 5 miles to the junction of

The North Cascades Highway–Marblemount to Mazama

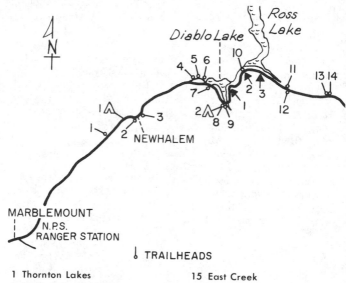

↓ TRAILHEADS

1 Thornton Lakes
2 Trail of the Cedars
3 Ladder Creek Falls
4 Stetattle Creek
5 Sourdough Ridge
6 Diablo Lake
7 Pyramid Lake
8 Colonial Creek
9 Thunder Creek
10 Ross Dam Access
11 Ross Lake—East Shore
12 Panther Creek
13 McMillan Park (Crater Mt.)
14 Canyon Creek

15 East Creek
16 Easy Pass
17 Cutthroat Pass—West
18 Lake Ann (Rainy Pass)
19 Rainy Lake
20 Bridge Creek (PCT)
21 Blue Lake
22 Washington Pass Meadow
23 Washington Pass Overlook
24 Cutthroat Pass—East
25 Driveway Butte
26 Cedar Creek
27 Sandy Butte
28 Goat Creek

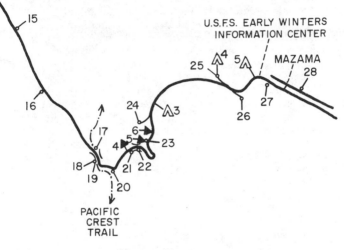

⚠ CAMPGROUNDS

1 Goodell Creek
2 Colonial Creek
3 Lone Fir
4 Klipchuck
5 Early Winters

↓ VIEWPOINTS

1 Diablo Lake; Colonial and Pyramid Peaks
2 Ross Dam
3 Ross Lake; Jack and Hozomeen Mountains
4 Whistler Basin and Mountain
5 Washington Pass
6 Kangaroo Ridge and Silver Star Mountain

Ruby Creek and Granite Creek and then climbs gradually an additional 13 miles up the Granite Creek valley. It reaches fairly level Rainy Pass, where there are several trailheads; from here the road descends slightly and then regains altitude to reach its highest point at Washington Pass, immediately beneath the granite massif of Liberty Bell and its associated spires. From here, the road switchbacks downward rapidly to reach Mazama and Winthrop.

In the Early Winters area, a Forest Service interpretive center is located about a mile west of Mazama.

The North Cascades Highway offers impressive views as well as access to thirty very fine trails, many of which are included in the trail guide section of this booklet. Heavy snows and avalanches force closure of the road normally between mid-November and mid-May.

Many people think the highway passes through the North Cascades National Park; that is incorrect. The highway passes through the Mt. Baker–Snoqualmie National Forest, the Ross Lake National Recreation Area, a small portion of the Wenatchee National Forest, and the Okanogan National Forest. The Park itself is both to the north and to the south of the highway.

TRAIL DESCRIPTIONS

There is a map for each trail chapter. Trails shown in dark dotted lines are described in the chapter. Some trails, such as the PCT, pass through two or more sections and link with trails listed in a given chapter; these trails are in parentheses at the end of the list of trails in each chapter, and are described in a different chapter. An alphabetical index of trails is at the end of this book.

In the text or in the beginning summary of each trail, an effort has been made to provide the reader with the following information: length of trail; walking time to the destination and walking time back (rarely equal in the North Cascades since almost always there is more altitude gain in than out); altitude gain, which includes ups and downs from the trailhead to the destination; and special features along the trail.

Even a steep, long trail can be fairly easy if one has a light pack and goes slowly. Conversely, a relatively easy trail can be difficult if one is carrying 80 pounds and is in a hurry to find a campsite before dark. If you know how far it is and how much altitude you must gain, you can determine how difficult the trail will be for you.

Almost always, hiking times are the estimate of the time an average hiker would need to walk the distance. After hiking one or two trails, you can compare your time to the hiking time given and establish a ratio that should be applicable to all the other trails in this book. This is more true for times going up than it is for times going down, since most of us are able to maintain close to a three-mile-an-hour speed when hiking on the level or going down.

All trail distances, given in miles, should be considered approximate. The following conversion table may be helpful to those who think in the metric system:

328 feet = 100 meters

0.1 mile = 528 feet = 161 meters

0.621 miles = 3,281 feet = 1,000 meters, or one kilometer

1.0 mile = 5,280 feet = 1.61 kilometers

Seasons for use normally extend from mid-July to mid-October in the high country. If the seasons for use are not stated at the start of the trail description, assume the foregoing.

MAPS

There are a plethora of maps covering the North Cascades, both topographic and nontopographic. The best overall map of the North Cascades National Park and the Lake Chelan and Ross Lake National Recreation Areas is the 1:100,000 topographic map (metric) published by the U.S. Geological Survey, available from the USGS Distribution Branch, Box 25286, Denver Federal Center, Denver, CO 80225. Topographic maps of the 7.5′ and 15′ series are available from the same source. An index and order form are available on request.

In 1980 the Park Service republished an expanded topographic map, "Main Trails and Back Country Camps, North Cascades Complex, Washington." This map gives elevations in meters. All designated campsites are shown, as is the route of the Pacific Crest Trail. This map is strongly recommended for those contemplating trips in the park complex.

Topographic maps of the Glacier Peak Wilderness and the Pasayten Wilderness are available from the Forest Service. These maps have metric contour intervals and trail distances in kilometers.

Topographic maps of the Canadian parks can be obtained from: Map and Air Photo Sales, Ministry of Environment, Parliament Buildings, Victoria, B.C., Canada V8V 1T7.

A topographic map is essential for any off-trail walking or climbing, and desirable for all visitors. The 7.5′ maps give great detail but are relatively bulky, and often two or three maps must be obtained to cover one trail or one area. Larger maps offer an advantage in cost and portability. Since maps are usually kept in outer pockets of packs, it is good to purchase a small plastic map container; soggy maps are difficult to read and fall apart easily.

The trail descriptions in this book provide the name of the USGS topographic sheet(s) and the Green Trail 15′ series topographic map(s) (available from P.O. Box 1272, Bellevue, WA 98009) that cover the trail area.

Planimetric (nontopographic) maps of each National Forest are available at district ranger offices and National Forest headquarters.

Compass angle of declination in the North Cascades is 22 degrees east of true north.

By 1982, the Forest Service will have changed their longstanding road-numbering system posted on access roads to the trailheads. The current four digits will be replaced by seven. Posting of roads, using the new system, began in the Mt. Baker–Snoqualmie National Forest in the fall of 1980. By 1982, updated forest maps will show the new road numbers. A guide for converting from one system to the other should be available in 1981, which should diminish the confusion during the transition years.

The new numbers are organized in a "trunk-branch-twig-leaf" manner, like this:

Arterial road	6100000
Collector road	6110000
Local road	6110110

The full seven digits will seldom be posted. In the example above:

<u>61</u>00000 would be posted as 61.

<u>6110</u>000 would be posted as 6110.

6110<u>110</u> would be posted as 110.

Abbreviations used in the trail descriptions include the following:

NCH—North Cascades Highway (Washington State Highway 20)

PCT— Pacific Crest Trail

WNF—Wenatchee National Forest

GPWA—Glacier Peak Wilderness Area

NCNP—North Cascades National Park

Very few trails in the North Cascades are crowded at any time. However, some on weekends suffer from overuse. Others are so rarely used that solitude can almost be guaranteed.

High-use trails are: Cascade Pass, Bridge Creek, Thunder Creek (near the Colonial Campground), Lakeshore (near Stehekin), Kennedy Hot Springs, Chain Lakes Loop and Table Mountain, Lake Ann (both near Mt. Shuksan and near Rainy Pass), Rainy Lake, Kulshan Cabin, Pilchuck, Blue Lake (between Rainy and Washington Passes), Cutthroat Lake, and other portions of the Pacific Crest Trail, particularly near road heads.

Low-use trails are: Sourdough Lookout, North Fork of Bridge Creek, Jack Mountain, Desolation Lookout, Pugh Mountain, Buck Creek Pass, Blue Lake–Johnson Mountain,

Summit Trail, Pyramid Mountain, Goat Peak, and trails in the Pasayten except for the PCT and Horseshoe Basin.

Finally, may the peace and tranquility of these most beautiful of all mountains be yours! As Mark Twain said, "There is no opiate like alpine pedestrianism."

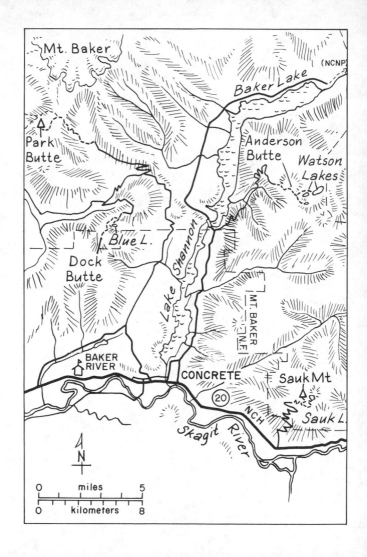

Mt. Baker

(NCNP)

Baker Lake

Park
Butte

Anderson
Butte

Watson
Lakes

Blue L.

Lake Shannon

Dock
Butte

MT. BAKER
N.F.

BAKER
RIVER

CONCRETE

Sauk Mt

20

NCH

Sauk L.

Skagit River

N

0   miles   5

0   kilometers   8

5

MOUNT BAKER–
SNOQUALMIE
NATIONAL FOREST
North Section

Trails:
Park Butte
Dock Butte (Blue Lake)
Sauk Mountain
Anderson and Watson Lakes and Anderson Butte

PARK BUTTE

DESTINATION: Park Butte Lookout, 5450'

TRAIL LENGTH: 4 miles

WALKING TIME (full pack): 2¾ hours in
1½ hours out

TRAILHEAD ELEVATION: 3350'

ALTITUDE GAIN, including ups and downs: 2200'

TOPOGRAPHIC SHEETS: USGS: Hamilton
Green Trails: Hamilton

Drive up Baker Lake Road from the NCH. Turn west just
past the concrete bridge 0.4 mile inside the National Forest
boundary. Drive 3.6 miles, take the right fork, and follow
signs to Schrieber's Meadow, about 9 miles from the Baker
Lake Road. There is parking for 10 to 15 cars in various areas
near the trailhead. The trail starts 100 feet down a side road
to the south and almost immediately crosses a bridge over
Sulphur Creek.

From the bulletin board and registration box, the trail
goes southwest, gaining altitude gradually. This is a good
place to pick blueberries and huckleberries in September.
After 0.6 mile the trail goes west, then north, through forest
and crosses three places where volcanic mudflows have devastated substantial sections of the forest and left boulder-
strewn, denuded areas. One of these flows occurred in 1911,
when enormous amounts of debris were released at the terminus of the Easton Glacier. An aluminum bridge, anchored
with cables, spans the worst of the torrents coursing through
these boulder-strewn channels. Passage can be difficult on
warm summer afternoons. After the trail crosses the third
devastated area and gains a bit of altitude, it crosses a small
creek; drink deeply and fill water bottles here. The path
steepens after the creek. About 800' is gained over the next
mile.

At 2.4 miles from the trailhead, the trail breaks into the lower Morovits Meadow; Mt. Baker and the Black Buttes can be seen easily from this point on. The trail goes northwest through splendid open meadow. At 2.6 miles is an unmarked trail junction. The right trail ascends a ridge to reach Baker Pass. The railroad grade can be seen on this trail. The left fork continues through the lower meadow, contours above a stream bed, crosses the stream, and enters the upper Morovits Meadow. There are superb campsites here. The trail goes west across the meadow to another trail junction marked by two posts. A faint way trail goes to the right and leads to Baker Pass. The main trail continues west across the meadow, turns south, ascends a ridge, and goes up to a bench. To the left (east) on this bench are two beautiful tarns and many potential campsites, but this area is too fragile ecologically for campfires.

The trail to Park Butte continues south, then curves west above Pocket Lake 400′ below to the southeast. The final half-mile ascent to the Park Butte Lookout follows. The lookout, leased and maintained by the Skagit Alpine Club of Mt. Vernon, is available for public use when not occupied by the club members.

The view from Park Butte is one of the best in the North Cascades; this may be one of the most beautiful places in the world. Dominating the scene is the ice-clad cone of Mt. Baker with its satellite peaks, the Black Buttes. The tip of Mt. Shuksan is barely visible. To the west is the valley of the Middle Fork of the Nooksack, and to the southwest the orange-tinted, snow-clad Sisters range. To the south are Loomis Mountain, Dock Butte, and in the far distance the snow-clad tip of Mt. Rainier. To the east and southeast are the great peaks including Blum, Hagen, and Sauk, and Glacier Peak in the distance. On clear days, Puget Sound can be seen to the west. As seen in the comments in the Park Butte Lookout register, reverence and awe are felt by visitors to this outdoor cathedral.

Returning to the junction in the upper Morovits Meadow, the hiker can proceed up to Baker Pass then drop to the west to Mazama Park, named by the Mazama Climbing Club of Portland at an outing in the early 1900s. Years ago, the club maintained a cabin in this meadow, the remnants of which can be seen. There are good campsites in this area.

An even better alternative is to continue north beyond Baker Pass, following one of the scrabble trails up. There are camping areas in the last trees. By ascending the steep, rough slopes of the railroad grade, the hiker can gaze down into the great cleft created by the Easton Glacier. In the early 1900s this glacier extended almost a mile further than it does now. Recently, the glacier has been growing again.

The experienced trekker can proceed northwest cross-country through trailless meadow. After about a mile is a viewpoint down into the Deming Glacier far below, and up to the summit of Mt. Baker to the northeast. Across this chasm are the Black Buttes where one can often see mountain goats foraging on the steep slopes. (Binoculars help distinguish goats from snow patches.) Further west 0.25 mile, and 250' lower, is Mazama Lake, a splendid alpine campsite. From here, it is a short scramble to the top of Meadow Point. Mountain goats are often seen on Meadow Point; deer and bear also inhabit the meadow.

The experienced hiker can also ascend the ridge above the last trees to about 8000' on Mt. Baker without venturing onto glacier, although snowslopes must be crossed. An ice axe is required. From this high point there are better views of Puget Sound and the San Juan Islands. Further ascent requires climbing skills and an adequate party.

A word of caution: Keep off the glaciers. They are dangerous places. Only roped-up and equipped climbers can safely traverse the ice fields of Mt. Baker.

(October 1980)

Geology

The Park Butte Trail is geologically interesting. About 2.5 miles from the Baker Lake Road turnoff, the Park Butte Road passes through vesicular andesite lava, known as the Sulfur Creek Flow. The rounded, forested hill to the left about 8 miles from the turnoff is a cinder cone. The orange material through which the trail passes is volcanic cinders, deposited downwind from the cone by the prevailing southwest winds.

West of Rocky Creek and Schreiber's Meadow is a shear-walled ridge composed of Yellow Aster Complex rocks, which are 460–2000 million years old.

West of the upper Morovits Meadow is a ridge of volcanic rock. This rock is not typical Mt. Baker hypsthene andesite porphyry, but is instead porphyritic olivine andesite and is believed to have originated from the Black Buttes.

At the southwestern end of the upper Morovits Meadow, 50 yards from the trail toward the Cathedral Crags, clay-rich lake sediments form a 25-foot-wide, 8-foot-thick sequence of horizontal strata. This deposit was formed by glacial outwash debris.

West of the upper Morovits Meadow is a ridge of volcanic rock of different composition, believed to be the remnant of an older flow originating at the Black Buttes.

(The author is indebted to Doug McKeever of the Department of Geology, Western Washington University, from whose masters thesis the above geologic information was abstracted.)

DOCK BUTTE (BLUE LAKE)

DESTINATION: Dock Butte, 5210'
TRAIL LENGTH: 1.8 miles

WALKING TIME (light pack): 1 hour in
                          45 minutes out
TRAILHEAD ELEVATION 3900'
ALTITUDE GAIN, including ups and downs: 1500'
FEATURE: Blue Lake, 4000'
TOPOGRAPHIC SHEETS: USGS: Hamilton; Lake Shannon
                    Green Trails: Hamilton

Drive east from Burlington on State Highway 20; turn
north 6 miles east of Hamilton, and follow Baker Lake Road
to the National Forest boundary. Half a mile beyond the
boundary, immediately after a bridge, turn sharply left
(west). Make a left turn at 3.6 miles onto the Loomis Mountain Road. Again, turn left at 7 miles at the Wanlick Creek
saddle. One mile further, make another left turn. The
trailhead is 10.9 miles from the Baker Lake Road turnoff.
There is parking for about ten cars at the trailhead.

From the trailhead, a way trail has been constructed
through logging debris for 0.1 mile; it connects with the old
trail just inside the forest boundary. Turn right (west) and
follow the old trail; 0.3 mile from the trailhead is a junction.
The upgraded and rerouted Blue Lake Trail turns left; the old
trail to Dock Butte continues to the right.

The trail to the lake runs about 0.6 mile. The trail is level,
but usually muddy and slippery. Excellent campsites are at
the east end of the lake. The area is fairly heavily used and,
unfortunately, littered; wood is difficult to obtain. Fishing in
the lake is sometimes good. A small peninsula extends into
the lake near the campsites; the water is deep enough here
for both bait- and flyfishing. There are sharp, rocky walls
above the lake to the south and west. The walking time to the
lake from the trailhead is about 20 minutes. Parents with
small children may find that Blue Lake offers a pleasant
one-day outing.

From the junction, the poorly maintained old trail goes up to Dock Butte. The tread is difficult to locate in places on the ridge above Blue Lake, but one can follow the ridge crest south to find the tread again. About 0.2 mile from the top of the butte, the trail to the right (west) looks easy, but it dead-ends and is not the right route. Make the fairly steep ascent to the left to the summit ridge; follow the scrabble trail on the ridge to the top. This is one minor Class 2 rock move, not normally difficult, but chancy if the rock is wet or icy. The view from the top is very nice, but marred by patch cuts in every direction. Glass and metal debris, remnants of the Dock Butte lookout, also detracts from the appearance at the summit. Still, it is a pleasant place. The valley of the Baker River lies to the east below. Loomis Mountain, Park Butte, and the Mt. Baker–Black Buttes massif lies to the north. To the west are the summits of the Twin Sister range. To the south is the Skagit Valley.

The Nooksack elk herd can sometimes be seen from the approach ridge or the summit. Binoculars may help in seeing these animals, uncommon in the North Cascades.

On the ridge above Blue Lake are several tarns and level areas that provide nice campsites. Although Blue Lake is often crowded, the Dock Butte area receives surprisingly few visitors.

(Lake—October 1974; Butte—September 1977)

SAUK MOUNTAIN

DESTINATION: Sauk Lookout, 5537'
TRAIL LENGTH: 2 miles
WALKING TIME (light pack): 1¼ hours in
                           1 hour out

TRAILHEAD ELEVATION 4350'

ALTITUDE GAIN, including ups and downs: 1300'

FEATURE: Sauk Lake, 4100'

TOPOGRAPHIC SHEETS: USGS: Lake Shannon
Green Trails: Lake Shannon

About 7 miles east of Concrete on the NCH, just before entering Rockport State Park, turn left and take a fairly rough logging road to the north. At about 6 miles, take the right fork in the road. At 6.8 miles, make a very sharp turn to the right and drive 0.2 mile up fairly steep road to the parking and picnic area on a bluff. Snow remains late on the last two switchbacks on the road; it may not be possible to reach the parking area until mid-July. The trail leaves from the east side of this area.

Gentle switchbacks go up the southwest side of Sauk Mountain, mostly in meadow. From afar, the meadow through which the trail ascends is a restful, deep green. Early in the season, glacier lilies and alpine phlox are very attractive. Later in summer, most of the wildflowers found in the North Cascades bloom alongside this trail.

The trail is fairly heavily used but rarely crowded. Logging is still going on, so those using the access road during the week must watch out for logging trucks. Extensive patch cutting around the mountain is, of course, not pretty. Because of the easy access and the relatively short and gentle trail, this is a very good hike for families.

If people are on the trail above, be careful where the trail crosses a slide area: rock fall in this area can be quite dangerous. Do not shortcut the switchbacks; this causes substantial erosion. The trail tops out on the southwest side of Sauk Mountain. It follows the east side of the ridge, then crosses, again, to the west side for the last hundred yards.

One can often climb to the ridge crest on Sauk in late June, encountering little or no snow; the trail from the crest to the lookout, however, is not snow-free until late July. The deteriorating lookout is still sufficiently intact to offer shelter from the elements. There are good views from the summit. The Skagit Valley lies below to the west. In the late afternoon sun, the Skagit River shimmers as it meanders toward Puget Sound. To the northwest, the Twin Sisters range is dwarfed by Mt. Baker. To the north is Mt. Shuksan, and to the northeast, the spires of the Picket Range. To the east is Hidden Lake Peak and beyond that, the peaks around Cascade Pass. To the southeast, the snow cone of Glacier Peak is visible; to the south is the Sauk Valley flanked by White Chuck and White Horse mountains.

One word of caution: Until the snow has melted completely, carry an ice axe. Also look up before crossing the chutes. Falls on steep snow, and head injuries from falling rock in the slide areas, have claimed several lives on this mountain.

At about 1.7 miles, 0.1 mile after the ridge crest, a fairly steep trail drops to the southeast, then to the northeast, passes through a notch, and again descends via switchbacks to the east side of Sauk Lake. This trail is about 1.5 miles long and loses about 1300'. The time down to the lake is only 35 minutes, but the time back up to the junction is one hour. There are fish in Sauk Lake. The nicest campsites are at the lake or on a bench above it.

There are campsites at about the 1.8-mile mark on the trail along the ridge crest extending east. After the snow has melted, water can be a problem in this area. There are no other camping areas.

(October 1980)

ANDERSON AND WATSON LAKES
AND ANDERSON BUTTE

DESTINATION: Anderson Butte, 5420'

TRAIL LENGTH: 1.8 miles

WALKING TIME (light pack): 1 hour in
45 minutes out

TRAILHEAD ELEVATION: 4300'

ALTITUDE GAIN, including ups and downs: 1200'

FEATURES: Anderson Lake, 4450'
Watson Lakes, 4550'

TOPOGRAPHIC SHEETS: USGS: Lake Shannon
Green Trails: Lake Shannon

The relatively easy access to this scenic area makes this a good trip for families. From the NCH about six miles east of the overpass at Hamilton, turn north and follow the county road past Grandy Lake to the Baker Lake Road about 4 miles north of Concrete. (If coming from the east, turn north a few blocks west of Concrete and follow a steep gravel road to this point.) The National Forest boundary is in about five miles; from the boundary, drive the main road 2.1 miles further. Turn right just before the ranger station and cross upper Baker Dam. Turn left 0.5 mile after crossing the dam. At about 1 mile, the road passes the Eastbank trailhead; this trail follows the lakeshore about 1.5 miles to Anderson Creek.

Continue about 10 miles from the east end of the dam to the not-too-obvious trailhead on the left (northeast) side of the road. There are parking areas, holding about 10 cars each, 100 yards above and 50 yards below the trailhead.

The trail winds up through dense timber about 0.5 mile before breaking into meadow. It climbs moderately through this meadow another half mile to a saddle under Anderson Butte. Here the trail divides. The left fork switchbacks up moderately about 0.8 mile to the summit of Anderson Butte, where fine views may be had (of Shuksan, Baker, Sisters, Baker River Valley, and the Pickets). The trail from trailhead to saddle gains about 600' and takes about 45 minutes. The walk to Anderson Butte from the saddle takes 25 minutes and gains about 500'.

The right fork drops about 100' and then ascends about 0.5 mile through a long meadow with spectacular views of Mt. Baker from the upper stretch. The path then plunges through a notch and drops steeply on a wooded ridge for about 0.5 mile, finally opening into a small meadow. There is a sign where the trail forks again; the right fork becomes a scrabble trail and progresses down through timber and talus about 0.5 mile, breaking into meadow around Anderson Lake. This is a very nice campsite with an excellent view of Mt. Baker. One can fish in the lake; bear or deer are often seen.

The left fork of the trail goes up over a rocky knoll about 200' and then drops about 500' via several switchbacks to lower Watson Lake. Fishing here is good. A scrabble trail follows the north side of the lake, crosses to upper Watson Lake, and continues around the north side of the upper lake to its east end. Tread is faint or non-existent in places.

These lakes are a deep, beautiful blue, with fine views of Bacon Peak. From the Anderson Butte saddle, it is about 1.5 miles (40 minutes) to Watson Lake and a bit less to Anderson Lake. Wood and water are plentiful at both lakes. Camping and fires at both Watson Lakes are allowed only at designated locations, of which there are nine (on the north side of the lower lake, between the lakes, and at the east end of the upper lake).

Hikers in good condition may visit all the lakes in a one-day trip. This is a very beautiful area, being visited more since the logging road improved access.

(August 1981)

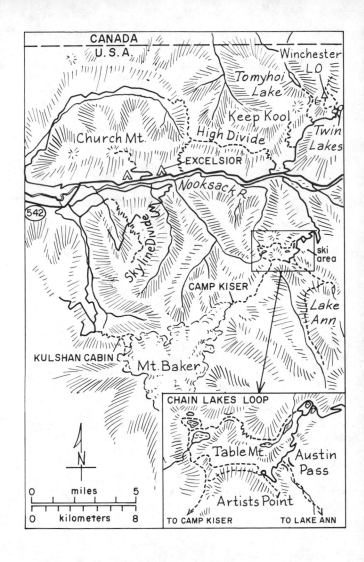

CANADA
U.S.A.
Winchester
LO
Tomyhoi
Lake
Keep Kool
High Divide
Church Mt.
EXCELSIOR
Twin
Lakes
Nooksack R.
542
Skyline Divide
CAMP KISER
Lake
Ann
KULSHAN CABIN
Mt. Baker
ski
area

N

0   miles   5
0   kilometers   8

CHAIN LAKES LOOP
Table Mt.
Austin
Pass
Artists Point
TO CAMP KISER   TO LAKE ANN

6

MOUNT BAKER–
SNOQUALMIE
NATIONAL FOREST
Northwest Section

Trails:
Church Mountain
Excelsior Ridge
Chain Lakes (Table Mountain)
Keep Kool Trail
Gold Run Pass
Winchester Mountain
High Pass (Twin Lakes)
Skyline Trail
Camp Kiser and The Portals
Lake Ann
Kulshan Cabin

CHURCH MOUNTAIN

DESTINATION: Church Mountain lookout site, 6100'
TRAIL LENGTH: 4.5 miles
WALKING TIME: 3 hours in
              1¾ hours out
TRAILHEAD ELEVATION 2600'
ALTITUDE GAIN, including ups and downs: 3500'
TOPOGRAPHIC SHEETS: USGS: Mt. Baker
                    Green Trails: Mt. Baker

Drive up State Highway 542 to 5.6 miles east of the town of Glacier. Turn north and drive up the logging road 2.5 miles to the trailhead. There is parking for 12 to 15 cars at the road end.

The last half mile of logging road must be walked. One creek en route to the trailhead cascades over the road and might be difficult to cross during the spring high-water runoff. After leaving the roadbed, the trail switchbacks up moderately through a patch cut, then through deep woods. At about 2 miles, it contours north, still through deep forest. At about 3 miles, it breaks into subalpine meadow. From here the trail passes through 1½ miles of alpine gardens. The trail turns west, climbs onto a ridge and switchbacks up the ridge to the old lookout site, about 4.5 miles from the trailhead. A toilet and old storage shed were in fair condition as of 1972; the latter could serve as emergency shelter. From this point, spectacular views can be had of Mt. Baker, Shuksan, and the Picket Range. The views of Mt. Baker are marred by extensive patch cutting on its north side. There are nice camping areas in the meadow below the lookout; there is also a level campsite just east of the last switchback below the top.

Two small pocket lakes lie about half a mile northwest of

the trail end; reaching them is not difficult, particularly if there is enough snow to glissade. The summit of Church Mountain is almost directly to the west; climbing either of its peaks from the lookout site does not appear difficult.

Experienced hikers may wish to contour to the right between the entrance and the middle of the meadow, and climb steeply to the east to the ridge. Do not attempt to climb the steep rock to the north. The ridge crest leads east; it is possible to walk the ridge for about ten miles to Yellow Aster Butte. One can descend either of the Excelsior Trails, the Welcome Pass Trail, or the Keep Kool Trail. There is a trail between Excelsior and Welcome passes. The rest of the ridge has no trail but is not difficult.

Vast fields of glacier lilies turn the upper meadows a golden yellow as the snow recedes. Other wildflowers often seen along the trail are the yellow violet, calypso orchid, and the trillium. Marmots are common in the meadows.

(July 1972)

EXCELSIOR RIDGE

DESTINATION: Excelsior Pass, 5350'
TRAIL LENGTH: 2.6 miles
WALKING TIME (light pack): 1¾ hours in
        1¼ hours out
TRAILHEAD ELEVATION 4150' (Canyon Creek)
ALTITUDE GAIN, including ups and downs: 1300'
FEATURE: Excelsior Ridge, 5800' (high point)
TOPOGRAPHIC SHEETS: USGS: Mt. Baker
                      Green Trails: Mt. Baker

There are two access routes to this area; both start by taking State Highway 542 from Bellingham. One trailhead is on the Mt. Baker Highway, 7.7 miles east of the gas station in Glacier. This trail switchbacks up steeply with no view for over 2 miles, breaks out briefly into meadow, then goes back into forest until 3.5 miles. About 100 feet of trail is obliterated, and one must go north-northeast to pick it up. The 4-mile sign is about 200' below the summit of Excelsior Pass. The site of the old lookout is a steep 0.25 mile to the right. The new High Divide Trail to Welcome Pass contours on the south side of the lookout ridge beneath the Excelsior Lookout site. The time up by this route is 3 hours to the lookout; time down 1½ hours. Altitude gain is 3,500'.

Camping in Excelsior Pass is pleasant, with splendid views of Shuksan and Baker. There are lovely wildflowers in July and August and brilliant fall color in late September and early October. There is plenty of water along the trail; wood is scarce in the meadows.

The easier access route is to take the Canyon Creek Road 2.2 miles past Glacier and drive 14.8 miles to a parking lot on the right, where there is space for 15 to 20 cars. The trail starts immediately north of this parking area, cutting across slash to the woods in about 200 yards. From the trailhead it is roughly 0.7 mile to the junction of the Canyon Ridge Trail, 0.8 mile to Damfino Lakes, and 2.6 miles to Excelsior Pass. The Damfino Lakes are too shallow for fish; there are nice scenic campsites at the lakes but also lots of bugs. From the lakes, the trail switchbacks up through forest to break into meadow below Excelsior Pass about 1.5 miles beyond the lakes; an additional 0.5-mile walk brings one to the pass with substantially less altitude gain, and with a saving of approximately 1.5 miles, from the first access route described. Bear and mountain goats are seen in this area occasionally. There is some wood but no water (except from snowfields) along the last half mile of trail and the ridge top. The lower portions of this trail can be quite muddy.

The High Divide Trail between Excelsior Pass and Welcome Pass was completed in 1971. It is approximately 5 miles long with 1000′ altitude gain and loss in each direction. The only water sources on this rather dry trail are (1) a spring one mile west of Welcome Pass; (2) a large tarn on the south side of the trail about 0.3 mile from Welcome Pass; (3) a shallow tarn 0.4 mile from Welcome Pass. There are several level areas for camping, but no water after snowfields have melted. Walking time one way is 2¾ hours.

The trail is in excellent condition and marked by tree-trunk cairns where it may be difficult to find. This is a magnificent trail, particularly lovely in early October at the height of the fall color. Though almost exterminated by hunters, bears are occasionally seen in this area. There are a number of areas along the route where one can sit and enjoy the splendid 360-degree panorama of mountains. From the Welcome Pass end, there is a splendid view of the Nooksack Cirque under Mount Shuksan, and of the crests of Icy and Ruth mountains.

It is also possible to walk the trailless ridge west as far as Church Mountain without much difficulty.

(October 1966—south approach; September 1979—north approach)

CHAIN LAKES (TABLE MOUNTAIN)

DESTINATION: Bagley Lake, 4200′

TRAIL LENGTH: 6.5 miles (add 2.5 miles to complete the loop on the road)

WALKING TIME (light pack): 3½ hours for the loop

TRAILHEAD ELEVATION 5100′ (road end on Kulshan Ridge)

ALTITUDE GAIN including ups and downs: 800′

FEATURES: High point, 5300' between Bagley and Chain
lakes; Iceberg Lake, 4800'
TOPOGRAPHIC SHEETS: USGS: Mt. Shuksan
Green Trails: Mt. Shuksan

Since this is a loop trail, there are alternative starting
points. For less altitude gain, start at the Artist's Point parking lot trailhead and end up at the trailhead to the right of the
road 0.1 mile from the Heather Meadow Ski Shop. If only
one car is available, the 2.5 miles between the trailheads
means an hour's walk, but it's usually possible to catch a ride
with someone driving up. The data given above assumes a
start at the higher trailhead.

From the Artist's Point parking lot, where there is substantial parking space, several trails gradually converge to
the west into one trail that contours under the south side of
Table Mountain, reaching a pass and trail fork at about 1.1
miles; turn right (north) at this fork. From here, it is 0.5 mile
losing about 400' to Little Mazama Lake, one of the four
Chain Lakes. This section of trail passes the trail descending
from Table Mountain. From the trailhead it is roughly 2.2
miles to the isthmus between Iceberg Lake and Galena Lake,
where there is a very nice campsite with adequate water but
limited wood. There are trout in the lakes.

From the lakes, the trail goes east, gaining about 800' to
reach the crest of the ridge north of Table Mountain at about
3.7 miles. There are spectacular views of Mt. Baker and Mt.
Shuksan from this ridge; indeed, mountains are in view almost all along this trail. From the ridge crest, the trail descends sharply in switchbacks over fairly rough talus in
places, losing about 1000' before reaching upper Bagley
Lake at about 5 miles. The trail then stays level along the
north side of the lakes until it reaches the trailhead near the
ski development.

Fall color is spectacular in the area. Camping areas are at all of the Chain Lakes. Bagley Lake is not very good for camping, nor are there quality campsites elsewhere in the loop. Marmots and pica are frequently seen. The trail is crowded, particularly on weekends and holidays.

This is an excellent trail for scenery, and is one of the few trails in the North Cascades where most of the altitude gain is by vehicle rather than on foot. For the less vigorous, a return from the Chain Lakes directly to Artist's Point makes a pleasant walk of just over four miles, gaining only 500' round-trip.

Another alternative is to make a loop from the Artist's Point trailhead via Table Mountain. The east trailhead starts north about 0.1 mile along the trail to Chain Lakes and goes up steeply to the north; it then turns and climbs the southeast slope of Table Mountain in exposed switchbacks. The altitude gain from the parking lot is about 500' to the flat top of Table Mountain. From here, the trail goes east about one mile. Near the west end, it is necessary to descend a 300-foot-long, moderately steep, semi-permanent snow slope; an ice axe and the ability to use it are essential for this snow traverse. Snow might not be present very late in the season some years. Be careful on the switchbacks on both sides of Table Mountain. Remember that snow is on the peak in places, much if not all of the summer season.

On the southwest side of Table Mountain are two small, beautiful tarns with fantastic views of Mt. Shuksan in one direction and Mt. Baker in the other. Level areas nearby are ideal campsites. The trail descending the west side of Table Mountain is marked near the top with cairns. Fairly steep, it switchbacks over talus, and, in places, is in disrepair. The trail on the west loses about 800' to the Chain Lake Trail. The hiker must regain about 300' returning on the circle loop to the Artist's Point parking lot, perhaps making a short trip

from the trail junction to the Chain Lakes. The 3.5-mile
Table Mountain loop takes about 2½ hours to walk; elevation gained is about 1000'. The hiker can retrace steps and
avoid the descent on the west, in which case the altitude gain
is only 500'.

There is no wood on top of Table Mountain; campfires are
both impractical and environmentally unsound; if camping,
carry a stove. Incredible views of the surrounding mountains
and valleys make this a fabulous, relatively short walk.

(October 1969)

KEEP KOOL TRAIL

DESTINATION: Yellow Aster saddle, 5300'

TRAIL LENGTH: 2.7 miles

WALKING TIME: 2½ hours in
              1½ hours out

TRAILHEAD ELEVATION 3100'

ALTITUDE GAIN, including ups and downs: 2250'

FEATURES: Tomyhoi Mountain, 7451' (high point)
          Yellow Aster Butte, 6100'

TOPOGRAPHIC SHEETS: USGS: Mt. Shuksan
                    Green Trails: Mt. Shuksan

Turn left off the Mt. Baker Highway immediately after the
highway maintenance shops; continue up the Twin Lakes
road for 3 miles. There is parking for 5 or 6 cars across the
road from the trailhead. The trail follows an abandoned logging road for about 0.25 mile, then switchbacks up moderately through deep forest until it reaches meadows at 2.2
miles. At about one mile there is a very fine tree-framed view
of Mt. Shuksan.

The trail continues across the lower meadow, which is bisected by a stream. There is a nice campsite here, but better ones are to come. The footpath, not always easily seen, goes north-northwest up a fairly steep slope to the ridge leading into the saddle between Yellow Aster Butte to the north and an unnamed butte to the south. In this saddle are six or seven tarns with level areas nearby: these are exceedingly scenic camping sites. Wood is limited.

From the Yellow Aster saddle, about 2.7 miles from the trailhead, one can climb Yellow Aster Butte, a cross-country meadow walk gaining about 800'. Wildflowers in the Yellow Aster Butte area are profuse and splendid. From Yellow Aster Butte, it is not difficult to climb the ridge and tor to the north. From the saddle, after climbing an unnamed butte to the south, it is possible to follow the trailless ridge to the top of the Welcome Pass Trail and descend via that route or proceed west on the High Divide Trail.

A scrabble trail continues from the saddle northwest, ascending progressively higher ridges to the base of Tomyhoi Peak.

In the upper Yellow Aster Meadows, mining excavations and the remnants of mining equipment recall gold-seekers.

Ptarmigan are common in the area, and mountain goats frequent the high ridges. Views from any of the high places are extraordinary. Mount Larrabee, American Border Peak, and Canadian Border Peak can be seen to the north. Winchester Mountain lies to the immediate east; beyond are the high peaks of the Picket Range in the North Cascades National Park. The twin summits of Goat Mountain can be seen to the southeast. Beyond Goat Mountain, Mt. Shuksan rears its splendid head. To the south is the snow cone of Mt. Baker. Below, to the north, is Tomyhoi Lake. It is hard to keep one's cool in so breathtaking a place!

(1972)

GOLD RUN PASS

DESTINATION: Tomyhoi Lake, 3700′

TRAIL LENGTH: 4 miles

WALKING TIME (light pack): 2½ hours one way

TRAILHEAD ELEVATION 3700′

ALTITUDE GAIN, including ups and downs: 1800′

FEATURE: Gold Run Pass, 5400′ (high point)

TOPOGRAPHIC SHEETS: USGS: Mt. Shuksan
Green Trails: Mt. Shuksan

Turn north off State Highway 542 13.1 miles past the gas station at Glacier, just beyond the highway maintenance shops. Drive up this narrow, rough road 4.6 miles to the trailhead. There is parking space for 6 or 7 cars in the area.

The path ascends about 400′ in switchbacks through a pleasant meadow, then plunges into forest. It runs level a half mile to the west, then ascends out of woods into meadow below Gold Run Pass. Take the well-used trail to the crest of the pass at 2 miles; an overgrown way trail also rambles through the upper meadow, leading to abandoned mining claims. The time up is just over one hour and the altitude gain about 1700′; the time down is 45 minutes. From the pass are most impressive views of Mt. Baker to the south and of Larrabee, American Border, and Canadian Border peaks to the north. A side trip 0.1 mile west of the pass brings the hiker to a knob; Tomyhoi Lake is seen below. This is the best view point on the trail.

It is two miles from the pass down to Tomyhoi Lake. The time down is about an hour, and time up about an hour and 25 minutes. The trail drops steeply on switchbacks, passing a campsite at about 0.5 mile. It then parallels a stream and crosses a meadow. There are several campsites in this area.

The path leaves the southwest end of the meadow, passes by a moss-covered, tree-supporting rock, and descends through forest 0.4 mile. The trail then breaks into the open and crosses a creek several times. Next to a creek just before the lake there are two campsites. The trail bears left here; a scrabble trail reaches the lakeshore, where there are 6 or 7 campsites. Wood and water are no problem at any of the camps. A rough way trail continues around the south side of the lake. In late fall, the lake may be as low as 20' below high-water mark. Larabee, American and Canadian Border peaks are visible, but there are unattractive clearcuts at the west end of the lake. The lake is visited mostly by fishermen.

The roughly 1800' must be regained en route back to the trailhead. This is one of the few North Cascade trails where walking time is the same in both directions.

Experienced wilderness travelers can cut off the trail about 0.6 mile north of Gold Run Pass and proceed cross-country to the Low Pass area. They can return via Twin Lakes.

(November 1978)

WINCHESTER MOUNTAIN

DESTINATION: Winchester lookout, 6521'

TRAIL LENGTH: 1.6 miles

WALKING TIME (light pack): 1 hour one way

TRAILHEAD ELEVATION 5200' (Twin Lakes)

ALTITUDE GAIN, including ups and downs: 1600'

TOPOGRAPHIC SHEETS: USGS: Mt. Shuksan
Green Trails: Mt. Shuksan

To reach the trailhead, turn left just past the highway maintenance buildings on State Highway 542, and proceed to the road end between the two Twin Lakes. There is parking for 25 or 30 cars here. In 1980, the road was open all the way to the lake, and it probably will remain open because of mining and logging on private lands in the area. The road is rough and steep with sharp curves, and should be driven only by experienced mountain drivers, preferably in cars with high clearance. Those who don't want to drive the road can park at the Gold Run Pass trailhead and walk about 2 miles of road to the Winchester Mountain trailhead; this walk gains 1500'.

The trailhead for both Winchester Mountain and Gargett Mine starts at the west end of the isthmus between the Twin Lakes. The trail forks in 0.1 mile, with the right fork leading to High and Low Passes, the Gargett Mine, and Mt. Larrabee, and the left fork leading to Winchester Mountain. The latter trail goes up moderately steeply through subalpine meadow. Early in the season, steep snowslopes without run-out block the trail in several places. Well into August hikers should carry an ice axe, and know how to kick steps in the snow and how to do a self-arrest, before attempting snow traverses. Later in the year, the only hazardous area is the 100-foot traverse of the "Red Band" of rock just before the ridge crest.

In 1980, the Winchester lookout was in deplorable shape with broken windows, loose shutters, dirt and debris. Nonetheless, it offers shelter from the inclement weather, which is frequent here. Perhaps someone will improve the lookout soon.

The 360-degree panorama includes: American and Canadian Border peaks, Mt. Larrabee, the Pleiades, the Pickets, the two peaks of Goat Mountain, Mt. Shuksan, and Mt. Baker. Tomyhoi Lake lies below to the west. Twin Lakes are azure pools to the east, Silesia Valley is to the north, and Swamp Creek to the south.

After the snow melts, there is no water on Winchester

Mountain. Those planning to stay on top for the sunset or sunrise should carry water and a good tent.

There are developed camping sites in the Twin Lakes area, which is good for family camping, although often crowded since it can be reached by car. The sunrise and sunset views of Mt. Baker reflected in the southern lake, and views of the Canadian mountains reflected in the northern lake, are quite elegant.

Another option for hikers is to take the gated road east of the north Twin Lake and follow the Silesia Creek Trail into the valley below. Cross-country hikers can head up to the southeast to an unnamed knob (above the picnic area) at 6100' and to a more scenic knob 400' higher and a half mile to the southeast. Climbers can also approach the north peak of Goat Mountain at 6891' via this route.

From the ridge crest before the lookout, at least early in the year when snow fills the gullies on the west side of Winchester Mountain, experienced cross-country travelers can descend from the ridge to below Low Pass, and cross country to the trail to Tomyhoi Lake, ascend Gold Run Pass, and return to the Swamp Creek Road.

(September 1980)

HIGH PASS (TWIN LAKES)

DESTINATION: Gargett Mine, 5800'

TRAIL LENGTH: 2 miles

WALKING TIME (light pack): 1¾ hours in
1 hour out

TRAILHEAD ELEVATION 5200' (Twin Lakes)

ALTITUDE GAIN, including ups and downs: 1000'

FEATURES: High Pass, 6000'; Ridge at end of trail, 6700'
(high point)

TOPOGRAPHIC SHEETS: USGS: Mt. Shuksan
                     Green Trails: Mt. Shuksan

See the Winchester Mountain Trail for information on reaching the trailhead.

After the junction 0.1 mile from the combined trailhead, turn right (north). The footpath contours under Winchester Peak, reaching Low Pass 1.5 miles from the trailhead and proceeding up to High Pass at 2.3 miles. The trail forks at High Pass; the left fork descends about 200' in 0.2 mile to the Gargett Mine. The trail to the right ascends the ridge; tread becomes less apparent and disappears at the ridge top, about 0.8 mile from the junction, having gained about 750' after High Pass. Another 45 minutes is required to reach the trail end on the ridge crest. There are blueberries in the area. The alpine floral display is quite splendid in season, and includes dwarf fireweed. There is evidence of mining throughout the area; old pipes and timbers mark the site of a glory hole on the shoulder of the Pleiades, a seven-spired peak near Mt. Larrabee. Beyond the ridge crest, a scramble requiring rock-climbing experience allows the hiker to reach the summit of Mt. Larrabee (Red Mountain).

There are a few springs along the trail and water is available from permanent snowfields. Wood is very scarce. There are fair campsites at High Pass. Grouse and ptarmigan are seen frequently; bear, mountain goats and deer are seen occasionally.

All trails in the Twin Lakes area are closed to motor vehicles. Current logging on patented mine claims may well leave scars for many years. The gold mines in the area may be reactivated. The Forest Service does not plan to maintain the road past the Tomyhoi Lake trailhead. If the timber or the ore run out, the road beyond that point will revert to a trail.

(September 1970)

SKYLINE TRAIL

DESTINATION: 5900'

TRAIL LENGTH: 3.5 miles

WALKING TIME (light pack): 2 hours in
1½ hours out

TRAILHEAD ELEVATION 4400'

ALTITUDE GAIN, including ups and downs: 2000'

FEATURE: Knob, south end of Skyline Divide, 6563' (high
point)

TOPOGRAPHIC SHEETS: USGS: Mt. Baker
Green Trails: Mt. Baker

Drive 1.1 miles on the Mt. Baker Highway past the gas station in Glacier, turn right on the Glacier Creek Road, and immediately thereafter turn left on Dead Horse Road. Drive 12.9 miles up this back road to the trailhead, where there is a large parking lot.

The trail switchbacks up through deep hemlock forest, remaining in the woods for about a mile. Over the next mile is a transition from timbered ridge to open meadow. At about 1.8 miles, a short side trip to the northeast leads to a scenic overlook above the Nooksack valley. Two miles from the trailhead, the footpath reaches the ridge crest, having gained 1500'. The walk to this point takes one hour. From here, a quarter-mile stroll east along the ridge top gives excellent views.

The trail goes south toward Mt. Baker. It meanders up and down for about 1½ miles over ridges, bluffs and knolls, gaining (and losing) about 500'. The trail ends at about 3½ miles in a small notch, marked with a cairn.

Damage from shortcutting switchbacks is growing in the meadows. Please stay on the trail!

Once the high open meadow is reached, the views in all directions are breathtaking! To the north is the high ridge extending from Church Mountain on the west to Winchester Mountain on the east. To the east are the rugged contours of Mt. Shuksan, one of the most beautiful mountains in the world. Looming to the south is the heavily glaciated Mt. Baker.

Both water and firewood are scarce, although snowbanks in the early summer are a water source. Water can also be obtained by descending about 500' to a small stream near the trailend. Given these limitations, there are excellent campsites along the ridge with spectacular views.

Unfortunately, mosquitoes, deerflies, and yellow jackets are prevalent. If the bugs are not too severe, the Skyline Trail is an excellent day hike for families; children over five should be able to walk to the end of the maintained trail without difficulty.

Most hikers will stop at the notch, then retrace their steps to the trailhead. Experienced alpinists have three options: (1) Descend slightly, continue around the point of a bluff, and meadow-walk 1.5 or 2.0 miles further, where the route reaches the precipitous Chowder Ridge on the north side of Mt. Baker. (2) Go west for about one mile, losing 750' on an unmaintained but clear-cut trail to reach a beautiful level alpine meadow with a small stream (an ideal isolated camping spot). (3) Follow a scrabble trail up along the Skyline Ridge to the south. It is about 0.3 mile to the first knob, 0.5 mile to the second knob, and one mile with a gain of about 750' to the third knob. From here, the hiker can continue on scrabble trail cross-country south about one mile. Then either a steep contour, or a drop, and a climb back of several hundred feet, will find the hiker in the meadows north of Chowder Ridge, from which he can return to the trail via the first route above.

CAMP KISER AND THE PORTALS

DESTINATION: The Portals, 6500'

TRAIL LENGTH: 6.5 miles

WALKING TIME (light pack): 2¾ hours one way

TRAILHEAD ELEVATION 5100'

ALTITUDE GAIN, including ups and downs: 1700'

SEASON FOR USE: August 1 to mid-October

FEATURE: Coleman Pinnacle, 6414'

TOPOGRAPHIC SHEETS: USGS: Mt. Shuksan; Mt. Baker
Green Trails: Mt. Shuksan; Mt. Baker

Drive past the Mt. Baker ski development on State Highway 542 to the end at the Artist's Point parking area, where there is space for perhaps 80 cars. Several way trails start at the west end of the lot, gradually merging into one trail that traverses the south side of Table Mountain, losing altitude then regaining it by the Chain Lakes Trail junction, 1.1 miles from the trailhead. This section of trail is popular and heavily used; however, most people either stop at the junction or turn north to Chain Lakes or the Table Mountain loop. The less apparent trail to Coleman Pinnacle, Camp Kiser (a misnomer since no camp is in this area), and The Portals (the rock and ice gateway to the slopes of Mt. Baker), drops to the left. The footpath contours under the rock ridge to the south for about half a mile, then climbs to the crest of a broad ridge.

A word of caution: This high ridge is exposed. Winds are common, and there is a significant risk of hypothermia. Only those experienced in traversing snow slopes and prepared for sudden inclement weather should walk this trail. For properly prepared hikers, the main trail is splendid, and side trips to lofty vistas beckon in many directions. Be sure to carry an ice axe, and take lots of extra clothes. Allow a full day if at all possible, to contemplate the fabulous scenery and to walk off the main trail.

The high trail is often lost under snow; without vibram lug boots and an ice axe you should not attempt it. Those experienced in self-arrest and wilderness high travel can proceed west on the south side of Ptarmigan Ridge. About three miles from the trailhead, the footpath reaches the south side of the Coleman Pinnacle (a Class 2 rock climb). From the Pinnacle, after the snow has melted, a very high, brilliant blue-green lake is visible half a mile to the south. Depending on snow conditions, this lake can be reached by either a snow traverse or cross-country travel, partly on a way trail. The area around the lake is exceptionally beautiful.

After Coleman Pinnacle, the trail passes through Camp Kiser, not a specific place but a section of the subalpine meadows. Losing altitude, and passing two campsites about 5 miles from the trailhead, the trail gradually peters out at about 6½ miles in a lava field near The Portals. The best views of Mt. Baker are 200 yards away from the rock on a permanent snow field. Beyond this point, only mountaineers should proceed across the technical ice and rock.

This is one of the most splendid walks in the North Cascades. There may be crowds at the trailhead, but there are few people beyond 1½ miles. Mt. Shuksan and Mt. Baker are in view throughout the walk. When the heather blooms around the Chain Lake junction, and in late September and early October when the fall color is at its height, views are also most impressive. From the Coleman Pinnacle you can see most of the great peaks of the North Cascades. To the north is Excelsior Ridge, Yellow Aster Butte, Winchester Mountain, Mt. Larrabee, and American and Canadian Border peaks. To the east, Ruth Mountain, and beyond it the Pickets. To the south, Blum and Hagen mountains, and in the far distance Glacier Peak. Pica, marmots, and ptarmigan are common. Occasionally, mountain goats and deer will be seen.

Campsites are limited. The eastern portion of Ptarmigan Ridge is flat but exposed. Later in the season there are campsites near an ice-fed lake south of the Pinnacle. (September 1977)

LAKE ANN

DESTINATION: Lake Ann, 4900′

TRAIL LENGTH: 4 miles

WALKING TIME (full pack): 2¼ hours one way

TRAILHEAD ELEVATION 4700′

ALTITUDE GAIN, including ups and downs: 1000′

TOPOGRAPHIC SHEETS: USGS: Mt. Shuksan
                    Green Trails: Mt. Shuksan

Drive State Highway 542 1.6 miles beyond the Mt. Baker ski facilities. Parking for about 10 cars is at the Austin Pass trailhead. The trail loses 500′ in switchbacks in the first half mile, to reach the valley floor. It follows the headwaters of Swift Creek southeast, losing altitude gradually, and after about 1½ miles crosses the Recreation Area boundary. The trail area within the Recreation Area is closed to overnight camping.

After traversing lovely meadow beneath Shuksan Arm to the northeast and Kulshan Ridge to the southwest, the trail reaches a junction at 3 miles. The right fork leads down the poorly maintained Swift Creek Trail. The more easily seen left fork switchbacks up to the east, gaining 1000′ and topping out on a ridge crest above Lake Ann. A short 200′ descent leads to the lake, 4 miles from the trailhead. There are a number of campsites around the lake, which is quite deep. Wood is scarce; a stove should be carried for cooking. Lake Ann is the base camp for mountaineers climbing Mt. Shuksan by the standard route; on weekends and holidays, the area is often overflowing with mountain climbers; campsites are at a premium.

It is possible to follow the scrabble trail from Lake Ann up toward Fisher's Chimneys. Those without climbing experience should not go very far, since the trail narrows and is quite exposed a mile or so beyond the lake.

The National Park boundary is about half a mile east of Lake Ann. The entire Lake Ann Trail lies within a game reserve. Pets are prohibited, and firearms may not be discharged anywhere along the trail between Austin Pass and Mt. Shuksan.

Views from Lake Ann east to Mt. Shuksan are quite impressive. Avalanches from the Upper Curtis Glacier occur frequently, making a noise like distant thunder. From the ridge above the lake, Mt. Baker is seen to the west.

Geology

Volcanic flows, presumably from Mt. Baker, are seen at Austin Pass. The rocks display columnar jointing and horizontal-flow banding. The rock is a porphyritic andesite. At 4400′, in one of many stream channels that cross the trail, is an outcrop of Chilliwack metavolcanic rock. The dark, fairly massive Chilliwack rocks also form the northeastern wall of the valley along Shuksan Arm.

At the Swift Creek log bridge is the first outcrop of the granodiorite Lake Ann stock. This rock can be seen in outcrops along the trail from here to Lake Ann; studies indicate it is one of the youngest exposed igneous intrusive rocks in the world.

The Shuksan metamorphic suite, formed by the Darrington phyllite and Shuksan greenschist, is exposed northeast of Lake Ann. There are no similar rocks in the northwest. The upper portion of Mt. Shuksan (the greenschist) may be a segment of sea floor basalt that has been metamorphosed along the boundary between colliding plates.

(The author is indebted to Eric James of the Department of Geology, Western Washington University, from whose master's thesis the geologic information was obtained.)

(August 1964)

KULSHAN CABIN

DESTINATION: Kulshan Cabin, 4700'

WALKING TIME (full pack): 1¼ hours in
45 minutes out

TRAILHEAD ELEVATION 3700'

ALTITUDE GAIN, including ups and downs: 1100'

FEATURES: Coleman Glacier snout, 4700'
Heliotrope Ridge, 6000'

TOPOGRAPHIC SHEETS: USGS: Mt. Baker
Green Trails: Mt. Baker

Drive State Highway 542 to Glacier. Turn south about half a mile east of Glacier; follow the initially paved logging road 8.1 miles to the trailhead, where a parking lot can accommodate about 35 cars.

This heavily used trail ascends gradually through deep forest. At about 1.5 miles, Kulshan Creek must be crossed; there is no bridge. In late spring and early summer, this crossing is difficult and can be hazardous.

The Kulshan Cabin, originally constructed by the Mt. Baker Club in Bellingham, has a stove, table, stretcher, and other amenities on the ground floor. Upstairs are bunk beds. Seven to ten campsites are within a hundred yards of the cabin. Water is available from a small creek to the west.

The cabin can usually be reached by late May or early June; the meadows above do not open until mid-July. Wood is quite limited; carry stoves for cooking. Do not expect solitude; this is one of the most heavily used trails in the North Cascades!

The cabin and its surrounding areas are base camps for mountaineers, who usually arise between midnight and 2 a.m. to begin their climb; these early departures often disturb campers sleeping nearby. The main trail crosses the creek 0.1 mile above the cabin. The trail forks 0.3 mile further; the right fork leads to the climber's scrabble trail up the hogback. This route, for the sure-footed only, goes south to a lobe of the Coleman Glacier, at an altitude of roughly 6000'. Views from here are quite splendid. The average hiker should not go further. The experienced cross-country traveler with an ice axe can continue up and west to a green knoll 0.9 mile from the top of the hogback. In late July, there are blooming lupine at this point. It is an ideal place for a picnic. The ability to kick steps in snow is required to visit this area safely.

From the trail junction, the left fork continues a half mile through alpine meadow to an overlook where the hiker can gaze down onto the broken ice of the Coleman Glacier. Ice-clad Mt. Baker looms above. It is a splendid place.

There are camping areas near the top of the hogback, close to the ice, and there is a good campsite near the junction of the hogback and glacier view trails.

From the Kulshan Cabin, there is also a scrabble trail going east. Several creeks must be forded, and the trail is slippery in places, particularly after rain. About 0.7 mile from the cabin, this trail ends at the lateral moraine of the

Coleman Glacier. A scramble over glacial debris allows access to the ice at the snout of the glacier, where the hiker can see a number of siracs (ice pinnacles).

Walking time from the cabin to the Coleman Glacier is 25 minutes; from the cabin to the glacier overlook is 30 minutes; to the top of the hogback is one hour.

Hikers without companions, mountaineering experience, ropes, crampons, and ice axes should never venture on to the Coleman (or any other) Glacier. To do so is to invite serious injury and disaster!

Carry binoculars: you can frequently see mountain goats on Bastile Ridge, across the valley from the glacier overlook. Magnification is also helpful for watching mountain climbers on the slopes of Koma Kulshan.

(July 1978)

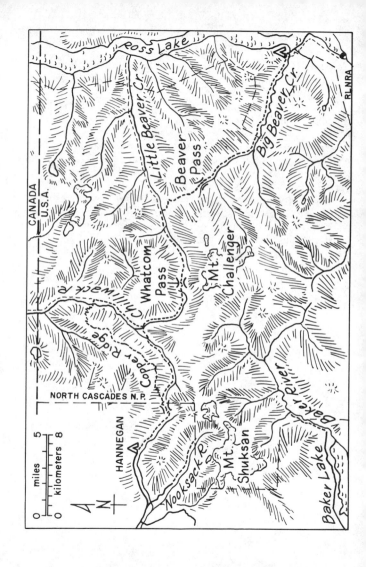

7

NORTH CASCADES NATIONAL PARK
North Section

Trails:
Baker River
Nooksack Cirque
Hannegan Pass—Whatcom Pass
Copper Ridge (Hannegan Mountain)
Big Beaver—Whatcom Pass

BAKER RIVER

DESTINATION: Sulphide Camp, 900′
TRAIL LENGTH: 2.4 miles
WALKING TIME (light pack): 1¼ hours one way
TRAILHEAD ELEVATION 780′
ALTITUDE GAIN, including ups and downs, 350′
SEASON FOR USE: March until December
TOPOGRAPHIC SHEETS: USGS: Mt. Shuksan
Green Trails: Mt. Shuksan

From the NCH, drive up the Baker Lake road to the bridge at Sulfur Creek just inside the Mt. Baker–Snoqualmie National Forest boundary. Follow the main paved road to the right after the bridge; a mile further, pass the Koma Kulshan ranger station on the left fork of the road (do not go right to Baker Dam). Continue on this paved, then graveled, road, crossing the Boulder Creek Bridge then passing the access road to the Baker Lake Resort. Swift Creek Bridge is 0.2 mile past the resort. From the bridge, it is 5.3 miles to the marked turnoff to the left (east); road quality deteriorates after the turnoff. Drive 0.3 mile to a junction. Straight ahead 0.1 mile is a trail shelter called Griner's Cabin.

Turn right; after 0.1 mile, turn left and continue 0.3 mile on rough road to the trailhead. A tenth of a mile before the trailhead there is space for 8 or 10 cars to park off the road.

The Baker River Trail is easily accessible from the road end. For orientation before the walk, the hiker can wander along the river or follow the old roadbed that leads east between the trail and the river. The surrounding peaks and ridges can be seen better from the river than from the forested trailhead.

At the trailhead there is a large Park Service sign, which incorrectly indicates that there is a bridge over the Baker River that allows access to the south side of Baker Lake.

Deep and glorious forest is a feature of this trail. At the

trailhead there are two splendid western red cedar trees. Moss is everywhere; sword ferns often grow from the trees, making this a true rain forest. Through the forest at the start of the trail are views of Hagan Mountain to the southeast.

At 0.5 mile, the footpath crosses a sandy flood plain, then goes over an immense fallen cedar. At one mile the trail crosses a creek. Near the crossing there are excellent examples of the nurse-tree phenomenon. First, there are large trees growing from the top of a huge log, through which the trail has been cut. A hundred feet further, there are hemlock seedlings growing on a cut tree to the left of the trail.

At 1.2 miles, the trail is washed out for a tenth of a mile. Cross cobbles, boulders, and gravel, fording several small creeks; the tread can be picked up slightly to the northeast of where it disappeared. The trail skirts a beaver pond at 1.6 miles; in the distance through a notch is high, snowy Pioneer Ridge. The boundary of the North Cascades National Park is at 1.7 miles; 0.2 mile beyond, the trail passes a large swamp/beaver pond. On sunny days this is a good location for eating lunch and enjoying the view.

The trail then enters deep woods. There are no views from 1.9 to 2.4 miles, until Sulphide Camp. Sulphide Camp is within the North Cascades National Park; camping permits are required, and pets are prohibited. The camp is a wide, grassy area on the west side of Sulphide Creek. There are two campsites on a small peninsula that extends into the creek and two campsites in the woods to the north, 50' and 100' from the creek. The campsites on the peninsula were silted in the great flood of December 1980. Wood supplies are limited.

The rocky bed of Sulphide Creek is about 50 yards wide; there are no bridges across the braided channels. Crossing requires a difficult ford. For this reason, the author did not check the scrabble footpath that once led from the east side of Sulphide Creek to Pass Creek some 4 miles further upriver. That trail has probably been reclaimed by the forest.

From the Sulphide campsite there are fine views to the north of a cliff of red rock, two spires to the right (Seahpo Peak), and to the left a long snow ridge on the southeast slope of Mt. Shuksan.

From the camping area it is possible with some difficulty, either following the creek bed or through the forest or both, to reach the junction of Sulphide Creek with Baker River. There is a pleasant, sunny gravel bar and a long, deep run in the Baker River which will tempt the fisherman.

The trail, usually open from March until December, can be hiked intermittently in the winter, when the surrounding peaks and ridges are more easily seen after the leaves of deciduous trees have fallen.

(January 1981)

NOOKSACK CIRQUE

DESTINATION: Nooksack Cirque, 3300'
TRAIL LENGTH: 5 miles
WALKING TIME: 2¾ hours one way
TRAILHEAD ELEVATION 2600'
ALTITUDE GAIN, including ups and downs, 700'
SEASON FOR USE: May to November
TOPOGRAPHIC SHEETS: USGS: Mt. Shuksan
                        Green Trails: Mt. Shuksan

This is a spectacular walk. It is recommended for experienced hikers capable of dealing with route-finding, poorly maintained trails, stream bed walking, and fording the Nooksack River. At high water in late spring and early summer, it may be very difficult to reach the Cirque. The best time to walk this trail is in the fall, when the river is low. Dippers (water ouzels) are often seen in and about the Nooksack River.

The access road leaves the Mt. Baker Highway (542) 0.2

mile past the highway maintenance buildings; turn left (east). Near the road is the Anderson-Bourn cabin, built about 1930 by prospector and mountain man Charlie Anderson. Two stories high and made from hand-hewed timbers, it is a relic of a bygone day.

The road forks at 1.3 miles; turn right. From the fork to the trailhead is 3 miles. There is a large Park Service sign at the trailhead and parking for 5 or 6 cars; do not attempt to drive further.

The trail goes to the right (south), crosses a creek and follows the bed of a logging road for 0.9 mile. The trail is brushy in places. At 0.4 mile, there are views to the north of the summit spire of Mt. Sefrit and a waterfall descending from the peak. To the southeast is Icy Peak, and the pinnacles of Mt. Shuksan can be seen to the south. After the road end in the patch cut, the trail deteriorates. It goes through deep woods, and is muddy in places, with tree roots in the tread. At 1.6 miles, cross a creek on a foot log.

The trail ends at the Nooksack River 2 miles from the trailhead; there is a campsite a few feet before the river bank and another 50 feet beyond. With moderate difficulty, timber bridges at this point allow access to the riverbed. There is no evidence of a trail for the next 100 yards, but by bushwhacking along the north bank of the creek, an easier foot-log crossing can be found, with a scrabble trail on the other side that goes through the woods to the National Park boundary about 0.7 mile upstream. This portion of the trail, like Topsy, appears to have "just growed." None of the deadfall has been removed; in places it is difficult to find. There are several campsites. The entrance to the trail from the river bank is not apparent, but it is marked by rock cairns.

At the point where the scrabble trail meets the river is a splendid view upriver of Icy Peak. Since scenery is limited from the forest trail, it is best to follow the riverbed upstream. Taking hip boots is highly recommended, since there are problems of crossing streams, side channels, etc., at many areas. Beyond the national park boundary there is no trail whatsoever, and the riverbed becomes the only access route to Nooksack Cirque. One mile beyond the park boundary is the bend in the river; from here it is approximately 1.25 miles to the base of the Nooksack Cirque. Walking becomes more difficult further into the Cirque; all but the most vigorous hikers will stop well before reaching the steep walls at the base of Mt. Shuksan.

It is a fabulous valley! Views improve as one proceeds upriver. The crags and spires of the Ruth Ridge, culminating in Ruth Mountain, are visible to the left. Turning south to the Cirque itself, the hiker is surrounded by peaks towering 4000'–6000'. The ice from the hanging glaciers of Mt. Shuksan occasionally tumbles and falls into the valley below, accompanied by a rumble like thunder. The headwall occupied by the East Nooksack Glacier is most impressive. Jagged Ridge extends from the Nooksack Tower on the west to Seahpo Peak on the east.

Since it is over a mile from a designated trail, camping is allowed any place in the Cirque. Wood is scarce, and because the area is ecologically fragile, fires are inappropriate; backpacker stoves should be carried.

(November 1980)

HANNEGAN PASS—WHATCOM PASS

DESTINATION: Whatcom Pass, 5206'

TRAIL LENGTH: 17.1 miles

WALKING TIME (full pack): 9–11 hours (2 days) in
8–10 hours out

TRAILHEAD ELEVATION 3100' (Hannegan)

ALTITUDE GAIN, including ups and downs: 4800' in
2600' out

FEATURES: NPS boundary, 4424'; Chilliwack ford (low point), 2468'

TOPOGRAPHIC SHEETS: USGS: Mt. Shuksan; Mt. Challenger
Green Trails: Mt. Shuksan; Mt.
Challenger

Take the Mount Baker Highway (542) east from Bellingham to Glacier. Drive 13.1 miles from Glacier to the highway
maintenance shops on the left (north) side of the road. Continue 0.3 mile further, and 100' or so before the bridge over
the Nooksack River, turn left off the pavement onto an unmarked gravel side road. The road forks at 1.4 miles; take the
left fork (the right fork is to the Nooksack Cirque). The Goat
Mountain trailhead is passed at 2.5 miles. The road ends at
5.4 miles; the last 0.1 mile of the road has been blocked off,
limiting parking and turnaround. At the trailhead is a trail
shelter and toilets.

For the first half mile, the trail follows an old wagon road;
the path then narrows and proceeds gradually upward on the
north side of the scenic, deep Ruth Creek Valley. Between 2
and 3 miles, the trail crosses several winter avalanche
slopes. At 2.9 miles a creek and slide area must be crossed;
this may be difficult early in the season. At about 3.5 miles
are the best camp sites near Hannegan Pass, in meadow just
to the right of the trail on a low ridge. There is another
campsite to the left of the trail at about 3.6 miles. Later in the
summer, water is scarce beyond the 3.5-mile mark.

It is between 4 and 4.1 miles to the summit of Hannegan
Pass, elevation 5066'. There are level areas at the pass for
camping if water can be obtained; well into July there is
water 150' east of the pass from snow fields. From the pass,
trails extend one mile north to the summit of Hannegan Peak
(6168'), and to Ruth Arm and thence to the base of Ruth
Mountain to the south. Although steep, both side routes are
not technically difficult and offer more impressive views as
altitude is gained. Mt. Sefrit (7179') is seen to the south, as is
the dome of Ruth Mountain (7106').

Leaving the pass going east, the main trail drops sharply

on switchbacks, losing about 500' in the first half mile; it then goes east over talus slopes. Five miles from the trailhead is the National Park boundary; the trail forks here. The left fork leads to Copper Ridge, Copper Ridge Lookout, and Copper Lake. A sharp right turn leads to Boundary Camp, below and 100' from the trail, immediately above the headwaters of the Chilliwack River.

The trail to Whatcom Pass goes less sharply to the right at the park boundary junction. Deep forest is entered at 5.4 miles. At 6.2 miles, the trail crosses the lower portion of Hells Gorge. Hells Gorge is a large rock slide area, starting almost at the Copper Ridge crest and extending down to the Chilliwack River. At 7.5 miles, the trail crosses Copper Creek, with waterfalls to the left, reliable sources of water. To the right, a substantial waterfall tumbles down the Chilliwack River. A designated camp is located here. The junction with the Easy Ridge trail is 9.3 miles, and the US Cabin campsite is 10.1 miles. (There used to be a substantial trail shelter at this site.) Water is available to the south of the camp. Bears and rodents are problems at this campsite, and all food must be protected.

It is 10.9 miles to the Chilliwack River. In 1980, the Park Service constructed a cable car crossing here. At 11.8 miles is Brush Creek, and 0.1 mile further is the junction with the Chilliwack trail extending north into Canada. At 14.1 miles is the watertight Graybeal shelter. This is a designated campsite. The best campsite is about 50 yards to the southwest on the bank of Brush Creek. From here, the trail climbs more steeply to Whatcom Pass (5206'). The Park Service is in the process of re-routing the trail in Whatcom Pass out of fragile areas.

At 15.8 miles is the Tapto Creek camp, the closest campsite to Whatcom Pass, 17.1 miles from the Hannegan trailhead. From the pass, the trail drops several hundred feet in meadow and then loses altitude via switchbacks, descending 2000' into the Little Beaver Valley.

On the Chilliwack Trail, it is 2.7 miles to the Indian Creek shelter, 3.5 miles to the junction with the north portion of the Copper Ridge trail, 9.1 miles to the Canadian boundary, and 10.6 miles to the trailhead at Chilliwack Lake.

Walking times are as follows: Trailhead to Hannegan Pass 2.3 hours; pass to Park boundary 0.5 hour; Park boundary to US Cabin campsite 2.3 hours, losing 2500′ from Hannegan Pass to US Cabin. From US Cabin to Graybeal is 2.3 hours, and from Graybeal to Whatcom Pass another 2.3 hours.

From Whatcom Pass, there is a scrabble trail going north to the Tapto Lakes for fishermen, and to Red Face Mountain for climbers. To the south, a walk of 0.2 mile and a gain of several hundred feet leads to a small pond with a magnificent view of Mt. Challenger to the southeast and Whatcom Peak directly south. Two faint trails lead off from this point: one stays level and leads to the access route to Mt. Challenger and Perfect Pass; the other goes fairly steeply onto the arm north of Whatcom Peak. Vistas improve as altitude is gained. Camping is not allowed in the Whatcom Pass area. (See information on Big Beaver Trail for the east access route to Whatcom Pass.)

Both Hannegan and Whatcom passes are quite splendid. The route between them is mostly deep-forest hiking and not too scenic.

(September 1972)

COPPER RIDGE (HANNEGAN MOUNTAIN)

DESTINATION: Copper Ridge Lookout, 6260′
TRAIL LENGTH: 5.2 miles
WALKING TIME (full pack): 3½ hours in
2¼ hours out
TRAILHEAD ELEVATION: 4424′ (NCNP boundary)

ALTITUDE GAIN, including ups and downs: 2750'
FEATURES: Hannegan Peak, 6186'; Egg Lake, 5200';
　　　　　Copper Lake, 5250'; Silesia Camp, 5690'
TOPOGRAPHIC SHEETS: USGS: Mt. Shuksan; Mt. Chal-
　　　　　lenger
　　　　　Green Trails: Mt. Shuksan; Mt.
　　　　　Challenger

See Hannegan Pass–Whatcom Pass for access to the National Park boundary five miles from the Hannegan
trailhead. At the boundary, the trail forks; the left fork, to
Copper Ridge, turns up and enters timber. After several
switchbacks, the trail breaks out of the timber briefly under a
large rock at about 7.6 miles, where there are views of Icy,
Ruth, and Shuksan mountains. A false top-out is 0.2 mile
further; 0.2 mile beyond that is a somewhat technical rock
and snow crossing over a slide area (the head of Hells
Gorge). A tenth of a mile further is the top of Copper Ridge.
Walking time from the junction with a full pack to the ridge
top is a little over 1.5 hours. The trail then goes up over a
knob; until August, it is possible to cut steps in the snow to
the left (north) and save some elevation gain, but there is
some exposure and an ice axe is required. The trail drops and
then immediately goes up and around a second knob. Near
the east side of the second knob a trail pole indicates Silesia
Camp to the right. There are two tent sites at the top of the
knob, excellent places to spend the night. Water can be obtained from melting snow by the trail post, 50 yards below
and northwest of the camp.

A post indicating Egg Lake Camp is 0.2 mile further down
the trail. The lake is 0.4 mile and about 300' below this post.
There are several designated campsites at the lake. (In July
1980, these tent sites were snow-free, although Egg Lake
was still 90% snow- and ice-covered.) There are mosquitoes
and no-see-ums, but deerflies are not a major problem.

The main trail goes up slightly, then drops several

hundred vertical feet, then gains roughly a thousand feet in altitude over the last mile to the Copper Ridge Lookout. From the lookout are unexcelled views, including Mt. Redoubt, Red Face Mountain, a portion of Mt. Challenger, Whatcom Peak, Mineral Mountain, Mount Blum, Icy Peak, Ruth Mountain, Mt. Shuksan, Mt. Baker, Hannegan Peak, and Copper Mountain.

Beyond the lookout, if you are interested in climbing Copper Mountain, drop to a saddle to the left. The ridge to the first summit (6855') looks fairly easy; there is further climbing, and the ridge looks more technical between the first summit and the second summit (7142').

The Copper Ridge Trail drops from the lookout through meadow and snow patches, losing 400' or so over the next 0.6 mile. There is a stopping point here where the hiker can look down 600' to Copper Lake nestled in its granite amphitheater. The trail switchbacks down steeply over a half mile to the lake. However, as of mid-July, the trail could be found only about 10% of the time, and the descent required glissading or plunge-stepping down fairly steep snow with occasional heather transits. The return involved kicking steps up steep snow slopes.

There is a trail post east of the lake saying the camp is to the left (west). There are dozens of trails in this area, certainly justifying the revegetation and rehabilitation project being attempted by the Park Service. There are several designated tent sites. The main trail turns right at the trail post; there is no visible tread for about a hundred feet. Look for a large boulder with a cairn on top, and expect the trail to go between several silver, dead trees on the left and a live tree on the right. The footpath, with tread more apparent, drops another 100', crosses the outlet creek from Copper Lake, gains a few feet, and then contours across a partially timbered area. About 0.5 mile past the lake, there is a stream ford; a very nice waterfall is 75' above.

About one mile past the lake, the trail crosses granite

talus through which runs a small creek. Follow cairns if tread cannot be found. Immediately beyond this area, switchbacks go up to the ridge top. Tread quality has been declining since Copper Lake. A half mile further, having gained a bit over 300', the footpath tops out on the ridge crest. Turn left (west) at this point and follow the trail upward another 100'. From here, the trail turns north and contours through snow and talus for half a mile, and then proceeds across a green meadow several hundred feet below a two-knobbed ridge. Beyond the knobs, the path continues north on the ridge crest for about 1.5 miles; it then descends rapidly over 3.9 miles to intersect the Chilliwack Trail in the valley to the east.

The walking time, with light pack, from Silesia Camp to the ridge top is 2.5 hours; the return time is a bit longer because of the climb up from Copper Lake. Fires are not allowed on Copper Ridge.

Loop to Hannegan Mountain

The scenery between the Copper Ridge Lookout and Hannegan Peak is superb. To reach Hannegan Mountain cross country, cut up off the trail 0.1 mile west of the second large rock above the trail, roughly 0.4 mile after beginning the descent from Copper Ridge. A scrabble trail is intersected 50' above; this can be identified by cut log ends. Follow this trail up to the ridge crest. Tread is faint or nonexistent in places. Once on the ridge crest, simply follow the crest over ups and downs on snow and heather. The route is fairly level for half a mile and then steepens. The last 100 yards upwards is steep, traversing snow and heather; use caution crossing a roughly 30-foot patch of scree and loose rock, which is a bit treacherous. As soon as possible, cut left out of this area to heather and more solid earth, and continue west on less steep and more solid ground to the Hannegan

Mountain trail immediately south of the summit. From here, it is a few feet to the top, where the hiker is treated to one of the splendid views in the North Cascades.

There are several campsites on top, one in the krummholz trees on the very summit. There is meltwater from snow patches 50' and 300' northwest of the summit.

Watch for mountain goats between Copper Ridge, Hannegan Peak, and Granite Mountain.

It takes a little over one hour to walk from the Copper Ridge Trail to Hannegan Peak. The trail from Hannegan Peak down to Hannegan Pass is steep, scrabbly, and not maintained. Halfway down there is one good campsite with water from a small tarn fed by a snow patch nearby. The time down from Hannegan Peak to Pass is 40 minutes; the time up is a bit over one hour. The time out from Hannegan Pass is just under 2 hours. The trail is rough, rocky, muddy in places, and not particularly pleasant walking.

(July 1980)

BIG BEAVER—WHATCOM PASS

DESTINATION: Whatcom Pass, 5206'

TRAIL LENGTH: 22 miles

WALKING TIME (full pack): 15–16 hours (2 days) in
11–12 hours out

TRAILHEAD ELEVATION 1618'

ALTITUDE GAIN, including ups and downs: 4750' in
1170' out

SEASON FOR USE: low trail: late April–late November
high trail: mid-July–mid-October

FEATURES: Beaver Pass, 3620'; Stillwell junction, 2450'

TOPOGRAPHIC SHEETS: USGS: Mt. Challenger 15';
Pumpkin Mt. and Mt. Prophet 7.5'

TOPOGRAPHIC SHEETS (cont'd): Green Trails: Ross Lake; Mt. Challenger

There are several access routes to the trailhead at Big Beaver Creek on the west side of Ross Lake. The easiest land route is the Ross Dam Trail from the North Cascade Highway. Turn left at the road, cross the dam, and follow the West Ross Lake Trail six miles from the dam to the bridge at Big Beaver Creek; there is a campground at the lakeshore near the trailhead. With advance reservations, lake transportation may be arranged at the Ross Lake Resort: turn right at the road, continue 0.3 mile to the lake shore and travel by charter motorboat to the trailhead at Big Beaver Campground. Other access routes include the West Diablo Lake Trail, the bridge below Ross Dam, and the road to Ross Dam, or the Seattle City Light boat from Diablo Lake to Ross Dam.

The Big Beaver Trail is roughly sixteen miles long. An additional six miles on the Little Beaver Trail reaches Whatcom Pass. The trail is fairly level for the first 8 miles, then goes upwards for about 1.5 miles, levels off for four miles, and then goes up again to cross Beaver Pass (3620'). The trail then descends, losing about 1100', to where it joins the Little Beaver Trail at Stillwell Camp. Going west, over the next 3 miles there is an altitude gain of about 500' to the Twin Rocks Shelter and campsite. From here, the final three miles to Whatcom Pass is steep, gaining 2200'. Until these last two or three miles, there is little to see except deep woods. The forest canopy is thick; the floor of this virgin forest is interesting and beautiful. From the Big Beaver trail, glimpses are brief and tantalizing of the Luna Cirque, Elephant Butte, and McMillan Cirque. An upward scramble east from the Beaver Pass camp allows views of the craggy, icy Luna Cirque, seen from the bare slopes above camp better than from the trail.

From Big Beaver Creek to the 39-Mile Creek Camp junction is 5.1 miles; the camp is 0.2 mile off the trail. From 39-Mile Creek to the Luna Camp junction is 3.4 miles; Luna Camp is 0.1 mile off the trail. It is 5.2 miles from Luna Camp to Beaver Pass Camp; the Luna horse camp is 2 miles from the Luna hiker's camp. 2.3 miles beyond Beaver Pass camp is Stillwell crossing where there is a campsite. From here, it is 2.5 miles to Twin Rocks Camp, 0.1 mile off the trail. Whatcom Pass is 3.6 miles beyond Twin Rocks.

Whatcom Pass is beautiful, isolated, and worth the substantial effort required to penetrate into the Picket Range. (The pass area and its western access are described under Hannegan Pass–Whatcom Pass.)

A permit is required for overnight stays in these areas; designated campgrounds must be used.

All campgrounds between Big Beaver and the Hannegan trailhead, except Boundary Camp, allow campfires. There is a water-tight trail shelter at Beaver Pass, and a shelter with a leaky roof at Stillwell Camp.

The Big and Little Beaver Trails are often brushy and/or muddy. Deerflies and mosquitoes are usually a problem along these trails; insect repellent is essential.

Trail relocation may be made in 1983 from Beaver Pass to Stillwell Shelter; this would increase trail distance half a mile or so.

The Big Beaver Trail will be substantially different if High Ross Dam is constructed. Some five miles of the lower end of the Big Beaver Valley, including impressive groves of huge western red cedar, will be flooded. At the time of this writing, it is not yet decided whether High Ross Dam will be constructed. Obviously, all footpaths in the Ross Lake area will be substantially different if the level of Ross Lake is raised 150'; most of the current campgrounds will be inundated. Should the dam be constructed, do inquire as to conditions at the NPS ranger station in Marblemount.

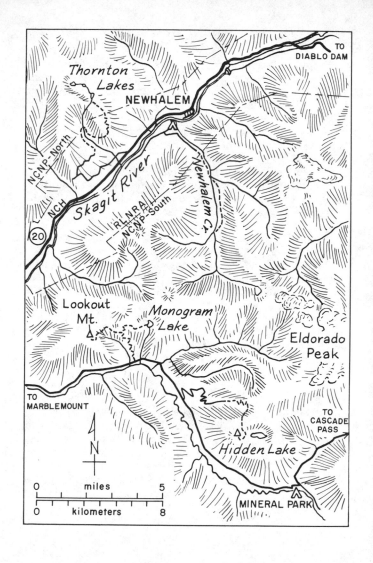

TO
DIABLO DAM

Thornton
Lakes

NEWHALEM

NCNP-North

NCH

Skagit River

Newhalem Cr.

R L N R A
NCNP-South

20

Lookout
Mt.

Monogram
Lake

Eldorado
Peak

TO
MARBLEMOUNT

TO
CASCADE
PASS

N

Hidden Lake

0   miles   5

0   kilometers   8

MINERAL PARK

8

NORTH CASCADES NATIONAL PARK
North and South Sections

Trails:
Hidden Lake
Thornton Lakes
Lookout Mountain and Monogram Lake
Newhalem Creek

HIDDEN LAKE

DESTINATION: Lookout shelter, 6890'

TRAIL LENGTH: 3.9 miles

WALKING TIME (full pack): 3½ hours in
2 hours out

TRAILHEAD ELEVATION 3560'

ALTITUDE GAIN, including ups and downs: 3400'

SEASON FOR USE: August 1 through September

FEATURES: Hidden Lake Peak, 7000'; Hidden Lake, 5733'

TOPOGRAPHIC SHEETS: USGS: El Dorado Peak and
Sonny Boy Lakes 7.5'
Green Trails: Diablo Dam and
Cascade Pass

Take the NCH to Marblemount, cross the Skagit River, and drive about 2 miles past the Marble Creek Bridge. Turn left and drive 5.2 miles to the road end. There is space for 7 or 8 cars, and turnaround space is meager. Follow the easily hiked logging road to timber at the end of the patch cut; from here, it is a moderately steep ascent for about 1 mile through deep woods, then it breaks into the Sibley Creek meadow. The trail is often difficult to find for the mile through the lush vegetation. If wearing shorts, watch out for stinging nettles. Forest Service trail crews brush back the meadow, but this work is often done late in the summer.

Switchback up 1.2 miles to the head of Sibley Creek, then cross the creek and traverse gradually up for about 0.5 mile through delightful meadow. (At the head of Sibley Creek there is an interesting juncture of granite with sedimentary rock and an abrupt botanical shift from verdant, thick meadow to alpine heather.) Another 0.9 mile of fairly steep ascent leads to a notch between Hidden Lake Peak and the spire on which the Hidden Lake Lookout sits.

The boundary between the National Forest and National Park is at this notch. There are impressive views of Hidden Lake below and of the Cascade Pass area to the east. The hiker can then drop over the trailless, fairly steep talus slopes to several good campsites on a bench midway between the notch and Hidden Lake. The altitude loss to the bench is about 400′, and to the lake itself an additional 400′. The safest access route to the lake bears to the far left (north) on descent, and is not the route directly below and east of the camping areas. There are no campsites near the shore at the west end of the lake. Water is no problem at the designated Hidden Lake campsite, since there is a creek nearby. Campfires are prohibited.

To reach the east end of Hidden Lake, where there are splendid campsites near the water, go one notch to the south after reaching the top of the Sibley Creek col. From here, go cross-country southeast; gain altitude and pass above a small lake. Turn south and proceed several hundred yards; two clear routes to the southeast lead to the south end of the lake, where there is an outlet stream, two good campsites with fire pits, and gorgeous views. This route to the lake is as easy as the route described above, and it offers the best fishing. The altitude gain to the lake via this route is roughly 2500′ in and 1000′ out. From the notch to the east end of the lake, it takes just under an hour down and one hour and 25 minutes out.

On the National Forest side of the crest, there is a campsite in the forest about 0.8 mile from the trailhead. Many campsites are available between Sibley Creek and the tarn 0.2 mile west of the saddle. Permits are required for overnight camping around Hidden Lake; no permit is required for camping in the National Forest.

Ptarmigan are often seen in and around the notch, campsites, and ridge crest. They are generally tame.

From the notch, the trail goes up another 0.3 mile to the Lois Webster Memorial Shelter (formerly the Hidden Lake Lookout). When not being used by work parties, the structure is available to the public as a shelter. The building is being maintained by a group of individuals both for its historic value and as a shelter. Assistance in maintaining the structure is welcomed; volunteers should contact The Friends of the Lois Webster Memorial Shelter, 1819 Hickox Road, Mt. Vernon, WA 98273. Please leave the building and contents in better condition than you found them. A register is inside the shelter.

Water is not easy to obtain on the lookout spire. Snow, 200' or so from the shelter, can be a water source well into August. After the snow melts, the closest water is the tarn 0.2 mile west of the notch, and about 200' south of the trail; a small way trail leads to the tarn. There is a good campsite at this location.

From the lookout on a clear day, you can see forever! Glacier Peak and, indeed, Mt. Rainier are visible to the south, as is Snowking Mountain in the foreground. Sauk, Bald, Lookout Mountain, Teebone Ridge, Mt. Shuksan, Eldorado, Mt. Baker, Hidden Lake Peak, and the Cascade Crest surround the mountaintop. The panorama of Boston, Sahale, Johannesberg, Spider, and Formidable mountains is most impressive. Cascade Pass itself cannot be seen from the lookout but can be seen from the top of Hidden Lake Peak or from the top of the Sibley Creek col.

An optional descent route is to climb Hidden Lake Peak and then follow the ridge crest down to the Sibley col, descending from the col to the trail at that point. This is easier early in the season, when snow is present, than later, when the steep meadow makes descent more difficult.

(October 1981)

THORNTON LAKES

DESTINATION: Thornton Lake, 4500'
TRAIL LENGTH: 5.2 miles
WALKING TIME (light pack): 3½ hours in
2¾ hours out
TRAILHEAD ELEVATION 2700'
ALTITUDE GAIN, including ups and downs: 2300'
FEATURES: Ridge above Thornton Lake, 4900' (high
point); Peak above lakes, 6234'
TOPOGRAPHIC SHEETS: USGS: Marblemount
Green Trails: Marblemount

The side road leading from the NCH to the trailhead is not marked. Turn west near Mile Post #117, 3.6 miles from the main intersection in Newhalem, or 11.2 miles from Marblemount. Three hundred yards up the road are signs, one of which states "Four wheel drive recommended." In July of 1981, this road was passable without difficulty in a standard car. Take the right fork 3.8 miles after the turnoff. The road ends abruptly, 5.3 miles from the NCH, where large boulders have fallen into the road; there is a bulletin board here. There is parking on the north side of the road. Turning around at the road end is difficult.

The trail begins at the road end and follows a deteriorating logging road. There is enough brush for the trail to be uncomfortable when the vegetation is wet. In places, the outer edge of the road is falling into the valley. The footpath goes up moderately for roughly one mile, crosses Thornton Creek, and goes up more steeply for another mile. There is a promontory here with good views. Follow the road past this point roughly 200 feet. There are several rock cairns and a trail post where the trail leaves the old road and enters the forest.

It is 2.1 miles from the trailhead to where the trail leaves the old road. There are views of the impressive peaks to the east (Teebone Ridge) along this section of the trail.

It is probable that the initial trail to the lakes was an informal trail created by high-lake fishermen. The portion of the trail within the recreational area remains a scrabble trail: the tread is slick and muddy, with many tree roots. This portion of the trail is in deep timber, without views. The North Cascades National Park is entered 3.4 miles from the trailhead.

A bridge crosses a small stream 0.3 mile further. There is a dependable water supply at this point. Beyond this point the tread substantially improves. The trail bypasses a bog, then switchbacks upward. After a half mile, go right at a trail post. There is jute netting, evidence of the rehabilitation efforts by the Park Service after the damage left around the old scrabble trail. Go left at a trail post 0.2 mile further. Go left at another trail post 0.1 mile along. The trail then tops out on the ridge above lower Thornton Lake. There is a splendid view of the lake below and the mountains in the distance. Trappers Peak (5964') is to the right of the lake. Mt. Triumph (7270') in the Picket Range looms beyond the lake to the northwest.

A steep, muddy, slippery descent, occasionally over steps blasted out of the granite, leads to the outlet creek of lower Thornton Lake. A mildly difficult descent on granite boulders brings the hiker to Thornton Creek, which is easily crossed. Just past the crossing is the designated campsite where there is space for five alpine tents; an additional site is 100 yards above on flat granite, for tents that do not require tent stakes. Campfires are prohibited at this location, and camping is not allowed anywhere else from the trailhead to snow on the ridges above the lakes.

From camp, it is possible to scramble up and down for several hundred yards to another gulch. An indistinct way trail contours around the lake, giving access to fishing areas. There are two higher lakes; to explore or fish them, or to climb to the peaks beyond, contour upward to the left from this last gulch, gaining about 1000'. It is possible to drop to any of the lakes in the basin below, or to continue on to the ridge west of the lower lake.

Views from the ridge are impressive: Thornton Lakes lie below. Mt. Triumph is to the north. Mt. Blum, Mt. Hagan, and Damnation Peak can be seen to the west. To the east are Pyramid and Colonial Peaks. Allow two hours from the lower lake to the high point of the ridge. The altitude gain is roughly 1700'.

In the spring, if there is ample snow pack, a more direct route is up through Thornton Creek Valley, from the point where the abandoned road crosses the creek, straight to the lower lake. Without snow this is a formidable bushwhack.

(July 1981)

LOOKOUT MOUNTAIN AND MONOGRAM LAKE

DESTINATION: Lookout, 5719'

TRAIL LENGTH: 4.7 miles

WALKING TIME (light pack): 3½ hours in
2 hours out

TRAILHEAD ELEVATION 1200'

ALTITUDE GAIN, including ups and downs: 4600'

FEATURES: Monogram Lake Trail Junction, 4300';
Monogram Lake, 4900'

TOPOGRAPHIC SHEETS: USGS: Marblemount
Green Trails: Marblemount

Follow the road as for Cascade Pass Trail; drive about 7 miles east of Marblemount and roughly 0.5 mile past the entrance to the Mt. Baker National Forest. The trailhead is on the north side of the road, just past a bridge. (In 1980, the bridge washed out; the creek is now bypassed by a detour; probably the bridge will be replaced by 1982.) There is no parking lot; there are several wide places to park on the south side of the road. The trail switchbacks up steeply through deep forest. At about one mile, there are large mossy rocks on which maidenhair fern grows. At 1.5 miles, water is available via a 50-foot scrabble trail to the west. At about 1.9 miles, the first possible campsite is at a spring, on the first level space along the trail. The elevation gained in the first two miles is about 2500'. The trail then goes about 0.3 mile through meadow, often overgrown in the summer. About 2.8 miles from the trailhead, the primary trail continues north and west of the lookout, breaking into a meadow at about 3.7 miles and switchbacking across the meadow and up the ridge to the lookout 4.7 miles from the road. The trail in the meadow is difficult to locate. It is difficult to maintain footing when the trail is wet. A flat area just beneath the lookout offers several good campsites. Water is available at a spring 0.3 mile below the summit and from the summit snowfields, which normally persist until mid-summer. The elevated lookout is in good enough condition to provide shelter in inclement weather.

The view from the lookout catwalk, though marred by patch cuts, is good in all directions. The Skagit and Cascade valleys lie below. The jagged summits of the Picket Range are seen to the north. Teebone Ridge, Little and Big Devil peaks, and Eldorado and Hidden Lake peaks are to the east; Sauk Mountain and Bald Mountain are to the west, and to the south, Snowking and Mt. Chaval.

The Monogram Lake junction, 2.9 miles from the trailhead, is marked by a trail post. There is little water between the road and the meadow, so a lot of water should be carried, particularly on hot summer days. The distance from the junction to the lake is 2.1 miles. The approximate walking time is 1½ hours up, and 1 hour back. The National Park boundary is about 0.2 mile from the junction.

The footpath scrambles up through forested hillsides for about one mile. After about one mile the trail breaks into a lovely high meadow, crosses a branch of Lookout Creek and angles south and up across a prominent ridge, gaining about 400′ in 0.4 mile. From the ridge crest there is an impressive view into the Monogram Lake Cirque below. From the ridge to the lake it is 0.7 mile, and a 300′ descent. There is a designated campsite at Monogram Lake with three tent sites: two near the outlet stream and one above the lake to the north. Fires are prohibited at this camp; stoves must be carried. There are also places to camp above and south of the lake, reached by a half-mile cross-country scramble. Fishing in the lake is good.

Little Devil Peak and Teebone Ridge can be reached cross-country from Monogram Lake without great difficulty.

Although fast hikers can make it to the lake and back out in one day, most parties prefer to make a two-day trip of it. The altitude gain from the junction to the lake is about 900′; from the road to the lake, 4000′ in 4.9 miles.

National Park restrictions apply to Monogram Lake, but not to the main trail and Lookout Mountain.

(August 1981)

NEWHALEM CREEK

DESTINATION: Newhalem Camp, 1800′
TRAIL LENGTH: 4.5 miles
WALKING TIME (light pack): 2 hours in
                                 1½ hours out
TRAILHEAD ELEVATION 1000′

ALTITUDE GAIN, including ups and downs: 1000'
SEASON FOR USE: early April to late November
TOPOGRAPHIC SHEETS: USGS: Diablo Dam;
Marblemount; El Dorado Peak
Green Trails: Diablo Dam;
Marblemount

Turn south 0.1 mile east of the bridge over Goodell Creek, just before entering Newhalem, on the NCH. Cross the Skagit River, pass the building on the left in the NPS campground, and follow a gravel road to the south. Turn left 0.7 mile from the bridge across the Skagit River. At 2.0 miles there is a dangerous hump in the road. There are no guard-rails, and it is difficult to see the road on the other side of the hump. Use great caution! At 2.2 miles, pass a dam and building on the left of the road. At 2.4 miles the road ends at the trailhead. There is parking for only one car; parking space for four or five cars is in the last 0.2 mile of road. There is a campsite, fire pit, and short footpath to Newhalem Creek under a huge cedar just east of the trailhead.

The trail follows an old logging road for its entire distance. There are several washouts through which the trail has been rebuilt. Because the road was originally graveled, there is little mud. Views are fair from about 2 miles onward, considerably better in late fall than in summer, when there are leaves on the alders surrounding the road.

The National Park is entered about half a mile from the trailhead. At 1.3 miles, the trail winds through flood-deposited boulders and debris. Newhalem Creek is crossed on a bridge at 1.6 miles. The trail then ascends on the east side of the creek, staying several hundred feet above it until it drops at trail's end. At about 2.8 miles, the scenery improves, both to the north and south. Little Devil Peak (6985'), Big Devil Peak (7055'), and Teebone Ridge are often visible from here on. The Picket Range can be seen to the northwest.

The trail passes through an area of regenerating clear-cut (logged before creation of the NCNP). At 3.2 miles, cascades and waterfalls can be seen descending from the peak to the west. There are two huge cedars 3.8 miles along the trail. At the 4-mile mark there is a junction of old logging roads; take the right fork. The trail descends gradually for a half mile, rounds a road washout at 4.3 miles, and then enters deep forest. The Newhalem Creek campsite is on the bank of the creek. At the campsite there is a horse bar, several open areas for tents, and a primitive toilet 100' to the east. There are several fire pits. A way trail leads through a deep, mossy glen to the creekside. Water is available from a creek descending from the east and from Newhalem Creek at the campsite. Firewood is plentiful.

This is a pleasant, gentle walk. The fisherman will want to take several way trails between the trailhead and the bridge to reach the creek. The trout limit in Newhalem Creek is five fish. This enjoyable walk is recommended in the spring or late fall, when snow lies heavy on the alpine meadows.

(November 1980)

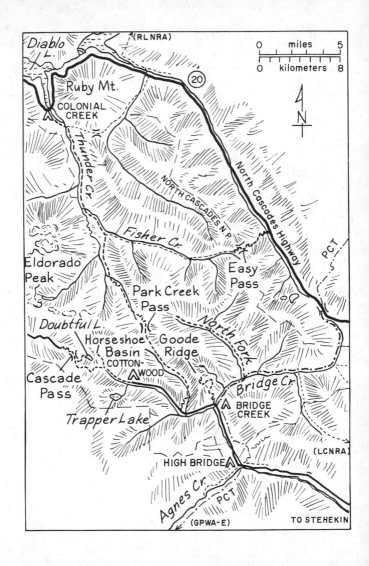

9

NORTH CASCADES NATIONAL PARK
South Section

Trails:
Cascade Pass
Horseshoe Basin
Park Creek Pass
Goode Ridge
Thunder Creek
Easy Pass (WNF)
Bridge Creek (PCT)
North Fork of Bridge Creek

CASCADE PASS

DESTINATION: Cascade Pass, 5400'

TOPOGRAPHIC SHEETS: USGS: Goode Mt.; Cascade Pass
Green Trails: McGregor Mt.;
Cascade Pass

The Cascade Pass area is one of the most spectacular in the North Cascades. If the visitor has only a short time in the North Cascades, this is one of the walks that should be made; however, expect company: this is one of the most popular areas in the range.

Camping is allowed at both trailheads, Basin Creek, and Pelton Basin. Climbers can obtain a permit for high camps on snow.

Aggressive attempts to replant damaged areas at Cascade Pass continue. There is a greenhouse for growing high alpine plants at the Marblemount Ranger Station. Green netting, placed in many areas of the pass, helps retain seeds and support plant growth; it is important not to walk on any areas where there is netting. All visitors to the area should remain on the designated trails.

East Approach

TRAIL LENGTH: 5.4 miles

WALKING TIME: 3½ hours in
2¼ hours out

TRAILHEAD ELEVATION 2750'

ALTITUDE GAIN, including ups and downs: 2900'

The east trailhead is at Cottonwood Camp at the end of the Stehekin Road. The trail ascends gradually along the

Stehekin River, detouring up briefly to avoid avalanche debris which dammed the Stehekin River and obliterated the old trail in the 1970s. It is 1 mile to Basin Creek Camp, where there are 5 or 6 scattered campsites. A bear cable is in this area to help preserve food supplies from marauding bruins.

Cross Basin Creek on a high plank bridge. The trail climbs more steeply from this point, switchbacking up on the deteriorating Mine to Market Road toward Horseshoe Basin. The trail to Cascade Pass is the left fork after several switchbacks; it traverses gradually upward to cross the waterfall of Doubtful Creek in one mile. Above this point there are 13 switchbacks ending in the woods above Pelton Basin. The trail then goes through timber for 0.4 mile, breaks out into open country, crosses a talus slope, and then zigzags up to Cascade Pass, 5.4 miles from the trailhead.

Water is easily obtained along the trail. Watch for pikas and marmots in the talus and meadow areas along the last mile of trail.

Moderately fast hikers can arrive on the first shuttlebus from Stehekin, reach Cascade Pass from the east in time for lunch, and return to catch the late afternoon bus back to the village. For a more leisurely exploration, those coming from the east should plan to spend the night at Basin Creek Camp or, better, the designated campsite for hikers in the timber near Pelton Basin, one mile east of the pass.

West Approach

TRAIL LENGTH: 3.7 miles

WALKING TIME: 2 hours in
1½ hours out

TRAILHEAD ELEVATION 3700′

ALTITUDE GAIN, including ups and downs: 1750′

Leave Interstate 5 at Burlington and drive the NCH to Marblemount. Cross the Skagit River and follow the road to its end; the last two miles are rough, steep, and inadvisable for trailers. The trail begins on the north side of the parking lot at the end of the road. This trail, constructed in 1967, switchbacks gradually but seemingly endlessly up, culminating in a half-mile level traverse, to Cascade Pass. The trail is almost always muddy. The thick forest cover obscures views until meadow at about 3.2 miles. Water is available along the entire route.

Views from the pass are extraordinary. Below to the east is Pelton Basin and the beginning of the Stehekin Valley. To the west is the valley of the North Fork of the Cascade River. Beginning in the west, the circle of peaks includes Hidden Lake, Eldorado, Forbidden, Sahale, Buckner Mountain, Booker, McGregor, Glory Mountain, Trapper Mountain, Magic Mountain, Mix-up Peak, the Triplets, and Johannesburg Mountain.

A variety of options confront the hiker and mountaineer after reaching Cascade Pass.

Doubtful Lake

One hundred yards east of the crest of Cascade Pass, the footpath to Sahale Arm and Doubtful Lake goes north from the main trail. This steep secondary footpath switchbacks up Sahale Arm, gaining 1000' in 0.7 mile. At the top of the arm, descend the steep north side of the arm and lose about 1000' to reach Doubtful Lake. Mining took place here in the late 1800's.

Fishing is generally good, although the lake is heavily fished in the summer. There are magnificent views of Sahale to the north and McGregor to the east. Distance from the pass is 1.5 miles.

Sahale Arm

Instead of descending to Doubtful Lake, continue higher on Sahale Arm by following the mountaineer's scrabble trail to an elevation of 8000'. At this point it is necessary to traverse a glacier, and those without experience in climbing should turn back. Sahale Arm features spectacular views of the surrounding "sea of peaks."

Cache Col

This is a dangerous trail and should be attempted only by climbers experienced on ice and snow. Follow a mountaineer's trail beginning at the pass, and traverse up and to the southeast across steep snow and talus slopes to a promontory 0.5 mile above the pass. From this promontory, descend slightly; after reaching the snow or ice, begin the 0.9-mile ascent over the glacier to reach Cache Col to the southeast. Just above this col is a spectacular but exposed campsite; there is also camping one mile further at Kool Ade Lake, 1000' lower. Again, snow and ice climbing training are required to reach the col safely.

Trapper Lake

To reach Trapper Lake from the pass, descend on the Lake Chelan trail 0.5 mile. Take the lower (right) fork and descend into Pelton Basin, crossing to the south side of the creek. Ascend a moderately visible scrabble path at the southeast side of Pelton Basin, gaining about 500', to a very nice camping area overlooking the Stehekin Valley. From here, two traverses over scrabble trail lead to the ridge overlooking Trapper Lake after another mile. A steep descent of 0.2 mile (easy early in the season over snow, but a difficult bushwhack late in the season) leads to the west end of Trapper Lake. Fishing and campsites are available at both ends of the lake. (The east end of the lake is best reached via a strenuous cross-country trek beginning at Cottonwood Camp.)

(August 1980)

HORSESHOE BASIN

DESTINATION: Black Warrior Mine, 4800'
TRAIL LENGTH: 1.5 miles (7 miles round trip from Cottonwood Camp)
WALKING TIME: 1 hour up; 35 minutes down (4 hours round trip from Cottonwood Camp)
TRAILHEAD ELEVATION 3650' (on Cascade Pass Trail)
TOPOGRAPHIC SHEETS: USGS: Cascade Pass
Green Trails: Cascade Pass

This is a less rigorous one-day trip from the Cottonwood trailhead than the trip to Cascade Pass, and although not scenically as splendid, it is an enjoyable alternative for those unable to make the trip to the pass between the first and last shuttlebuses of the day.

Horseshoe Basin can be reached by continuing on the abandoned Mine to Market Road (now a trail) two miles west of Cottonwood Camp, three miles before Cascade Pass. Climb, gaining 1150' in 1.5 miles, into the large cirque beneath Sahale and Boston mountains, Ripsaw Ridge, and Mt. Buckner. A dozen waterfalls cascade down from the snow and ice fields above. The trail ends at the Black Warrior Mine, with extensive tailings below the mine shaft entrance.

Much of the summer, there is a snowfield just below the mine that may offer problems to the inexperienced; be careful in this area. If in doubt, go down about two switchbacks, cross the snow field at that point, and work your way back up the talus slope, staying to the right of the creek and to the left of the mine tailings.

This mine is now in the National Register of Historical Places. It has been restored by the Park Service and is safe to explore. At least two flashlights should be taken. Watch your head and your feet: the shaft in places is only five feet high, and there are pipes and rough areas over which you could easily trip. Allow your eyes to adjust to the darkness. The shaft penetrates the mountain perhaps 150', then the main shaft turns left an additional 75'; further penetration is unsafe, and the Park Service has put up a screen prohibiting passage.

Before leaving, let your imagination wander to the winter of 1909, when miners wintered here, going between cabin and mine shaft through tunnels dug underneath the 30-foot snowpack.

Although there is lumber and metallic debris outside the mine area, there are no cabins standing since avalanches have decimated the area. There are wild flowers, particularly mimulus, in profusion along the trail. The jagged "sawteeth" of Ripsaw Ridge above are impressive. The area is restricted to day use only; the nearest camp is at Basin Creek, roughly 2.3 miles away. The intermittently muddy trail is brushed annually. Tread is vague where the path follows stream beds. There is no problem obtaining water in the basin.

In late July, 0.2 mile from the junction with the Cascade Pass Trail there is a splendid proliferation of succulent yellow blooming rock plants along the trail.

(July 1980)

PARK CREEK PASS

DESTINATION: Park Creek Pass, 6100'
TRAIL LENGTH: 8 miles

WALKING TIME (full pack to 5 miles; light pack beyond):
4½ hours in
3⅓ hours out

TRAILHEAD ELEVATION 2340'

ALTITUDE GAIN, including ups and downs: 4200'

FEATURES: 2-mile Camp, 3300'; 5-mile Camp, 4100'

TOPOGRAPHIC SHEETS: USGS: Goode Mt. 7.5'
Green Trails: McGregor Mt.

Park Creek Pass is a magnificent area! Relatively isolated and uncrowded, it is a place for experiencing the breathtaking impact of the wild high country.

Take the shuttlebus (or walk) 18.5 miles up the road from Stehekin, or 4.5 miles down the road from Cottonwood Camp, to the trailhead. There is a sign where the trail takes off north of the road; there is an unimproved camping area near the creek to the right of the trailhead.

After 100 yards, the trail climbs moderately. At 1 mile, there is a small spring from which water can be obtained. One tenth of a mile beyond and a 50-foot walk to the right, a rocky knob permits splendid views up the Flat Creek Valley. One hundred yards or so beyond this, the trail tops out, and there are views over the Stehekin Valley.

From this point, the trail drops gently to 2-mile Camp. Hiking time to the camp, fully packed, is 1 hour from the trailhead. There is a toilet on the hillside above the camp, and adjacent to Park Creek there is space for about 2 tents.

The trail forks at this point, with the horse trail going left. The hiking trail crosses a sturdy bridge to the north side of Park Creek. It then climbs, sharply for several hundred yards and gradually thereafter. Fully packed, it takes another 1¾ hours to reach 5-mile Camp. Water is available at 4 miles.

Most of 5-mile Camp is in timber without views, but Campsite #4, 50 yards beyond, is in open meadow with a spectacular view of the great cirque beneath Booker and

Buckner mountains. Wood is scarce. Water is available from a small creek. Bear cable is available, without stringers.

(The hiker and horse camps at 5-mile Camp have been separated. The hiker camp is now 0.3 mile further along the trail to the pass.)

From 5-mile Camp to Park Creek Pass takes about 1¾ hours, lightly packed. The trail first goes through the brushy valley floor for 0.5 mile, then goes up the hillside, crosses a stream, and at 7 miles breaks into meadow. After it leaves the valley floor, it goes up steeply. It is a long 8 miles to the 0.2-mile-long pass, which is snow-filled at the bottom.

The trail contours above and on the northeast side of the pass. Views down Thunder Creek, from the north side of the pass, are quite spectacular. The lowest peak in sight is Mt. Booker at 8280'. Storm King (8515'), Mt. Buckner (9112'), and Mt. Goode (9197') complete the circle of mountains around the trail.

Camping is prohibited at the pass itself. Camping must be 1 mile off the trail for 3 miles on either side of the crest of Park Creek Pass. To the west, on the high ridge approach to Mt. Buckner, camping is allowed ½ mile or more off the trail. The time down from the pass to 5-mile Camp is a little over an hour, and from 5-mile Camp to the Stehekin Road is 2 hours. There is adequate water between 5-mile Camp and the pass.

Beyond the pass, the trail follows Thunder Creek north 20 miles to the Colonial Creek campground near the North Cascades Highway. It is also possible to travel cross-country higher onto Buckner Mountain for ever-improving views.

(August 1978)

GOODE RIDGE

DESTINATION: Lookout site on ridge, 6760'
TRAIL LENGTH: 5.4 miles

WALKING TIME (light pack): 3½ hours in
                            2½ hours out

TRAILHEAD ELEVATION 2200'

ALTITUDE GAIN, including ups and downs: 4600'

TOPOGRAPHIC SHEETS: USGS: Goode Mt.; McGregor Mt.
                     Green Trails: McGregor Mt. (trail
                     not shown in 1980)

The unmarked trailhead is 16.5 miles from Stehekin, 0.1 mile beyond the Bridge Creek bridge. The initial few feet of tread is fairly apparent, but after that the trail is difficult to locate for approximately 200 feet. Go west 50 feet, then northwest to the left of a dead tree, and at about 200 feet the path becomes clear. Look for surveyor's flagging tape if the route is unclear. Sawed log ends may also assist.

This trail, abandoned for a number of years, was worked by a trail crew in 1980, and major impediments were removed. The trail is still considered a scrabble trail for its entire length, and in a few places it is difficult to locate.

Before starting up, drop below the road to Bridge Creek. There are two splendid pools just below the trailhead; drink deeply and fill water bottles. It is 1.5 miles, about 55 minutes hiking, to a small spring where more water may be obtained. There is no water thereafter until snow patches near the high point; after mid-August, little or no snow will be left even at the site of the lookout. Two full water bottles are recommended in late summer and early fall.

The trail goes up steeply and remorselessly. It is in woods with minor views for the first 2.5 miles (1½ hours hiking, moderately packed). The trail then breaks out of the forest and there is a fine view of Bridge Creek. Alpine flowers bloom from here to the end of the trail. Views improve as one gains altitude. At about 3.8 miles (an hour later), the trail re-enters woods for 0.3 mile; there are two campsites in this area, one dry, and one near a small snow patch.

The trail again breaks out of the timber and goes north to

the east side of Goode Ridge, switchbacks up, and then contours to the south side of the ridge. Between 5.0 and 5.1 miles, there are many campsites with (as of late July) water available from snowfields. The top of the ridge, at about 5.3 miles, is level, and there are many good campsites along the summit ridge, with water available from patchy snow. Green View Lake is to the northwest, nestled between Memaloose and Goode ridges. Below are the deep, green valleys of Bridge Creek and the Stehekin. Azure Trapper Lake fills the cirque beneath Glory, Trapper, and Magic mountains to the west. The Flat Creek valley leads to the peaks of the Ptarmigan Traverse. Close by loom Goode, Booker, McGregor, and Tolo mountains. In the distance are Dome and Glacier peaks. Truly a spectacular 360-degree panorama!

At the high point, a rock platform, cables, glass, metal, etc., mark the site of the old fire lookout.

Fast hikers can make the round trip between the first and last shuttlebuses of the day, and have lunch at the high point. (July 1980)

THUNDER CREEK

DESTINATION: Park Creek Pass, 6100'

TRAIL LENGTH: 19.1 miles

WALKING TIME (full pack): 9–12 hours (2 days) in
6–8 hours (1 day) out

TRAILHEAD ELEVATION 1220'

ALTITUDE GAIN, including ups and downs: 6300'

TOPOGRAPHIC SHEETS: USGS: Ross Dam; Forbidden
Peak; Mt. Logan 7.5'
Green Trails: Diablo Dam; Mt. Logan

The trail begins about 0.1 mile south of the North Cascade Highway off the paved Colonial Creek Campground road.

There are places for about 35 cars in the large parking area east of the trailhead. The trail runs along the west shore of the Thunder Arm section of Diablo Lake to the lake end at about 1 mile. At about 0.7 mile, there are a number of beautifully burnished silver cedar trees still standing which died due to flooding from the lake. At 1.3 miles, a new large metal bridge crosses Thunder Creek. Watch for harlequin ducks here in the late spring. From the bridge, the trail proceeds on the east side of Thunder Creek, gaining altitude gradually.

The trail forks at a signed junction at about 1.7 mile; the right fork goes 0.1 mile to a gauging station where there is a cable crossing of the river, a hiker camp (Thunder) with three sites with fire grates, and a wilderness guard cabin. This section of the river offers good fishing, using waders or hip boots, after the spring runoff.

The left fork at 1.7 miles is the main trail. Two miles from the trailhead, the 4th of July Pass footpath departs eastward and upward. From about 1.5 miles, the trail remains high on the east canyon wall for 2.8 miles; access to the river is very difficult over this stretch. From 4.3 miles on, the river can be reached with relative ease. The trail crosses a number of small creeks that must be forded, but these are not difficult even at high water. At about 5.3 miles, there is easy access to the river over a very nice grassy knoll. Maidenhair fern is on the riverbank.

Other campsites on this trail include Neve Camp at 2.3 miles (3 sites); McAllister Camp at 6.5 miles (5 sites); Tricouni Camp at 7.6 miles (3 sites); Junction Camp at 9.7 miles (5 sites); Skagit Camp at 13.6 miles (4 sites); and Thunder Basin Camp at 16.5 miles (3 sites; no campfires).

McAllister Creek

The way trail to McAllister Creek leaves to the right at about the 6-mile mark. (When last checked, the McAllister

Creek trail was poorly maintained and difficult to find, and it gradually petered out about three miles beyond the bridge over Thunder Creek.) The altitude gain to McAllister Creek is about 700' in total; many ups and downs make the actual altitude gain easily 1000'. Walking time to McAllister Creek is about 3 hours in and 2½ hours out. This is an enjoyable walk, mostly through deep forest and lush undergrowth. There are occasional views of the surrounding peaks through clearings in the forest. Bunchberry, trillium, calypso orchids, and very large cedars and Douglas firs are found here. Wood and water are plentiful.

Seattle City Light contemplates a possible new dam at about the 5.3 mile mark. Construction of this dam would, of course, markedly change the area!

From McAllister Creek, the trail runs about two miles on the level; for the next two miles it switchbacks up steeply to a junction with the Fisher Creek trail. (From this point, via the Fisher Creek trail, it is 9.1 miles to Fisher Basin and 10.5 miles to Easy Pass; it is 3.7 miles from the pass to the North Cascades Highway.) The next 0.75 mile is fairly level; a way trail descends steeply to Meadow Cabin from here. The main footpath contours down and proceeds on a slight gradient to Skagit Queen Camp at the junction of Skagit Queen and Thunder creeks, 4 miles from the Thunder-Fisher junction. From this campsite an unmaintained trail leads to the Skagit Queen mine and the base of the Boston Glacier. (The mine area is currently being acquired by the park through condemnation.)

From the Skagit Queen Camp, a brisk climb up switchbacks for one mile leads to the USGS cabin. Views improve beyond the cabin. Three more miles of fairly easy walking brings one to the mouth of Thunder Basin and to Basin Camp. One more mile of trail leads to the headwall of the basin. There are some steep portions in this mile, and the tread is extremely marshy, even after several weeks of dry weather. A final 0.75 mile brings the hiker to the top of Park

Creek Pass. There is abandoned mining equipment along the last 4.75 miles of trail.

Views are limited until the Fisher Creek junction. Tricouni, Primus, and Klawatti mountains and the Klawatti Glacier can be seen across the Thunder Creek valley. Further to the south, Forbidden and Boston peaks and their glaciers come into view as one goes higher. On the left, in the upper valley, Mt. Logan towers above with the Fremont Glacier clinging to its steep side. Directly south, the Thunder Glacier seems almost to overhang the trail. A tremendous view back down the valley can be had by turning around just before reaching Park Creek Pass.

The entire trail lies within the Ross Lake National Recreation Area and the North Cascades National Park. The boundary between the two is at about 6.8 miles; park rules apply beyond this point. Permits are required for overnight camping in both areas, and camping is restricted to designated campsites. Camping is not permitted in the Park Creek Pass alpine area.

(To McAllister Creek, May 1969)

EASY PASS (WNF)

DESTINATION: Easy Pass, 6500'

TRAIL LENGTH: 3.7 miles

WALKING TIME (light pack): 2½ hours in
                                        1½ hours out

TRAILHEAD ELEVATION: 3700'

ALTITUDE GAIN, including ups and downs: 2800'

FEATURE: Fisher Camp, 5200'

TOPOGRAPHIC SHEETS: USGS: Mt. Arriva 7.5'
                                       Green Trails: Mt. Logan

Since the trail contours under a north slope and is shaded by a steep rock ridge, it opens late and closes early due to snow. An ice axe is essential until about Labor Day in most years.

The trailhead is 46 miles east of Marblemount off the NCH. A paved road extends 0.1 mile west of the NCH, then dead-ends at the Easy Pass trailhead. There is parking for 8 to 10 cars near the road end and parallel parking along the spur road for 20 more. The footpath goes west, dropping a few feet and then proceeding on the level 0.15 mile to Granite Creek. The creek must be forded (uncomfortable at any time and dangerous in spring high water); there may be foot logs upstream or downstream. After the stream, the trail proceeds up on a moderate grade through deep forest; at about 1.5 miles from the trailhead it breaks into an avalanche meadow. From here on, there are views all the way to Easy Pass.

The trail crosses the meadow and proceeds south toward tall trees. Past the trees is a ford of Easy Pass Creek. The trail turns southeast, gaining altitude. Shortly thereafter it passes through avalanche debris, then contours up beneath a peak to the south. From about 2.0 to 2.4 miles, the trail crosses beneath a headwall to the west; the next 0.6 mile switchbacks up the headwall, topping out by a small creek in a level area where there are possible campsites. The trail proceeds up through meadow and eventually switchbacks under a rock face; it then contours west over talus slopes to Easy Pass.

The views from the pass are elegant, particularly in late September and early October, when the larch are golden yellow. Ragged Ridge to the northwest, Mt. Logan to the west, Mt. Hardy to the east, and Mt. Arriva, Fisher Peak, and Black Peak to the south are most impressive. There is room to ramble southeast on progressively higher ridges. A trailless walk to the north, gaining about 800', leads to a splendid viewpoint on the east end of Ragged Ridge.

There are few good campsites along the Forest Service portion of the trail. Easy Pass itself is closed to overnight camping. Those desiring to camp overnight can proceed down 2 miles from the pass (losing 1300′) to the Fisher campsite in deep timber in the valley below. One can cross country southeast into the Fisher Creek basin. Any campsite more than a mile from the trail in the basin is acceptable. At either location, overnight camping permits are required. Campfires are prohibited at Fisher Camp and within the Fisher Creek basin; backpacker's stoves should be carried. The walking time down to Fisher Creek is 50 minutes; time up is 1 hour and 25 minutes. There are alpine flowers in the area and an open subalpine meadow for about a mile west of the campsite.

From the pass it is 22 miles to Diablo Lake via the Fisher and Thunder Creek trails.

(August 1976)

BRIDGE CREEK (PCT)

NORTH TRAILHEAD: NCH, 4400′; Rainy Pass, 4800′

SOUTH TRAILHEAD: Stehekin Road, 2200′

TRAIL LENGTH: 12.4 miles Stehekin Road to NCH (low point between Washington and Rainy passes)

13.9 miles Stehekin Road to Rainy Pass

WALKING TIME (light pack): 5–6 hours down, NCH to Stehekin Road; add 35 minutes from Rainy Pass

6–7 hours up, Stehekin Road to NCH; add 45 minutes to Rainy Pass

TOPOGRAPHIC SHEETS: USGS: McGregor Mt.; McAlester Mt.; Washington Pass

Green Trails: McGregor Mt.; Stehekin; Washington Pass

This trail is a section of the Pacific Crest Trail. A substantial portion of the trail is in deep forest, particularly at each end. It does pass through avalanche slopes and open areas with views. In season, lupine and Indian paintbrush bloom along the route. The trail is muddy in places, but well maintained throughout. Wood is adequate at all campsites, and water is not a problem. Bird songs speed your way along the trail; there are often many butterflies.

South Trailhead

From the Stehekin valley, the trailhead is 0.2 mile before the Bridge Creek bridge. The trail ascends through deep forest, then drops to a bridge over Bridge Creek. From here it switchbacks up, gaining 400', to the junction and the North Fork Trail at 3 miles. The North Fork Camp is at the junction of Bridge Creek and the North Fork; there are good campsites here beside the rushing water. There is a small, scenic campsite 0.2 mile before Maple Creek on a rocky shelf above the gorge; this is the prettiest camp on the trail, but one must obtain water from Maple Creek, and it is exposed in inclement weather.

Cross Maple Creek on a bridge 50' above the old ford. The access trails to the bridge on either side may not be apparent, but the bridge can be seen from either direction as one approaches the creek. Six-mile Camp is indeed at 6 miles. The trail to this camp goes down to the river, where there are a number of campsites beneath the trees. Mud is a problem here in wet weather.

For better campsites, continue 0.8 mile to South Fork Camp, where there are several campsites by Bridge Creek. A foot log permits access to Rainbow Lake 6 miles away. (See Rainbow Lake Trail.) At 8.5 miles, Hideaway Camp (on Bridge Creek) is recommended only as a bivouac site. A bridge crossing 0.5 mile further allows access to Fireweed

Camp. Here is the junction to the trails to Twisp Pass, McAlester Pass, Stiletto Meadow and Peak, and Copper Pass. In another 0.8 mile is a campsite and an old cabin near the Bridge Creek Mines. The cabin could provide emergency shelter for up to 12 people.

At 10.8 miles is the north border of the National Park. Cross Bridge Creek at 11 miles on a footlog downstream from the horse ford. Remnants of mining are apparent in the area. Just above this is the spur trail to Copper Pass and the Stiletto Meadow bypass trail. From this point, it is 1.2 miles to the North Cascades Highway and 2.7 miles to Rainy Pass.

North Trailhead

If walking in from the North Cascades Highway, park your car at the lowest portion of the highway between Rainy and Washington Passes; this saves 1.5 miles of deep woods walking by taking the 100' way trail from the road to reach the Pacific Crest Trail.

Of the two access routes to the valley from the west, the Cascade Pass route (described earlier in this chapter) is shorter and more scenic than Bridge Creek.

(July 1977)

NORTH FORK OF BRIDGE CREEK

DESTINATION: Trail end, 4200'

TRAIL LENGTH: 7 miles

WALKING TIME (light pack): 4 hours in
3 hours out

TRAILHEAD ELEVATION 2800' (Bridge Creek—PCT)

ALTITUDE GAIN, including ups and downs: 1400'
TOPOGRAPHIC SHEETS: USGS: Mt. Logan; McGregor
Mt.; Goode Mt.
Green Trails: Mt. Logan;
McGregor Mt.

The trailhead is three miles up Bridge Creek from the Stehekin Road, on a bluff 0.4 mile beyond the Bridge Creek bridge and North Fork Hiker's Camp. The junction was well marked in August 1980.

Many trees in the area are dead or dying, probably from spruce budworm infestation. At 0.8 mile a small pond with lily pads can be seen to the left; at the same place there is a view of the mountains at the head of the North Fork Valley. Water is available at one mile. At 1.9 miles is an excellent view of Mt. Goode to the south. The trail breaks into Walker Park at 2.1 miles; there is another excellent view of Goode and of the waterfall cascading down its side. Water is available here. This area, about 0.3 mile wide, is the creation of the massive avalanches that cascade down the north face of Goode and extend up the north side of the valley and decimate tree growth, leaving an open area at a far lower altitude than is usual in the Stehekin area.

At the Walker Park (horse) camp (3100') are a table, fire pit, and camp sites, and water is available 100' further along the North Fork Trail. There are also, unfortunately, lots of flies on hot days.

The trail continues up gently through forest cover to Grizzly Creek Camp, three miles from the trailhead. Here there are four tent sites, three in deep woods, with fire pits and grills. The fourth tent site is 200' upstream from the ford. On the bank of Grizzly Creek, this site allows good views of the peaks at the head of the valley. The liability of this site is the noise that Grizzly Creek makes as it tumbles past. A wilderness toilet is 100' to the left of the main trail near the tent sites. It is difficult to find a good location to hang food bags around this campsite to protect them from bears, but the Park Service advises that bear problems at this campsite have been negligible.

The walking time from the trailhead to Grizzly Creek Camp with a full pack is under 2 hours. Since there are no designated campsites further up the trail, most people establish camp at Walker Park or beside Grizzly Creek, and do the rest of the trail light-packed. Walker Park is the more scenic of the campsites, but there may be a conflict between hikers and horseback riders. The Grizzly campsite is for hikers only.

The trail crosses Grizzly Creek via a horse ford 150' past the campsites. As of 1980 people can cross 200' downstream, where there is a crude log bridge. If Grizzly Creek cannot be crossed on a downed tree, it must be forded. During spring high water this ford could be hazardous.

It is best to check with the Park Ranger staff to be sure that the trail has been brushed; much of the trail for the next 2 miles is in dense, tall brush, and the going could be uncomfortable in dry weather and miserable in wet.

At 3.5 miles views improve, and shortly thereafter there is water from a creek crossing the trail. At four miles, there is a good view of Goode and Storm King mountains and their hanging glaciers. If wearing shorts, watch for nettles in the brushy areas. At 4.1 miles, a 40-foot-long flooded area in the trail must be bypassed. A few feet further is a pretty campsite to the left of the trail. At 4.3 miles is an open area where one can rest and enjoy the splendid scenery. Water can be obtained from the North Fork of Bridge Creek, although there is glacial flour in it. At 4.6 miles is a waterfall to the left, close by the trail, which is better heard than seen since it is obscured by brush.

At 6.2 miles a timbered ridge ascends on the right of the trail ahead; along the footpath there are occasional level areas. Most of the brush has disappeared by now, and the area is grassy meadow. At 6.8 miles the meadow is splendid. Twin waterfalls cascade off a mountain ahead. At 6.9 miles the tread becomes vague. At 7 miles the trail turns a corner and ends where there is a splendid view north of Mt. Logan and the Douglas Glacier. A wide pass with a waterfall cascading hundreds of feet is framed by Mt. Logan and its hanging glaciers on the left and a rock spire on the right. In the foreground a tumultuous waterfall, formed by the North Fork of Bridge Creek, cascades from the pass above. There is interesting red rock with quartz crystals in this area. The altitude here is about 4200'.

This is a splendid place, and well worth the effort to reach it; plan time to remain in this area. Since this trail is little used, particularly to the end, a hiker can almost always get a sense of magnificent isolation.

The distance from Grizzly Creek Camp to the trail end is 4 miles. The time up light-packed is 2 hours; time down is 1.7 hours. The time out from Grizzly Creek Camp (with a full pack) to the junction with the main Bridge Creek trail is an hour and 20 minutes; the total round trip time is 7 hours.

(August 1980)

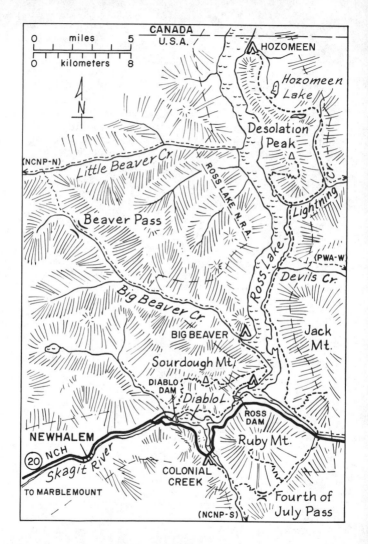

10

ROSS LAKE NATIONAL RECREATION AREA

Trails:

Ross Lake, East (East Bank; Hozomeen to Nightmare
Camp; Nightmare Camp to Ross Lake)

Fourth of July Pass (Ruby Mountain)

Ross Dam–Big Beaver

Diablo Dam–Ross Dam

Desolation Lookout

Jack Arm

Sourdough Mountain

(Devil's Dome)

If Seattle City Light builds the controversial High Ross Dam, raising the existing dam 122 feet, it would affect all the trails in the Ross Lake area, particularly Big Beaver (see Chapter 7), East Bank, Hozomeen–Nightmare Camp, and Ross Dam–Big Beaver.

ROSS LAKE, EAST (EAST BANK; HOZOMEEN TO NIGHTMARE CAMP; NIGHTMARE CAMP TO ROSS LAKE)

TRAIL LENGTH: 30.1 miles

WALKING TIME: 2–3 days one way

TRAILHEAD ELEVATIONS: 1800' (NCH); 1650' (Hozomeen)

ALTITUDE GAIN, including ups and downs: 2800'

SEASON FOR USE: April to November

FEATURES: Willow Lake, 2900' (high point); Hidden Hand Pass, 2500'; Nightmare Camp, 2150'; Lightning Creek Trail, 2500'; Deer Lick Cabin, 1920'

TOPOGRAPHIC SHEETS: USGS: Hozomeen; Skagit Peak; Pumpkin Mountain; Ross Dam; Crater Mountain
Green Trails: Ross Lake; Jack Mountain; Diablo Dam; Mt. Logan

It is 30.1 miles between the two trailheads. Since most hikers will go from one trailhead to the other, rather than making the round trip, the south portion of the trail will be described to Lightning Creek. The north portion of the trail from Hozomeen to Lightning Creek will be described next.

Since this is a lowland trail, it is generally snow-free from April to November. In light snow years, it may even be accessible during the winter. There are fine views of Jack

Mountain, Hozomeen Peak, the Pickets, and, of course, Ross Lake from the trail.

It is possible to arrange (in advance at the Ross Lake Resort) water transportation to and from the trailheads, but generally not before July 1. Parties using two cars can exchange car keys at midpoint on the trail.

East Bank Trail

The south trailhead is on the NCH 8.2 miles east of Thunder Arm Bridge and 33 miles east of Marblemount. There is parking for 50 or 60 cars on the north side of the highway.

From the highway the trail drops to the Ruby Creek Bridge 0.2 mile away. Turn left here and follow the trail along the north shore of Ruby Creek. After about 0.1 mile, the trail forks; take the upper, broader trail. A 2.6-mile walk, taking about an hour, leads to the junction with the East Bank trail. The Hidden Hand campsite is about 0.7 mile beyond this junction, toward Ross Lake.

From the junction, the East Bank Trail goes up into a saddle at about 1 mile, gaining about 800'. It then gradually loses altitude until it reaches the Roland Creek campsite 3.7 miles from the junction. Beyond Roland Creek the trail remains near the lakeshore, with good scenery to Lightning Creek. It is 1.3 miles from Roland Creek to the May Creek campsite, 0.9 mile from May Creek to the Rainbow Point campsite, and 2.3 miles from Rainbow Point to the Devil's Creek campsite. From Devil's Creek it is 1.4 miles to the junction with the Devil's Dome Trail. From this junction to Lightning Creek is 3.5 miles, then 0.1 mile to the Lightning Creek Trail junction, and another 0.1 mile to the Lightning Creek Camp. From the trailhead to the Lightning Creek Trail junction is 16 miles.

A few yards past the junction with the Lightning Creek Trail is the junction with the Desolation Peak Trail. It is 2.1

miles up this trail to Jack Point. (See Desolation Peak Trail for information beyond the Jack Point lakeshore.) Hiking time is 7 hours from the trailhead to the Lightning Creek Camp, with another hour to the Desolation trailhead.

Two precautions: First, ticks are prevalent in the area. Hikers should inspect each other frequently and remove the critters before they embed themselves. Second, giardia, a protozoan parasite which causes diarrhea and other symptoms, seems particularly prevalent around Ross Lake. All water should be boiled, or treated with iodine, before drinking.

Water and firewood are not problems, and campfires are allowed at all designated campsites. Bears are fairly common, particularly at the Lightning Creek Camp.

(1970 and 1971)

Hozomeen to Nightmare Camp

The north trailhead at Hozomeen is reached by driving the Trans-Canada Highway east from Vancouver; shortly before the town of Hope, turn right (south) on the Silver-Skagit Road immediately before a highway bridge (in 1975 there was a sign for Ross Lake). It is 39 miles from this turnoff to the trailhead. Immediately after passing the old City Light bunkhouse, follow the side road that goes up, turns back to the north, and passes through the Hozomeen Campground; the trail begins immediately east of a cabin at the road end loop, about 0.2 mile on the turnoff from the main road.

From the trailhead, it is three miles (1¼ hours) to the Hozomeen Lake Trail junction. The side trail to the lake is 0.6 mile long and ends in a campground on a promontory in the lake, where there is space for about ten campsites. This is the nicest campsite on the trail, although wood is scarce. The two peaks of Hozomeen dominate the view from this promontory. Fishing is good in the lake; fly fishermen will want to bring a raft, since the forest comes right down to the lakeshore. Campfires are allowed at all campsites on this trail.

Two miles (40 minutes) away from the junction is the Willow Lake campsite; this is the high point of the trail (2850'). There is a cabin at the lake with bunk space for two; the roof is waterproof. There is also a toilet and an area for a tent.

East of Willow Lake the snow tends to stay late in the spring; look for yellow metal blazes on the trees to help with route finding. The trail drops fairly sharply, follows a mossy stream about 0.2 mile through a beautiful little canyon, and then abruptly breaks out high above a valley. Near this point, off the trail 20' to 30' under a grassy knoll, there is an excellent view of Mt. Hozomeen to the northwest. The only good views of Hozomeen are at Hozomeen Lake and at this point. One hour or 2.7 miles from Willow Lake is Nightmare Camp, set in a grove of huge cedars close by Lightning Creek. Here is a bridge across the creek, and the intersection with Lightning Creek Trail. Skagit Peak can be seen to the east.

Experienced hikers can walk the lakeshore in early spring, when the water is low, for about nine miles on beaches, ledges, and occasionally Class 2 rock between Hozomeen and Lightning Creek. This route is impossible when the lake is full.

If the controversial High Ross Dam is constructed, substantial changes will occur on this trail.

(1975)

Nightmare Camp to Ross Lake

The trail crosses Lightning Creek on a bridge east of Nightmare Camp and proceeds south along the east side of the river. The river can easily be reached for fishing along most of the route. The path is mainly within deep forest; views of the surrounding peaks are rare. From the bridge it is about 2.5 miles to Deerlick Camp. Walking time is one hour; altitude loss is a bit over 200'.

A trail post marks the way trail west to Deerlick Camp; an 0.1-mile side trail leads to the river. There are two campsites by the creek, dank even in good weather, and two campsites on a bench above the creek.

Two-tenths of a mile further is the trail post marking the junction with the Boundary (3 Fools) Trail. From this point, it is 0.8 mile to the Pasayten Wilderness boundary, 3 miles to the Little Fish Shelter to the east, and 4 miles to Ross Lake to the west. The east trail gains about 500' in the first half mile, and then stays level to the wilderness boundary (and all the way to the shelter).

The west trail drops at this point, crossing a small bridge and then the sturdy bridge across Lightning Creek. On the other side is the Deerlick Cabin, a horse-hitching area, and level, although muddy, ground for a tent. The cabin roof is mossy, with a few holes, but it could serve as a reasonable rain shelter. It is often used by Park Service trail crews. This is a pleasant, scenic area; two huge cedars tower above the cabin and bridge.

Going west from the bridge and cabin, the trail climbs for roughly 0.9 mile, gaining about 350'. Near the cabin the trail is in dank, deep forest. Shortly thereafter it is in very dense young forest, probably regrowth following a burn.

The trail levels off about 500' above Lightning Creek and continues west for a bit over 2 miles. Over the next mile, it descends via switchbacks to Ross Lake. At the high point there are good views of the lake to the west and south, of the East Bank Trail bridge over the mouth of Lightning Creek directly below, and of Mt. Prophet to the west. Close to the campground, marked by a trail post, is the junction with the Desolation Peak Trail. A few yards further, also marked, is the junction with the East Bank Trail, which runs to the south and in a few feet crosses the suspension bridge across the mouth of Lightning Creek. A short way trail leads from this junction to the Lightning Creek Campground, where there are tables, restrooms, and 5 or 6 campsites.

Water is not a problem between Deerlick and Ross Lake early in the season, but later water is probably scarce. Birds are frequent along the trail, and bird song echoes through the trees in June. Grouse are common, and deer, and occasionally bear, are seen at the Lightning Creek Camp. Wild flowers, particularly Indian paintbrush, are common along the trail in late spring. Walking time from cabin to campground is 1½ hours; in the opposite direction, allow an extra 15 minutes for the switchbacks above Ross Lake.

(June 1980)

FOURTH OF JULY PASS
(RUBY MOUNTAIN)

DESTINATION: Fourth of July Pass, 3700'

TRAIL LENGTH: 3 miles

WALKING TIME (light pack): 2¼ hours in
1¼ hours out

TRAILHEAD ELEVATION 1300'

ALTITUDE GAIN, including ups and downs: 2500'

SEASON FOR USE: May through November

FEATURE: Ruby Mountain, 7408'

TOPOGRAPHIC SHEETS: USGS: Ross Dam; Crater Mountain
Green Trails: Diablo Dam; Mt. Logan

This trail gives access to Fourth of July Pass, Ruby Mountain, and to the Panther Creek Trail, which descends to the North Cascades Highway. The trailhead is 2.1 miles from the Colonial Creek Campground on the Thunder Creek Trail; see Thunder Creek Trail for access to the trailhead.

The trail starts to the left (east), ascending moderately via switchbacks on fair tread for about 0.7 mile. After crossing a creek, the trail traverses to the southeast for 0.4 mile, and then switchbacks up moderately, topping out at about 2.9 miles from the junction (on the Thunder Creek Trail). A large rock left of the top-out point offers excellent views of Colonial and Snowfield peaks to the west. A walk 0.1 mile up the trail, then 100 feet south to a knoll, offers striking views of the Eldorado massif to the southwest. The designated Fourth of July Pass campsite is about 100 yards after the top-out point, roughly 3 miles from the junction.

Several creeks cross the trail, so water is no problem, at least in the spring. Calypso orchids bloom in profusion; trillium, flowering Oregon grape, and yellow wood violets also bloom along this trail in May.

Diablo Lake is glimpsed through breaks in the forest cover. In warm weather, heat can be a problem while ascending the trail.

Although the average hiker and camper will stop at Fourth of July Pass, there are other options. The hiker can proceed east; the trail gradually loses altitude. About one mile beyond the top-out point is a junction. The trail to the right continues down Panther Creek to the North Cascade Highway, about 5 miles away. The less apparent trail to the left leads to the summit of Ruby Mountain. In 1973 this trail was marked "no longer maintained"; further down was a sign on a tree saying "Hoot Owl Trail."

Parties with two cars could make the loop down Panther Creek. The hiker can take his chances on hitchhiking back to the trailhead at the Colonial Creek Campground from the Panther Creek trailhead; the road distance between the two trailheads is 8.5 miles.

From the Panther Creek Trail junction to the Ruby Mountain summit is about 5 miles and takes about 3½ hours. From the summit back to the Colonial Creek campground takes roughly 4 hours. The altitude gain from Colonial Creek is about 6300'. Although very strong hikers can do this as a day trip, most will want to pack in to the campsite at Fourth of July Pass, and ascend light-packed to the summit, with the option of spending a second night at Fourth of July Pass.

Only the experienced hiker in good condition should attempt the ascent of Ruby Mountain. The trail is indeed not maintained, and the tread is quite difficult to locate. There are a few level places for camping, but there is no water. The trail is considerably harder to locate descending than ascending; it would be wise to mark areas without tread with blazes or surveyor's flagging tape during the ascent. Alternating between level stretches and switchbacks, the trail to Ruby Mountain goes north. Views begin when the trail reaches 5000'. The trail leaves the timber on the west side of Ruby Mountain, goes north without gaining altitude for about a half mile, and then switchbacks up a beautiful meadow with fine views of Colonial and Pyramid Peaks, Mt. Baker and Mt. Shuksan, and other spires to the west. The trail finally peters out in a little notch at about 6700'. The hiker should go northeast up a moderately steep meadow, bypassing talus if possible, to the col between two false summits at roughly 7300'. From this col there is a splendid view of Ross Lake below and a permanent snowfield from which to obtain water. Follow the ridge crest north, bypassing on the east the first summit a few feet below the top, and walk a quarter mile to the true summit. The last 50' up are on talus. The summit is cairned, with a summit register.

The view from the Ruby Mountain summit is incredible. All of Ross Lake is spread out to the north. Jack Mountain, Hozomeen Peak, Sourdough Ridge, the Pickets, Colonial, Pyramid, and Snowfield peaks, the peaks in the Cascade

Pass and Black Peak areas, are all visible in a stunning 360-degree panorama.
(September 1973)

ROSS DAM—BIG BEAVER

DESTINATION: Big Beaver Camp, 1610'

TRAIL LENGTH: 7 miles

WALKING TIME (light pack): 2¾ hours in
                          3½ hours out

TRAILHEAD ELEVATION 2050' (NCH)

ALTITUDE GAIN, including ups and downs: 300' in, 700' out

FEATURE: Ross Lake, 1600'

TOPOGRAPHIC SHEETS: USGS: Ross Dam; Pumpkin Mountain 7.5'
                    Green Trails: Diablo Dam; Ross Lake

The trailhead is on the left (west) side of the North Cascade Highway 3.8 miles beyond the Thunder Arm bridge over Diablo Lake. The area is well marked. While there is space for 35 cars at the trailhead, the parking area is often inadequate on summer weekends.

The trail drops moderately, crosses over a rustic bridge, and passes rocky cliffs with ferns and flowers. In about 0.7 mile, the trail loses 350' and comes out on the road that goes to the Ross Dam powerhouse below the dam. To get to the lakeshore, turn right on the road, walk 0.3 mile, losing 175', to the boat launching area.

To get to the dam, turn left and drop almost as far, cross the dam, and continue north along the lakeshore. From the dam, it is a half mile to the trail down to the Ross Lake Resort. Another half mile leads to the Green Point junction;

from here, a side trail leads half a mile to the Green Point Campground, on a peninsula extending into Ross Lake. From the Green Point junction, it is 2.3 miles to the junction with the eastern access to Sourdough Ridge and Lookout, sometimes called Pierce Mountain Way because the trail circles Pierce Mountain. (Via this route, it is 4.2 miles to the Pierce Mountain campsite and 5.1 miles to the lookout.) From this junction it is 3.2 miles to Big Beaver Creek. About 4.5 miles from Ross Dam, the trail enters a glen. Nearby Pierce Creek cascades in a spectacular waterfall. Continue one mile north to reach the bridge over Big Beaver Creek. Immediately north of the bridge, the trail forks; a short way trail to the right (east) extends 0.2 mile to the Big Beaver Campground. The trail to the left (west) ascends Big Beaver Creek.

Between Ross Dam and Big Beaver Camp the trail occasionally breaks out onto the lakeshore, with good views of Ross Lake and of Jack Mountain to the east. Most of the trail is in deep forest, though. The trail from Ross Dam to Big Beaver is fairly level and takes about 2 hours to walk. Allow 20 minutes down to, and 30 minutes up from, the dam or lakeshore.

(Highway 20 to Ross Lake, 1980; Dam to Big Beaver, 1967)

DIABLO DAM—ROSS DAM

DESTINATION: Ross Dam bridge, 1225′
TRAIL LENGTH: 3.8 miles
WALKING TIME: 1½ hours one way
TRAILHEAD ELEVATION: 1250′
HIGH POINT: 2000′
ALTITUDE GAIN, including ups and downs: 800′

SEASON FOR USE: March through November
TOPOGRAPHIC SHEETS: USGS: Ross Dam
                    Green Trails: Diablo Dam

From the North Cascades Highway 21.7 miles east of Marblemount, turn north, drop on a steep road, and cross Diablo Dam. Drive east about half a mile to the parking area 0.2 mile west of the Diablo Lake Resort. There is space for 6 or 7 cars at the trailhead. The trail begins on the east side of the Sourdough Creek Bridge and runs northeast, bypassing the resort. It crosses Deer Creek in half a mile; at about the same point, way trails from the resort join the main trail. The footpath goes through forest, gradually gaining altitude and emerging on a bluff about 500′ above Diablo Lake. From this point there is a view of the NCH across the canyon. Pyramid Peak, Colonial Peak, and Ruby Mountain can also be seen from here. Approaching Ross Dam, the trail switchbacks down through deep timber, breaking out occasionally into the cleared powerline right-of-way. A footbridge crosses Diablo Lake, offering access to the Ross Dam powerhouse. To extend the walk, go up the truck road to the top of Ross Dam itself; or cross the dam and walk along Ross Lake; or go up to the North Cascades Highway.

There are no campsites along the trail (day use only). Some water is available from springs. This is a good fall or spring conditioning walk, offering some views. The hiker may turn around at the high point, 2.8 miles from the trailhead, rather than descending to Ross Dam.
    (1972)

DESOLATION LOOKOUT

DESTINATION: Desolation Lookout, 6100′
TRAIL LENGTH: 4.7 miles

WALKING TIME: 4¾ hours in
2¼ hours out

TRAILHEAD ELEVATION: 1600′

ALTITUDE GAIN, including ups and downs: 4500′

TOPOGRAPHIC SHEETS: USGS: Hozomeen Mountain 7.5′
Green Trails: Ross Lake

The easiest access to the trailhead is by water; boats may be chartered at the Ross Lake Resort. It is a two-day, one-way walk to reach the trailhead from either Hozomeen or the North Cascades Highway.

The trailhead is on the east shore of Ross Lake, 2.1 miles from the junction with the Lightning Creek Trail; it is about 0.3 mile south of Jack Point, and 1.25 miles north of Cat Island. Four switchbacks up from the lakeshore, the way trail meets the trail from Lightning Creek. The Desolation Lookout trail then switchbacks moderately steeply through dry, fairly open country for about one mile, offering good views up and down Ross Lake. The trail then enters brush and small trees, with minimal views until it breaks into meadow between 2.5 and 3 miles. The only water is at one small spring at about 2.5 miles. The fourth mile is in meadow, switchbacking up to the ridge crest. From here, the trail swings north through gorgeous wildflowers to the false summit of Desolation Peak, dips slightly into a saddle, and then ascends several hundred feet to the true summit where the lookout is. Grouse, hummingbirds and crickets are common along the trail.

The lookout is manned in summer. Except for the fire watcher, people are scarce because of the difficult access. There is a sense of remoteness and isolation.

In a normal year, all snow melts from the summit ridge by August. As it is difficult to find water later, June and July are the best months for visiting. The Park Service has established a campsite on the summit ridge near the lookout. Fires are not allowed at this campsite; a backpacker's stove should be carried. A permit is required for overnight camping.

From the summit, there are magnificent views down into the Ross Lake basin and into the Little Beaver Valley to the west. Ruby, Colonial, and Pyramid peaks are easily seen to the south. To the north are the spires of Hozomeen Mountain. To the east and south in the Pasayten Wilderness are Castle Peak, Skagit Peak, Spratt Mountain, Devil's Dome, and Jack Mountain. Mt. Baker and Mt. Shuksan are visible beyond the Pickets to the west. Surprisingly, the hiker may hear water plunging into Ross Lake from falls on the far side of the lake, at least three miles away. Tame deer are common in the lookout area. Unfortunately, deerflies are a problem in midsummer.

Warnings: (1) Ticks are common on the lower part of the trail; (2) Giardia often infests the water here; boil the water or treat it with iodine.

It is possible to cross country down the north slope of Desolation and climb two lower peaks to the north.

(1967)

JACK ARM

DESTINATION: Jack Arm, 6000'

TRAIL LENGTH: 5.7 miles (8.5 miles from NCH)

WALKING TIME: 4½ hours in
2 hours out
(9 hours round trip from NCH)

TRAILHEAD ELEVATION: 1800'

ALTITUDE GAIN, including ups and downs: 5400'

TOPOGRAPHIC SHEETS: USGS: Ross Dam and Crater
Mountain 7.5'
Green Trails: Diablo Dam; Mt. Logan

The trailhead is 2.8 miles from the NCH at the junction of the Ruby Creek and East Bank trails. At this point the East Bank Trail goes north and the less obvious Jack Mountain Trail goes east-northeast. The trail does not lead to Jack Mountain itself; it leads to a high ridge about 2.5 miles south of Jack Mountain. In its first three miles it switchbacks up moderately. After about a half mile the footpath breaks out of forest cover, allowing views of the countryside, including the NCH below, Ross Lake, Ruby Mountain, and Sourdough Ridge. Meadow is between three and four miles from the trail junction. The switchbacks continue upward.

Water supplies are very limited, particularly later in the year, so a substantial amount of water should be carried. The Little Jack designated campsite is 4.5 miles from the junction and 1.2 miles from the trail end above. Campfires are prohibited; carry a portable stove. A permit is required for overnight camping.

The trail ends on the ridge crest at a rocky knob, which was cairned in 1974. There are amazing views of Jack Mountain, Crater Mountain, Granite and Panther creeks, Ruby, Colonial and Pyramid peaks, Ross, Diablo and Gorge Lakes, and the Big Beaver Valley. Even the tips of Mt. Baker and Mt. Shuksan rise beyond the mountain crests to the west.

In 1974 the trail was not well maintained and was badly overgrown in places, but it was not difficult to locate.

(July 1975)

SOURDOUGH MOUNTAIN

DESTINATION: Lookout, 5997'
TRAIL LENGTH: 5.2 miles to lookout (3.8 miles to camp)

WALKING TIME: with full pack to camp: 4 hours in, 2
hours out
with light pack, camp to lookout: 2 hours
up, 1¾ hours down
TRAILHEAD ELEVATION 900′
ALTITUDE GAIN, including ups and downs: 5250′
FEATURE: Sourdough campsite, 5000′
TOPOGRAPHIC SHEETS: USGS: Diablo Dam and Ross
Dam 7.5′
Green Trails: Diablo Dam

There are few trails in the North Cascades more miserable than the first 2 miles of this route. Only those in excellent physical condition should attempt the hike, preferably on a cool day. In midsummer, in addition to heat, there are deerflies. The best time to explore this area is late September and early October, when it is cooler, there are fewer bugs, and the fall color is splendid.

Take the North Cascades Highway from Marblemount toward Diablo; take the left fork where the highway crosses Gorge Lake and continue into Diablo proper. The trail begins immediately behind the plastic-covered swimming pool in Diablo. Monotonous, steep switchbacks make the first 2 miles unpleasant. At about one-half mile the trail breaks out over a rocky bluff, giving a nice view of the town of Diablo and Gorge Lake. At about 0.9 mile there is scrabble access to water from a small creek to the west. About 1.5 miles there is a small stream that crosses the trail. At about 2.2 miles, a way trail marked by blazes and a cairn indicates where to leave the main trail for a 100-yard side trip leading to a rocky bluff overlooking Diablo Lake. This is an excellent stopping point for lunch.

The trail enters the National Park at 2.5 miles. There is water at 2.6 miles. At about 2.7 miles, the trail breaks into meadow and becomes less steep, although tread quality deteriorates thereafter.

The trail now goes north, reaching the cleft between the access ridge and Sourdough Mountain at about 3.8 miles. Here is the Sourdough campsite at about 5000'. Water is available from Sourdough Creek, which is easily crossed. In the fall this is the last available water. Earlier in the season, water can generally be had from snowfields along the summit ridge and small creeks en route.

From the campsite, the footpath to the lookout ascends the meadow via switchbacks, goes moderately up and east until about 0.25 mile west of the lookout, then switchbacks up through the meadow to the top of the ridge; for the last quarter mile, the trail traverses the ridge crest.

The view from the lookout is spectacular. Five great valleys (Upper and Lower Skagit, Ruby, Thunder, and Big Beaver) radiate like the spokes of a wheel. Diablo Lake below sparkles in the afternoon sun. Ross Lake is an azure ribbon to the north. Sourdough Lake is to the northwest. Grouse, eagles, bears, marmots, pikas, ptarmigans, and hawks frequent the area. Deer are common and may be pests in the camp areas. In the fall the ridge blazes red and yellow in the sun. Meadow flowers are superb.

The lookout house was built in 1917 and rebuilt in the mid-30s. The structure, in excellent condition, is manned only at times of high fire danger. If a fire watcher is on duty, you will usually be welcomed inside.

Cross-country travel from the Sourdough campsite up the Sourdough Creek col leads to the ridge crest without great difficulty. From here, there is a very fine view of the Picket Range to the northwest. It is possible to reach Sourdough Lake by dropping down about 1000' and traversing to the northeast.

(July 1981)

Approach via Pierce Mountain Way

> TRAIL LENGTH: 4.4 miles to Pierce Camp
> 5.1 miles to Lookout
> TRAILHEAD ELEVATION 2100′
> ALTITUDE GAIN, including ups and downs: 4100′
> FEATURE: Pierce Camp, 5100′
> TOPOGRAPHIC SHEETS: Green Trails: Diablo Dam and
> Ross Lake

An alternative, longer route to the lookout involves dropping from the NCH, crossing Ross Dam, and proceeding along the Big Beaver Trail to the Pierce Mountain Way trailhead, roughly 3.8 miles from the highway. From here it is 4.4 miles to Pierce Camp (5100′) and another 0.7 mile to the lookout. The altitude gain is roughly 600′ less, but the distance is about 3.7 miles greater.

Using two cars, or hitchhiking along the North Cascades Highway, it is possible to make a two-day loop trip. Starting at the top, head for the flat area with tarns below and to the northeast. Tread is faint to nonexistent between the lookout and the Pierce Mt. Campsite; follow cairns, or simply descend on rock, heather and snow. Below the campsite, the trail may be difficult to locate where it traverses a recently ravaged burn area. Inquire beforehand at the Marblemount Ranger Station about this Pierce Mountain access route, since it is a secondary trail and maintenance may vary from year to year.

Estimated hiking times from the highway to the lookout via the Pierce Mountain Way is six to seven hours up, and four to five hours out. Campfires are not allowed at the campsites in the area; carry a small stove. In July 1981 both designated campsites were substandard. The walk between the two camps, however, is glorious. Experienced back-country travelers can also follow Sourdough Ridge west for a mile or so, and then descend cross-country to the Sour-dough campsite. This is a longer but more scenic alternative to following the trail.

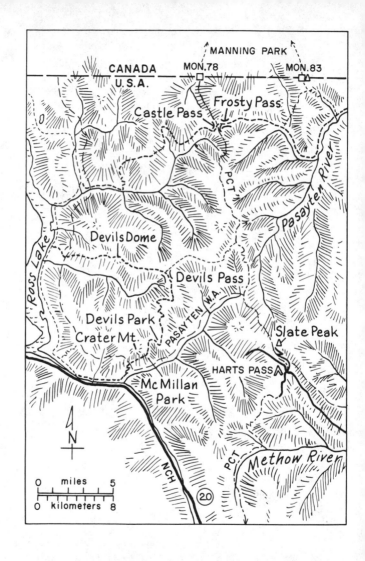

11

PASAYTEN WILDERNESS
South Section

Trails:
Devil's Dome
McMillan Park and Devil's Park
(Boundary Trail)
(Pacific Crest Trail)

DEVIL'S DOME

DESTINATION: Bear Skull Shelter, 5800'

TRAIL LENGTH: 6 miles

WALKING TIME (full pack): 5 hours in
2¾ hours out

TRAILHEAD ELEVATION 1800'

ALTITUDE GAIN, including ups and downs: 4200'

FEATURES: Dry Creek Pass, 6000'; Devil's Dome, 6980'
(high point)

TOPOGRAPHIC SHEETS: USGS: Pumpkin Mt.; Jack Mt.
Green Trails: Ross Lake; Jack Mt.

This area opens about July 1 in an average snow year, about two weeks earlier than the more western portions of the range. Because of the difficult access and the altitude gain, the area is uncrowded: solitude is practically guaranteed. It is a splendid place to experience the North Cascade wilderness.

The trailhead is 12.4 miles from the NCH, on the east side of Ross Lake. If arriving by boat at the lakeshore (where there is a good campsite), walk north parallel to the lake 0.1 mile, then switchback up 0.2 mile to reach the East Bank Trail. Do not take the left fork to the horse camp; turn right. The trail proceeds up steeply and crosses, at 1.2 miles, the boundary between the Ross Lake National Recreation area and the Pasayten Wilderness area. The trail is in good condition to the boundary.

Beyond the boundary in the Pasayten Wilderness the trail may be poorly maintained and occasionally difficult to locate; the tread is particularly faint between 1.8 and 3.3 miles.

There is no water from the lake to approximately the 1.8-mile mark, where water may trickle from a spring; canteens should be filled at the lake before starting up. There are good-sized streams at about 3 miles, 3.8 miles, and 4.5 miles. At 1.9 miles is the first good view of Ross Lake and the mountains to the west. From the 2.6-mile mark on, views improve as altitude is gained.

The trail goes east, gaining altitude, sometimes in switchbacks. About 5.5 miles from the trailhead, after three steep switchbacks, the trail tops out on a ridge crest. The main trail turns right (east) up the ridge crest for 0.3 mile to an obscure trail junction. A small alpine fir was blazed at this junction in 1972; immediately to the south (toward Jack Mountain) there is a tall, four-trunked tree. If going to the Bearskull Shelter, turn north at this point and follow the way trail about 0.2 mile, then go northwest 0.1 mile, losing about 200'. If you have trouble finding the shelter, look for a trail running across the steep meadow to the north; the shelter is at the base of this trail.

In 1972 the shelter was in good condition, with a stove, bunks for four people, a table, and many rodents. Nailed above the entrance is a bear skull. About 0.2 mile up the ridge crest is a level campsite. Water is available from a stream issuing from a snowfield a few feet from the Bearskull Shelter. A toilet is 100 feet to the north.

From Bearskull, there are three possibilities for exploration. The first is to continue east on the main trail to Devil's Dome. This path contours gradually uphill in beautiful meadow country, with fine views of Jack Mountain, Crater Mountain, Jackita Ridge, and Devil's Park. The footpath rises into the saddle between Devil's Dome and a peak to the north. The distance from the Bearskull junction to the saddle is 1.2 miles, gaining about 700′. It is about 5 miles further to Devil's Pass.

The second trail is a scrabble trail proceeding north from the Bearskull Shelter, and contouring upward beneath a rocky bluff. Views from this trail to the west are very fine. This trail peters out in high meadow, leaving the hiker many options, including scrambling to the summit of either rocky bluff from a saddle about one mile from the shelter. There are magnificent displays of alpine flowers in this area.

The third option is to turn left immediately on the ridge crest and follow a scrabble trail up and west about 0.2 mile, drop another 0.2 mile, then scramble up to a flat ridge, gaining altogether some 500′ in the approximately 0.7 mile. From here one can walk gently up and west for 1½ miles, following a faint tread or simply wandering in the glorious open meadow. From this ridge there are splendid views of Desolation Peak, Hozomeen Mountain, Ross Lake, the northern Pickets, and the Canadian Mountains. From the end of the ridge there is an amazing view practically straight down into Ross Lake.

Wildlife in the area includes the bald eagle, grouse, ground squirrel, and deer. Of geologic interest is conglomerate, unusual in the North Cascades.

A long loop returning to the trailhead can be made by going south from Devil's Pass along Jackita Ridge, and leaving via McMillan Park, returning to the starting point at the NCH via the Ruby Creek Trail. (See McMillan Park and Devil's Park Trail.) It is also possible to reach the Pacific Crest Trail or the road at Chancellor by continuing east from Devil's Pass.

(July 1972)

McMILLAN PARK AND DEVIL'S PARK

DESTINATION: Devil's Park, 5850'

TRAIL LENGTH: 7 miles

WALKING TIME (full pack): 7½ hours in
4½ hours out

TRAILHEAD ELEVATION 1650' (Panther Creek Bridge)

ALTITUDE GAIN, including ups and downs: 4900'

FEATURES: Crater Mt. lookout site, 7054' (high point);
Confluence of Granite and Ruby creeks,
1900'; McMillan Park, 5500'; High point on
Jackita Ridge, 6840'

TOPOGRAPHIC SHEETS: USGS: Crater Mt.; Shull Mt.;
Jack Mt.; Azurite Peak
Green Trails: Mt. Logan; Jack Mt.

The trailhead is just west of Panther Creek Bridge on the North Cascades Highway, 32.8 miles east of Marblemount and 55.1 miles west of Winthrop. There is a large parking area at the trailhead. The trail drops and crosses Ruby Creek on a large foot-and-horse bridge. Turn right at the junction immediately after the bridge. Ruby Camp is 50 feet away, by the river; there are two nice tent sites close to the rushing water. A toilet is on the hill above the camp.

From the bridge, it is 0.9 mile to the recreational area boundary and 3.5 miles to the McMillan and Devil's Park Trail. The trail follows the north side of Ruby Creek, gradually gaining altitude. Walking time to the McMillan Park trailhead is about 1½ hours.

A shorter alternative may be available to reach this trailhead. Drive 2.9 miles further east on the NCH to the junction of Canyon and Granite Creeks. There is a bridge allowing the hiker to cross Granite Creek. Follow the trail on the east side of Granite Creek to the confluence. At low water in the fall it is possible to ford Canyon Creek without great hazard; at times it is also possible to cross the creek on a foot log. If this route is feasible and safe, it saves about 2.5 miles. The ford is impossible in late spring and early summer.

From Granite Creek, the trail switchbacks up steeply, with water available at 1.2 and 3.3 miles. This is a steep, hot climb, topping out at 3.8 miles where the trail forks; the right fork leads to McMillan Park, and the left fork to Crater Mountain.

Crater Mountain

To explore the Crater Mountain area, switchback up through beautiful alpine meadow. Five miles from Ruby Creek the trail forks, with the right fork leading to the Crater Mountain ridge 1 mile further. From this high ridge there are good views. The left trail (at the 5-mile junction) goes to the summit of Crater Mountain. This trail is less well maintained, difficult to locate in places, and requires a Class 2 to Class 3 rock climb for about 400 feet to reach the summit; route finding is facilitated by fading yellow paint marks on the rocks. Distance from the junction to the summit is about 2.7 miles.

The view from the summit of Crater is one of the best in the Cascades. The hiker-climber can see portions of Diablo and Ross Lakes, Jack Mountain, Mt. Baker, Mt. Shuksan, and the entire sweep of the western and eastern Cascades.

There is a dramatic climatic demarcation along the Granite Creek Valley. The mountains to the west are heavily glaciated; by contrast, those to the east contain far less snow and ice. Most of the precipitation brought by storms from the Pacific Ocean has been deposited on the mountains to the west.

Mountain goats are often seen in the Crater Mountain area. There are campsites on the ridge crest (water is scarce late in the season) and in the lower meadows.

McMillan Park

From the 3.8-mile trail junction, the right fork leads to McMillan Park, 4 miles from Canyon Creek. The Park is 1½ square miles of high alpine meadow with many campsites with water available. Deer are common in the area, and mosquitos are ubiquitous. Visitors are few.

A word of caution: McMillan Park is hunted heavily during the High Cascade hunting season. Check the dates of the season (usually begins about September 10th), and visit the area before the hunting parties arrive.

The footpath continues through McMillan Park. The time up from Canyon Creek to McMillan Park is about three hours; another two hours is required to reach the Crater Ridge; to reach the summit of Crater Mountain, allow three hours.

After reaching the northeast portion of McMillan Park at about the 5-mile mark, the trail drops about 500′ in a half mile. From the crossing of the creek bottom to the Devil's Park shelter is another 1.4 to 1.5 miles with an altitude gain of 1000'. After McMillan Park, water is scarce until the shelter, where there is a small, reliable stream 100 feet to the east. Wood for campfires is available in the Devil's Park area. The shelter sleeps four people, and there are excellent campsites in the surrounding meadow. The Devil's Park meadow extends about 0.8 mile and offers spectacular views of Slate Peak, Harts Pass, Crater, Jack, and Hozomeen mountains, and the Pickets to the west.

From the shelter the trail goes southeast through the meadow approximately 0.4 mile. It is marked by stakes flagged with fluorescent tape. The trail makes a fairly sharp curve to the east, again flagged, and is easy to pick up as it turns south and begins to climb Jackita Ridge. If unable to follow the trail, go directly east from the Devil's Park shelter and climb the meadow. You will meet the trail after about a half mile and an altitude gain of 600'. From here the trail gradually climbs along the ridge for two miles. A barely discernible trail takes off about 1.5 miles after the trail turns south, and contours steeply up to the ridge top and then down the other side into the Cascade Basin. The main trail, immediately below the first of two prominent knobs, drops sharply, losing about 500', then goes through woods. The trail meanders west, going almost on the contour line out on the ridge. It returns east to near the ridge crest and follows the ridge crest closely to Devil's Pass.

The views from Jackita Ridge are superb, and since this area is seldom visited, wild game is seen frequently. The ridge is too steep and dry to permit camping.

From the junction of the Crater Lookout and McMillan Park trails to the Devil's Park shelter is slightly over three miles and takes about 2 hours. From the Devil's Park shelter to the point on the ridge where the trail drops sharply is another 2.5 miles, taking 1¼ hours. With full packs, allow 5 hours from Granite Creek up to the Devil's Park shelter; the descent can be done comfortably in 3 hours.

Deerflies and mosquitoes are a problem at Devil's Park; do carry repellant.

(August 1969)

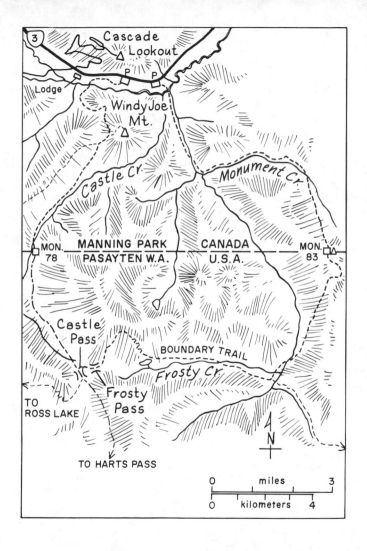

12

MANNING PARK—
PASAYTEN
WILDERNESS

Trails:
Monument 78
Monument 83
(Boundary Trail)
(Pacific Crest Trail)

MONUMENT 78

DESTINATION: Monument 78, 4400'

TRAIL LENGTH: 7.9 miles

WALKING TIME: 4 hours in
3½ hours out

TRAILHEAD ELEVATION: 4200'

HIGH POINT: 5380'

ALTITUDE GAIN, including ups and downs: 1250'

SEASON FOR USE: late June to late October

TOPOGRAPHIC SHEETS: Manning Provincial Park PS-M1
25-meter contour
USGS: Castle Peak and Frosty
Creek 7.5'
Green Trails: Jack Mountain and
Pasayten Peak

The main reason for walking this trail is to complete the northernmost section of the Pacific Crest Trail or to make the loop trip via Monument 83.

The trailhead is roughly a mile east of the Manning Park administration office. There is parking for about 40 cars. The Monument 78 trail starts on the south side of the lot and parallels Canada Highway 3 for a half mile. The trail passes the sewage plant and drops to cross the Similkameen River. (There are no signs around the plant.)

After the bridge, the trail proceeds up on a fire road for about 2.4 miles until it intersects the Frosty Mountain trail on a sharp curve. Walking time to this point from the trailhead is about 1.5 hours. The altitude gain is about 1250'. There is no water for about 2 miles after the river. Leave the fire road and follow the Frosty Mountain trail approximately 0.7 mile to a fork. The right fork continues to the summit of Frosty Mountain; take the left fork to Monument 78.

There is another fork 0.1 mile further. The left fork leads 0.1 mile to a campground; water of inferior quality is available near the trail junction. Take the right fork over a path which gradually descends as it proceeds north. Logging scars can be seen in the valley to the east. About 7.6 miles from the trailhead, a bridge crosses a delightful creek; there are several campsites in the deep woods on the east bank. Walking time to this campsite with a full pack is 3½ hours.

Monument 78 on the U.S.–Canada border is 0.3 mile further. The triangular brass monument is a few feet west of the trail; a cleared swath 10′ on either side of the border clearly delineates the international boundary. At this point, the trail enters the U.S. and the Pasayten Wilderness. Customs regulations on both sides of the border must be observed. People crossing the international boundary must report to the nearest customs house in the country into which they have crossed.

Overnight stays in the Pasayten Wilderness require wilderness permits, obtained from either the officials of the Okanogan National Forest, or at the administration office in Manning Provincial Park.

The trail makes two fairly steep switchbacks immediately after entering the United States, and then contours gradually up through timber and burn areas to reach Castle Pass, 4 miles from the monument and 11.9 miles from the trailhead. The altitude gain over this four miles is 1000′. There is a fair campsite with water 50 feet east of the trail 2.8 miles from the monument. The trail enters subalpine meadow 0.3 mile north of Castle Pass. A way trail to the right (west) descends 0.1 mile, where there is a good campsite next to a small stream. There are level but waterless campsites at the pass itself. At the pass is the junction with the Boundary Trail going west; from here, Big Face Creek is 10 miles and Ross Lake 25 miles. Walking time from the monument to the pass is an hour and 45 minutes; the time back is an hour and 20 minutes. On the second switchback 0.2 mile south of the Pass, the trail meets the Frosty Creek Trail (the Boundary Trail going east). (See Monument 83 Trail.)

The Pacific Crest Trail continues south from this point to Hopkins Pass and Hopkins Lake. (See the northern portion of the PCT.)

(September 1979)

MONUMENT 83 (MANNING PARK)

DESTINATION: Monument 83, 6500'
TRAIL LENGTH: 9 miles
WALKING TIME: 4¾ hours in
3½ hours out
TRAILHEAD ELEVATION: 4200'
ALTITUDE GAIN, including ups and downs: 2300'
SEASON FOR USE: late June to late October
TOPOGRAPHIC SHEETS: Manning Provincial Park PS-M1
25-meter contour
USGS: Castle Peak and Frosty
Creek 7.5'
Green Trails: Jack Mountain and
Pasayten Peak

The trailhead is 2.5 miles east of the Manning Park lodge. A large parking area is at the trailhead; the trail starts at the east end of the lot. Turn right at a road junction at 0.2 mile, and parallel BC Highway 3. Turn right in 0.1 mile, cross a bridge, and 0.1 mile further cross another bridge. Take the left fork in the road 0.2 mile further, and again take the left fork after another mile. Ten minutes further, the trail crosses another bridge; there is access to water at this point. There is a campsite on the north side of the trail 2.4 miles further, with water 100 yards below along the access road. A half mile further there is again a small campsite. The last water is 5.5 miles from the trailhead and 3.5 miles below the summit; water containers should be filled here. At 8.4 miles is the junction with the Cathedral Lake trail on the left (east). At 8.8 miles, the trail emerges on the summit ridge. Views, practically nonexistent until now, are splendid.

On the Canadian side of the border, a log cabin, the original fire lookout, still stands in remarkably good condition. It can be dirty and rodent-infested but it has a rainproof roof. A hundred feet to the south is Monument 83, next to a lookout on stilts, in good condition but usually locked. Between the two structures is a carved wooden headstone bearing the inscription "Pasayten Pete. Shot by J. E. Lael, 8/26/61." The ridge crest has been logged to facilitate views from the lookouts; this has resulted in a grassy alpine ridge, which early in July is thickly carpeted with alpine flowers.

Views from Monument 83 are splendid. The swath cut east and west along the U.S.–Canada border is clear. To the east is Bunker Hill, and in the distance, Cathedral Peak. To the south, Ptarmigan Peak and Point Defiance. To the southwest, Blizzard Point and Mt. Winthrop. To the north, Chuwanten Mountain, and the northwest, Windy Joe Mountain, Frosty Mountain, and the Three Brothers. The valleys of the three forks of the Pasayten River are below.

The U.S. boundary and the Pasayten Wilderness area boundary are at this point. Customs regulations cannot be ignored; people crossing the international boundary must report to the nearest customs house in the country into which they have crossed. A Wilderness Permit is required for overnight stays in the Pasayten Wilderness; fortunately, Manning Park can issue the necessary papers, or they may be obtained from officials at the Okanogan National Forest.

The trail passes Monument Spring 0.6 mile from the boundary. There is a good campsite at this location. In late fall water trickles from the spring, but with patience water supplies can be replenished here. The junction with the north loop of the Boundary Trail is 0.5 mile further. To the left (east) the trail extends to Bunker Hill. To the right (west) it proceeds down, losing approximately 1900' in four miles. The trail crosses Chuckuwanteen Creek 2½ miles from the junction. A half mile of new trail follows. About 3 miles from the junction is a campsite in the deep timber, which can be reached in 0.2 mile by following a way trail east and down through the avalanche slope. This is the only camping area since Monument Spring. One mile further there is another campsite just above Frosty Creek, which must be forded. In 0.2 mile is a major junction: the trail to the left crosses Frosty Creek, and the trail to the right proceeds up Frosty Creek toward Castle Pass. There are campsites here in the deep woods.

Continuing west, the left trail ascends gradually through dense forest. After about 1.6 miles there is a difficult ford of Frosty Creek. During spring high water, crossing the stream here could be a major problem. There is a campsite 3.6 miles from the junction, 0.1 mile south of the trail, but the creek must be forded to reach it. At 3.7 and 4.3 miles the creek must again be forded. The junction with the easily-missed side trail to The Parks is at 4.4 miles. This way trail is overgrown; look for a sign on a tree about 50 feet from the junction. The trail to The Parks is about 3 miles long, and gains roughly 1200'.

One-third mile along the main (right) trail is the Frosty Lake campsite, 100 yards north of the lake. From the Chuckuwanteen–Frosty Creek junction to this point has been about 4½ miles, gaining 700'. (There is considerable discrepancy between Forest Service figures and this author's experience on this section of trail; the actual distance may be as short as 3.5 miles or as long as 6 miles. Reader input is requested.)

From the campsite the trail switchbacks up fairly steeply. Roughly 1.5 miles from the Frosty Lake Campsite is a superb campsite in high alpine meadow, with water from a stream 0.2 mile down the trail. Half a mile further is Frosty Pass, elevation 6500′. This level ridge offers level campsites, but there is no water available after the snow has melted off the ridge crest. To the north rises Mt. Winthrop, 7860′, an easy climb from the pass. Immediately below is a small tarn, the source of Frosty Creek. Blizzard Peak is to the south. Joker and Castle peaks rise to the west. Plan to spend some time here.

The trail to the west descends steeply on badly eroded tread to reach the Pacific Crest Trail 0.2 mile south of Castle Pass. Approximately 1000′ is lost in the 1.2 miles covered. (See Pacific Crest Trail and Monument 78 Trail for routes after this junction.)

Walking time for the 1.2 miles from the PCT to Frosty Pass is 50 minutes with a full pack; allow 30 minutes in the reverse direction. From Frosty Pass to the Frosty Creek–Chuckuwanteen junction, again full packed, over 7.5 miles takes 3½ hours; the reverse direction takes 4½ hours.

If making the 35-mile loop from Manning Park via Monument 83, Frosty Pass, Castle Pass, and Monument 78, a minimum of three days and two nights should be allowed. Four days allows more comfortable hiking and a chance for exploration. Allow a full day for the side trip to The Parks. Remember, the Manning Park trailheads are a mile and a half apart.

(September 1979)

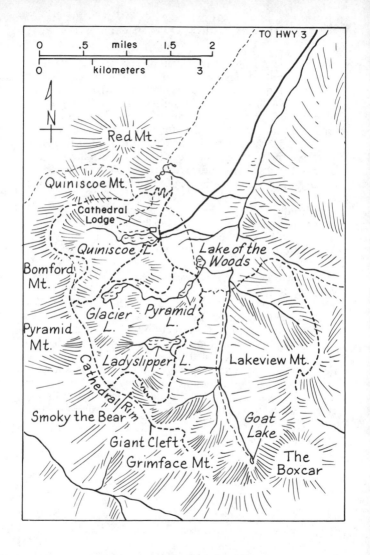

13

CATHEDRAL PARK (BRITISH COLUMBIA)

Trails:
Cathedral Rim (North Section)
Cathedral Rim (South Section) via Ladyslipper Lake
Lakeview Mountain

CATHEDRAL LAKES

The turnoff from Canada Highway 3 is 15.2 miles east of Hedley, or 2.6 miles from the Keremeos left turn to Osoyoos. Almost immediately, cross a one-lane bridge over the Similkameen River. Base camp for the Cathedral Lakes Resort is 13.5 miles from the turnoff. The trailhead is reached by turning left at 14.8 miles and proceeding 0.4 mile to a parking area for 25 cars. There are several campsites by the Ashnola River, 100' from the parking area. The trail crosses a footbridge and joins the jeep road about 0.5 mile uphill after the river is crossed. From this junction it is about 8.5 miles to Quiniscoe Lake by private jeep road, and perhaps 9.5 miles by trail, with an altitude gain of about 4000'.

The jeep road is nine miles from base camp to the lodge at Quiniscoe Lake. Road log is as follows. 1.0 mile: road joins trail. 1.1 miles: trail to left of road; this does not go to the lakes. 2.0 miles: Lakeview Creek is crossed on a bridge, where hikers should obtain water since there is no more water until Lindsey Creek, several miles further. 2.6 miles: trail goes to the right; jeep road to the left. 4.4 miles: Sheep Camp; water is available from a creek to the east. 8.4 miles: Lake of the Woods–Scout Lake Trail junctions. 9.0 miles: Cathedral Lodge.

The people who run the lodge will take hikers to the lake (with advance reservations) for $28 Canadian per person round trip (in 1980). There are usually three trips a day, at 10 a.m., 2 p.m., and 4 p.m., with extra trips on heavy-use weekends or holidays.

Hikers may use either the trail or the road. The trail takes seven to eight hours. The jeep road takes six hours to walk. There is a campsite on the trail at Lindsey Creek, and there are places to camp at Scout Lake.

Driving up the jeep road saves a full day up, and a half day down, through areas that are usually hot and not scenic. I recommend paying the fare and being driven up the road.

There are many trails in the area offering loops and circle hikes. The lakes, in order of beauty, are Ladyslipper, Glacier, Quiniscoe, Scout, Pyramid, and Lake of the Woods. The Cathedral Rim Trail, from its start at Lake Quiniscoe to its end near Grimface Mountain, and the Lakeview Mountain–Centennial Trail are the best footpaths and are described here.

(There are discrepancies between names used by the lodge, by the provincial park, and on the British Columbia map. Sometimes I use two names if they match the location; where there are different names for one location, the name on the B.C. map is used.)

CATHEDRAL RIM (NORTH SECTION)

DESTINATION: Bomford Mountain, 8369′
TRAIL LENGTH: 7.4 miles (loop)
WALKING TIME (light pack): 5 hours
TRAILHEAD ELEVATION: 6775′ (Quiniscoe Lake)
ALTITUDE GAIN, including ups and downs: 2000′
FEATURES: Quiniscoe Mountain, 8100′; Glacier Lake,
       7250′; Scout Lake, 6950′
TOPOGRAPHIC SHEET: Ashnola River 92 H/1, British Columbia

Take the trailhead to Scout Lake on a side road 150′ north of Cathedral Lodge. A 15-minute walk through the woods leads to the junction of the trail to Scout Lake and the Cathedral Rim Trail. It is 0.2 mile further north, plus 0.2 mile on a side trail west, to Scout Lake. (A trail to the right goes to the jeep road.) Scout Lake has good campsites, but camping in the area is discouraged. Lots of lupine grow around the lake.

From Scout Lake, return to the junction and proceed up in switchbacks along Cathedral Rim Trail. Switchbacks ascending a half mile lead to the treeline, and views are splendid thereafter. After another 0.4 mile the tread disappears. Follow the rock cairns upward. Scout Lake can be seen below. A sign 0.2 mile further indicates the junction of the Centennial and the Cathedral Rim trails. Again there is a good view of Scout Lake below. The Centennial Trail crosses high meadow near a tarn, where there is a good campsite, contours under Quiniscoe Mountain, which the Cathedral Rim Trail is about to ascend, and goes west several miles through meadow before dropping to the Ashnola River.

The Cathedral Rim Trail continues up through high, flowered meadow. Follow the cairns, since in most places there is no tread. One can wander in this and most other high areas, since they are above timberline. Red Mountain, the peak 0.5 mile north of the Centennial Trail, can be climbed without difficulty.

The Cathedral Rim Trail requires a talus scramble, then runs the ridge crest for 0.5 mile, mostly in meadow but occasionally on rock. There are several summits in the area, all about the same altitude. Ptarmigan are often seen here. The trail drops 300′ in 0.3 mile to a broad saddle, and then ascends Bomford Mountain, gaining perhaps 550′ to the 8369′ summit. The summit may be bypassed to the west, saving 200′.

Descend, following rock cairns, through meadow and talus slopes, to the Glacier Lake Trail junction in a saddle 0.6 mile to the south. One can roam on the broad fingers of meadow extending west. From the junction descend fairly steeply on scree, meadow, talus, and snow to the shores of Glacier Lake. This larch-lined, splendid alpine lake, altitude 7250′, is a day-use area only; camping and fires are prohibited. It is about a mile from the ridge crest to the lake exit stream; 0.9 mile, through meadow and then woods, to the junction with the Pyramid Lake Trail; and 0.7 mile through woods back to the start at Quiniscoe Lake.

Wind is frequently cold on the Cathedral Rim; carry extra clothes even if the weather is warm at Quiniscoe Lake. Snow may fall in this area any day of the year, so take precautions against hypothermia before any hikes in the Cathedral Lakes area. This loop takes four to five hours; most people will want to make it a full day trip to allow time for lunch, exploration, and photography. Over 200 varieties of wildflowers have been described in the Cathedral Lakes area by botanists from the University of British Columbia. In early August, the height of the flower season, flowers are everywhere. There is a striking change in flowers at timberline. Below timberline, lupine and paint brush predominate. Near timberline, shrubby cinquefoil is most common, and higher up, tundra flowers, including the moss campion and golden fleabane, predominate.

Once the rim is reached, the vista of the peaks of the Pasayten Wilderness lying to the south and west unfolds dramatically. Peaks and ridges stretch forever, like waves in a stony sea. Glacier Lake is an aquamarine gem surrounded by larch.

(August 1980)

CATHEDRAL RIM (SOUTH SECTION) VIA LADYSLIPPER LAKE

DESTINATION: End of Rim Trail, 8000'

TRAIL LENGTH: 12 miles (loop)

WALKING TIME (light pack) 8½ hours

TRAILHEAD ELEVATION: 6775' (Quiniscoe Lake)

ALTITUDE GAIN, including ups and downs: 3200'

FEATURES: Highest point of Cathedral Ridge, 8570';
Ladyslipper Lake, 7200'

TOPOGRAPHIC SHEET: Ashnola River 92 H/1 British Columbia

Follow the trail from Cathedral lodge 0.1 mile, crossing the outlet stream of Quiniscoe Lake to the Pyramid Lake Trail. It is one mile through woods to the Lake of the Woods Trail junction, and another 0.3 mile, passing the north end of Pyramid Lake, to the junction with the Ladyslipper Lake–Lakeview Mountain Trail. The trail loses perhaps 120′ to this junction, then climbs moderately. It is about 1.1 miles to Ladyslipper Lake. The trail breaks into meadow at about 0.7 mile, and a half hour from the junction there is a fine view from a knoll above the lake. The trail goes up to a high point of 7500′ and then drops down to the lake at 7200′. This is the prettiest lake in the Cathedral Lakes and is also the best for fishing. Camping and campfires are prohibited at this lake.

Follow the trail a half mile around the east side of the lake and cross the outlet stream; get plenty of water here. The cairned footpath continues south, with tread faint in places. It remains almost level for a half mile, then switchbacks up steeply to the west, turns northwest, and terminates with a final scrabble up scree and talus to the Cathedral Rim. This trail segment is about 1.5 miles long and gains about 1000′. Walking time from the lake is about one hour. Watch for mountain goats on this segment of trail.

The junction with the Cathedral Rim Trail is 0.1 mile from the top-out point. From here, turn left (southeast) and follow the rim trail through granite formations. About 0.5 mile from the junction is Smokey the Bear, a granitic formation resembling the legendary fire fighting bear, or Yogi the Bear. One can climb above this formation for a photograph without difficulty. It is another half mile to a giant cleft. The trail immediately preceding the cleft is vague, and in one place, descent of 150′ or so of Class 2 rock or scree is necessary to bypass a ten-foot obstruction, which can be climbed up with difficulty but which the average hiker can not climb down. The trail ends on a knoll about 0.1 mile from Grimface (McKeen) Mountain. This is a good spot to eat lunch, and water, scarce on the ridge, may be obtained from nearby snowfields.

From this knoll, there is a splendid panorama of The Boxcar, Lakeview Mountain, the Deacon, Orthodox Mountain, and across the border, Cathedral Peak, Remmel Mountain, Sheep Mountain, and the other peaks of the Pasayten Wilderness Area. The adventurous could drop to the south into a valley, ascend a ridge, follow the ridge crest, crossing what appears to be a difficult pass, drop into the valley on the other side, and go cross-country to join the Boundary Trail near Cathedral Lakes or Cathedral Pass. The adventurous can also drop down a scree slope to Goat Lake below. (The lake cannot be seen from the knoll.) Most, however, will retrace their steps to the junction, from where the rim trail goes northwest. It passes through an area of eroded granite called Stone City. Shortly thereafter on the ridge crest is the Devil's Woodpile, a fractured lava dike. There are views down to Ladyslipper Lake, and mountain goats are frequently seen in the meadow and talus below. The trail then goes up to the summit of Pyramid Mountain, where, again, goats are often seen, and then drops to the junction with the Glacier Lake Trail. The distance between these two junctions is about 2 miles. Descend the rather steep first stretch of the Glacier Lake Trail (as described under Cathedral Rim–North) but, midway along the lake, turn left and cross country along the alpine ridge to the northeast. You can go straight north for a view down to Quiniscoe Lake. Eventually you will pick up the flagged and blazed but less-than-obvious trail that descends directly to Quiniscoe Lake. It is about 0.7 mile to the ridge cutoff, and one mile from the cutoff to the lake via this route, saving a mile compared to the return route discussed under the north section.

This is a moderately strenuous walk; hikers should be in good condition.

(August 1980)

LAKEVIEW MOUNTAIN

DESTINATION: Lakeview Mountain, 8622'

TRAIL LENGTH: 4.5 miles

WALKING TIME (light pack): 2¾ hours in
2 hours out

TRAILHEAD ELEVATION: 6775' (Quiniscoe Lake)

LOW POINT: 6300' (Lakeview Creek)

ALTITUDE GAIN, including ups and downs: 2400' in, 400'
out

TOPOGRAPHIC SHEET: Ashnola River 92 H/1 British Columbia

Follow directions for the south section of Cathedral Rim to the Ladyslipper Lake–Lakeview Mountain junction. Turn left and follow the switchbacks down. At the south end of a switchback at 0.5 mile is the flagged and cairned junction with the Goat Lake Trail. From the junction to the lake is about 2 miles. At 0.8 mile is the bridge across Lakeview Creek; this is the low point of the trail. There is a fair campsite on the east side of the creek. Walking time from Quiniscoe Lake to the bridge is 20 minutes.

Going up, the trail is muddy and in poor condition in several places. Two areas of puncheon must be crossed. When wet or frosty it can be quite slippery. Fifteen minutes after starting up is a small bridge and water. There is water on the left as the creek from the meadow is first reached. From here on, there are splendid alpine flowers. The trail parallels the creek up and then breaks into full meadow. From the bridge to this point is about 1.2 miles. The creek at the breakout point has no obvious snowfield source, but quite adequate water. There are also a few small tarns on the crest near the Centennial Trail, where water is also available.

Tread becomes faint. The Centennial Trail follows the creek up to the crest, and then turns left in the high meadow, passing beneath the Twin Buttes and ultimately descending to Mountain Goat Creek; it does not go down to Mountain Goat Lakes, easily seen from the crest.

The Lakeview Mountain Trail goes southeast. There are several good campsites at the meadow and in the nearby tree-line area. Walking the route up to the mountain the hiker may follow cairns, but any way is the right way. Perhaps easiest is to go directly up the ridge, rather than left to the saddle and then up the ridge. It takes a little over 1 hour for the 1.5 miles from tree line to the summit. The summit is cairned and has a post on top. It can be best reached by contouring around the east side and going up the south side over talus. The views are truly splendid. To the southeast is Haystack Mountain. Immediately to the south are the two elevated ends of The Boxcar. To the north is a broad, grassy ridge that invites one to roam among the miles of high alpine flowers. Best of all, to the west is the entire Cathedral Rim, from Grimface Mountain on the south to Red Mountain on the north. Ladyslipper, Glacier, Quiniscoe, and Pyramid Lakes are visible.

To look down to Goat Lake, from a bit west of the crest go south half a mile. By clambering out on a rock knob at this point, Goat Lake can be seen nestled in its cirque beneath The Boxcar–Denture Ridge, Matriarch Mountain, Macabre Tower, and Grimface Mountain. There is a chute to the left of this rock knoll, to the right of the main ridge, which leads down, allowing a cross-country scree, talus, and meadow traverse to the lake. A round trip is possible from there via trail back to the trail junction above Lakeview Creek.

More enjoyable, however, is to walk down the ridge crest to the saddle, enjoying the view of Mountain Goat Lakes below. From there, wander over the high ridge, with splendid panoramas and seemingly infinite varieties of flowers.

Wild flowers change dramatically at timberline where clusters of foot-high lupine give way to small tundra flowers. Unfortunately, there are mosquitoes and no-see-ums too.

(August 1980)

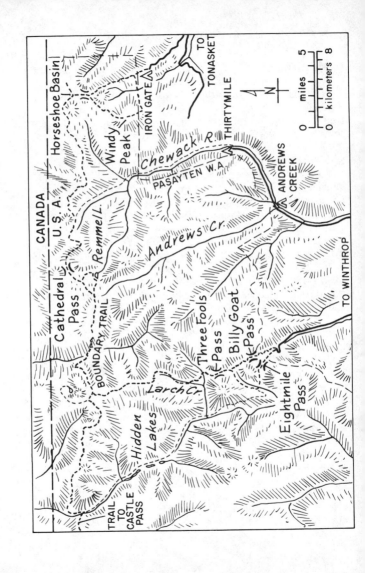

14

PASAYTEN WILDERNESS
Northeast Section

Trails:
Horseshoe Basin
Boundary Trail
Larch Creek Trail
Windy Peak

HORSESHOE BASIN (PASAYTEN WILDERNESS)

DESTINATION: Louden Lake, 7100'

TRAIL LENGTH: 6.6 miles

WALKING TIME (full pack): 3½ hours in
3 hours out

TRAILHEAD ELEVATION: 5800'

ALTITUDE GAIN, including ups and downs: 1500'

FEATURE: Sunny Pass, 7200' (high point)

TOPOGRAPHIC SHEETS: USGS: Horseshoe Basin
Green Trails: Horseshoe Basin

Leave U.S. 97 at Tonasket and drive 11.6 miles to Loomis. From the post office at Loomis, follow the paved road northwest. Turn left at 2.2 miles, left again at 10.8 miles at Toats Creek (stay on the pavement); enter the Okanogan National Forest boundary at 15.5 miles, and then turn north 16.2 miles from Loomis on a primitive side road marked Iron Gate. The trailhead is 5.9 miles up this one-lane road; use caution in wet weather. There is parking for about 30 cars, campsites, and toilets at the trailhead.

The trail first follows the Tungsten Mine Road and enters the Pasayten Wilderness at 0.2 mile. At half a mile, there are junctions with trails leading east to Deer Park and 14-Mile Camp, and west to the Windy Creek Trail. At 2 miles is a water source. At 3 miles the hiker must bypass a wooden fence. The trail breaks into meadow at 4.5 miles, where there is a good campsite. From here, the trail goes up more steeply to reach scenic Sunny Pass, 5 miles from the trailhead. The left trail at this point is part of the Windy Peak Loop. The Horseshoe Basin or Boundary Trail continues north and slightly east, reaching Horseshoe Pass 6 miles from the trailhead. A creek and tarn are at this junction. The Long Draw Trail goes east toward Goodenough Peak. There is an 0.8-mile way trail to Smith Lake, perhaps the only water source in the area in the late summer or early fall. At Horseshoe Pass the Boundary Trail turns left and passes through splendid meadow; 0.75 mile further is Louden Lake, with several splendid camping areas. North of and below the trail 0.2 mile past the lake is another good campsite.

From base camp at Louden Lake, one can cross country north to a high plateau. Here are border markers #103 and #104 and the 20' slash across the border. A half mile north of the border and some 500' below are two beautiful lakes containing fish. Scenery is good from the mile 103 marker west, and east from the mile 104 marker. It is possible to continue along the Boundary Trail to the west as far as time and energy permit.

Mountain goat, big horn sheep, and deer may be seen in the Horseshoe Basin area. The splendid high meadow of Horseshoe Basin is best visited in late June or early July. Later in the year, water is a problem. Grazing is still allowed by the Forest Service in this area. Flocks of sheep can intrude on the wilderness experience. After July 15th, check at the Winthrop ranger station to determine if domestic animals are in the area.

(July 1975)

BOUNDARY TRAIL

EAST TRAILHEAD: Iron Gate, 5800'
WEST TRAILHEAD: Ross Lake, 1600'; Castle Pass, 5500'

TRAIL LENGTH: 94 miles (Iron Gate to Ross Lake)

WALKING TIME: 7 to 10 days

HIGH POINT: Cathedral Pass, 7600'

LOW POINT: Pasayten River, 3900'

ALTITUDE GAIN, including ups and downs: about 14,000'
(east to west)

TOPOGRAPHIC SHEETS: USGS: Horseshoe Basin; Bauer-
man Ridge; Remmel Mt.; Ash-
nola Mt.; Ashnola Pass;
Tatoosh Buttes; Frosty Creek;
Castle Peak; Ross Lake; Skagit
Peak
Green Trails: Pasayten Peak; Jack
Mt.; Coleman Peak; Billy Goat
Mt.; Ross Lake; Horseshoe
Basin

The peace and quiet of deep wilderness, the fantastic
beauty of the hills, and excellent opportunities for photography enhance this unusual true wilderness route. Good
lake and stream fishing is available in many areas.

Although access is nowhere easy, the trail can be done in
segments rather than in one sustained march. The east access to the Boundary Trail from Iron Gate Camp to Louden
Lake is described under Horseshoe Basin. The section of the
trail from one mile south of Monument 83 to Castle Pass is
described under Monument 83. The trail from Castle Pass to
Ross Lake is considered part of the Boundary Trail and is
described here. The last several miles of the trail are discussed under Lightning Creek. (The author has not walked
the sections from Peeve Pass to one mile south of Monument
83, and from Castle Pass to the boundary between the Ross
Lake NRA and the Pasayten Wilderness; information was
obtained from maps and from other hikers.)

Louden Lake to Scheelite Pass

From Louden Lake, it is 0.3 mile to a good campsite north of and below the trail. A mile beyond the lake is a campsite near a tarn. At 3 miles, the footpath rises; there is a table and a good tent site near a tarn in an insect-infested meadow. At 5 miles, the trail crosses a stream; there is a good campsite 50 yards to the northwest. Half a mile further is another stream; nearby is a nice campsite located under some dead silver-colored trees. Snow Sled camp is 1.3 miles further in a small meadow. Another mile brings the hiker to the crest of a ridge with a magnificent stand of bleached tree trunks on both sides of the ridge crest. Alpine larch are also in this area. There is a campsite 50 yards south of the trail; it is not obvious. For the next 2.2 miles, there are no places to camp. Water is scarce; water bottles should be filled at any opportunity.

The trail turns to the north 0.7 mile past the ridge crest; Cathedral Peak comes into view. A mile and a half further is a campsite with a table; water is available from a spring about 100 yards to the south. A hundred-yard bushwhack to the west leads to a beautiful tarn, where there are level, pleasant campsites if the hiker wishes to camp further from the trail. Elevation at this point is 6800'. From the camping area, the Boundary Trail switchbacks down fairly steeply, losing approximately 500' in about 0.6 mile. The footpath passes about 200 yards from Scheelite Lake.

Walking time, light-packed, for the ten miles from Louden Lake to Scheelite Pass is about 4 hours. It is high and scenic most of the time, making this portion of the Boundary Trail very memorable. The trail is free of snow by early July. Finding water can be a problem in late summer and early fall. The ideal time for walking this segment of the trail is mid-July. No-see-ums, mosquitoes, and deerflies are a constant problem along the trail.

(July 1975)

Scheelite Pass to Peeve Pass

West from the Scheelite Lake area, the trail drops a bit into forest, crosses a small creek, then ascends to a high ridge in 1½ miles. The trail stays high for a splendid 1½ miles to the Tungsten Mine. Here is the junction with the trail from the end of the Chewack River Road. Buildings in the area are full of rodents but have water-tight roofs; they're good to head for in a downpour. There are campsites around the buildings. There is a nice campsite on the left, half a mile west of the mine buildings. It is 1.8 miles from the mine area to Apex Pass, where there are alpine larch and a level area for a dry camp. From this point, it is a fairly easy (Class 2) walk to the top of Apex Peak, from where there are spectacular views to the west of the triangular spire of Cathedral Peak (8600′).

After crossing the pass, the footpath makes a long gentle descent to below Cathedral Pass, crosses Cathedral Creek, and then switchbacks up to reach Cathedral Pass, the highest point on the Boundary Trail. It is 2.5 miles between Apex and Cathedral Passes.

From Cathedral Pass, descend to perhaps the most beautiful lake in the North Cascades: past a shallow tarn, a way trail to the left leads to the east shore of Upper Cathedral Lake. The main trail passes tarns and the exit stream to a campsite on the west side of the lake. The lake lies beneath the sheer granite scarp of Amphitheater Mountain 0.8 mile from the pass. The lake and streams abound with trout. The granite ramparts glow in the evening sun. Plan at least one overnight camp in this lovely area.

The trail loses altitude below Upper Cathedral Lake and crosses under a granite cliff. After 0.7 mile is the junction to the half-mile-long trail to lower Cathedral Lake, about 400′ below. There is a high meadow campsite about 2½ miles west of the upper lake. Three miles from the upper lake is a junction with the trail to Remmel Lake. The hiker has two options. The shortest route west is the Boundary Trail directly to Spanish Camp. The more scenic route is on the Remmel Lake bypass.

In slightly over a mile is the junction with the Andrews Creek Trail. There are many campsites in this area.

Down the trail 3.3 miles is a high pass (7400') on Bald Mountain. If time permits, leave packs here and enjoy a glorious ridge saunter east.

After a mile or so over a high plateau, the trail enters timber and switchbacks down into the valley of the Ashnola River. From the high point at Bald Mountain, almost 2400' is lost in this jarring descent.

Near the bottom of the valley is the junction with the trail to Black Lake 14 miles away. A half mile further is a trail shelter, in excellent condition, that sleeps four. One-tenth of a mile further is the Ashnola River, which one must ford. It is about 4.1 miles from the high point on Bald Mountain to this ford. The water was about 18 inches deep in a low snow year; the ford could be difficult if the water level was higher.

Beyond the ford there is a miserable slog upward in deep woods, as the altitude lost on the east is regained on the west. Two miles from the ford is a fair campsite. After about 3 miles (1½ hours) the trail breaks into meadow after regaining about 2000'. There are a number of unmarked trails in this meadow. At the first fork, take the upper trail. There is a good campsite a bit over 3 miles from the ford, to the south about 100' below the trail.

The main trail, marked with pointed stakes, contours north around the meadow, gradually gaining altitude. There are no good campsites after the one mentioned above until Peeve Pass (6800'), 4.6 miles from the ford of the Ashnola River. There are several level camping areas at Peeve Pass, with water from a small stream 0.2 mile south on the Larch Creek Trail to Billy Goat Pass.

From the junction with the Larch Creek Trail, it is a bit over 18 miles to the Billy Goat Corral, 13 miles to Hidden Lake, and 14 miles to the Pasayten River. (See Larch Creek Trail.)

(July 1977)

Peeve Pass west

The 8 miles west of the Peeve junction is perhaps the most enjoyable segment of the Boundary Trail. About one mile west of Peeve Pass is the junction with the trail to Park Pass and Ramon Lakes to the north. The main trail proceeds west, intersecting the one-mile way trail to Quartz Lake 1½ miles further. There are campsites at the lake. Proceeding west, the main trail contours beneath the south and west faces of Quartz Mountain, at an elevation of slightly over 7000'. Further west, Dean Creek is forded. The footpath then gains about 600' to reach the summit of Bunker Hill, 7239'. All of the trails described in this paragraph run through splendid high alpine meadows.

Such elegance does not continue. The junction with the trail descending into Dean Creek is 0.3 mile west of Bunker Hill. A half mile further is a high meadow campsite. The trail then descends, first in meadow, then in timber. There is another campsite 3.2 miles from the top of Bunker Hill. Five miles below the summit, Bunker Hill Creek must be forded. Another 1.7 miles further is the junction with the trail to Hidden Lakes and a bridge crossing the east fork of the Pasayten River. The Pasayten River itself is crossed on a bridge 0.6 mile further. This is the low point on the Boundary Trail, elevation slightly above 3900'. The trail runs along the river for a mile or so to a junction. If the hiker wants scenery at the cost of gaining altitude, he should proceed northwest up Harrison Creek, gaining about 2100'. A way trail near the high point leads to Monument Spring Campsite and to the splendid views from Monument 83. (See Monument 83 Trail.)

The hiker can walk about the same distance but gain considerably less altitude by proceeding southwest, following the valley of the Pasayten River, then turning west, at the north end of the Pasayten airstrip, up Soda Creek, and going northwest past Dead Lake to the trail junction in the Chuckuwanteen Valley.

(See Monument 83 Trail for information on the Boundary Trail from this point to Castle Pass.)

Castle Pass to Ross Lake

The trail west from Castle Pass loses about 400' into the Castle Fork Valley, then switchbacks up to slightly over 6000'. The trail stays high for several miles, then descends rather steeply into Big Face Creek (so called because it is below the big face of Joker Mountain). The descent out of meadow into lower country is boring. Tread is faint or nonexistent in the Big Face Valley. After the creek crossing, the footpath gradually, then steeply, ascends into the Elbow Basin. It again stays high, up to slightly over 6600', and works its way along or just south of the ridge between Welcome and Elbow basins. Tread is faint in these areas. There are good views of Skagit Peak and of Hozomeen and Jack mountains. At the southwest end of the ridge the trail descends sharply into the Three Fools Creek Valley, then turns west to the Little Fish shelter. From this point, the trail follows the river valley west to the boundary between the Pasayten Wilderness and Ross Lake National Recreation Area. From this boundary it descends to the Lightning Creek Trail. (See Lightning Creek Trail to get from this point to Ross Lake.)

The distance from Castle Pass to Ross Lake is between 19 and 25 miles. (The former mileage is from the USGS maps, the latter from Forest Service data.) This section of trail is for experienced wilderness travelers only, since route-finding can be a problem in places. If it is solitude you seek, it is unlikely that you will see anyone between Castle Pass and the Little Fish shelter. (I am indebted to Mr. David Ryeburn of Burnaby, British Columbia, for providing information on this segment of the Boundary Trail.)

LARCH CREEK TRAIL

DESTINATION: Peeve Pass, 6900'

TRAIL LENGTH: 18 miles

WALKING TIME (full pack): 10–12 hours in
8–9 hours out

TRAILHEAD ELEVATION: 4800'

ALTITUDE GAIN, including ups and downs: 4100'

FEATURES: Larch Pass, 7100' (high point); Three Fools Pass, 6000';
Billy Goat Pass, 6600'

TOPOGRAPHIC SHEETS: USGS: Billy Goat Mountain; Ashnola Pass; Ashnola Mountain 7.5'
Green Trails: Billy Goat Mountain

To reach the trailhead, drive north on the west Chewack Road, beginning just west of Winthrop. Turn off on the Eight Mile Creek road and follow it 16.5 miles to the end. The last 0.9 mile of road is rough and difficult. Parking is quite limited at the trailhead, with space for three or four cars. There is a flat area near a stream 0.9 mile from the road end for easier parking.

At 0.2 mile the trail forks. The left (west) fork goes 1.5 miles to crest at 8 Mile Pass, gaining about 700'. The boundary of the Pasayten Wilderness is at the crest of the pass. There are good views of Big Craggy Peak and of 8 Mile Peak from this trail. The day hiker can make a triangular loop hike; after crossing 8 Mile Pass, descend to the trail junction across Drake Creek and turn right. Follow this trail to its junction with the Larch Creek Trail, and return to the trailhead.

The right fork goes to Billy Goat Pass, 2.8 miles from the trailhead. (The time up to the pass is 1½ hours; time down, one hour.) "Kid Camp" is a half mile beyond the pass: it is an excellent campsite with a splendid view of Billy Goat Mountain to the southwest. A mile and a half from the pass, the hiker must ford Drake Creek. There are campsites on the north side of the creek by the crossing. Two Bit Creek is 0.5 mile further. A tenth of a mile beyond the crossing is the loop trail junction. From this point, it is about 5½ miles back to the trailhead via Billy Goat Pass, and 7 miles via the loop along Drake Creek and then over 8 Mile Pass.

To reach the Larch Creek Trail, continue north almost a mile to Three Fools Pass, slightly over six miles from the trailhead. A half a mile north of the pass is a campsite. In another half mile is the Larch Creek Trail junction. Diamond Creek is crossed at 8.1 miles. The trail then curves around the base of a bluff and begins its ascent of the Larch Creek valley. At about 9.6 miles it crosses Larch Creek. There is a campsite here: another good campsite is one mile further. There is a nice campsite in a small meadow below Larch Pass. The pass, the high point on the trail, is about 13 miles from the trailhead. A dry camp is located about 0.6 mile north of Larch Pass.

The junction with the Coral Lake Trail is about 14.5 miles from Billy Goat Corral. A way trail of less than a mile leads to Coral Lake. The main trail drops over a pass to reach the Timber Wolf Creek campsite at 15.6 miles. The junction with the Sand Ridge Trail is 1.7 miles further. The distance to the summit of Sand Ridge is about 0.5 mile, and the altitude gain about 300'. The views from Sand Ridge are quite impressive. The Boundary Trail can be seen contouring around the side of Quartz Mountain. Peaks and valleys seem to stretch to infinity. Vegetation on the ridge is like arctic tundra. This way trail is well worth walking; leave packs at the junction, but do carry a camera.

There is another campsite north of the junction with the Sand Ridge Trail. The Larch Creek Trail joins the Boundary Trail at Peeve Pass roughly 18.7 miles from the Billy Goat Corral trailhead. There is a campsite 50 yards south of the junction, with water from a stream along the trail 0.1 mile further south.

(See Boundary Trail for information after Peeve Pass.)

Three Fools Pass is not particularly scenic. Billy Goat Pass is pleasant and enjoyable. From Larch Pass northward to Peeve Pass, the trail rambles through splendid meadowland. One can walk long lovely miles in the Pasayten without seeing another person. Between Larch and Peeve passes, solitude is practically guaranteed.

(July 1977)

WINDY PEAK

DESTINATION: Windy Peak, 8384'
TRAIL LENGTH: 6.5 miles
WALKING TIME (light pack): 3 hours in
                          2⅓ hours out

TRAILHEAD ELEVATION: 5800'

ALTITUDE GAIN, including ups and downs: 3100'

FEATURE: Junction of Windy Peak and Boundary trails, 7200'

TOPOGRAPHIC SHEETS: USGS: Horseshoe Basin
Green Trails: Horseshoe Basin

Although many people visit Horseshoe Basin, few visit the Windy Peak area. Winter comes early to this area because of its elevation. The area is most scenic in late September when the larch needles are turning gold.

See Horseshoe Basin (Pasayten Wilderness) for access to the Windy Peak trailhead. Continue up the Boundary Trail half a mile to the cleared rectangular area containing granite rocks. The way trail to Windy Peak has no sign but is cairned, and leaves near the northwest end of this cleared area; the connecting loop is called the Clutch Trail. (One can also reach Windy Peak from the Long Swamp Campground at the end of the pavement of Long Swamp Road via the Windy Creek Trail.)

The Clutch Trail drops moderately, losing about 600' in 0.7 mile, to the middle fork of Toats-Coulee Creek. There is a campsite here. Cross the creek on a footlog, or ford it. About 0.2 mile beyond the creek, there is an unmarked trail junction; take the left, more heavily used fork. Midway up the canyon the trail breaks into clear areas with grass and flowers. Contour up on switchbacks to the top of one ridge, cross it, and continue upward, eventually crossing the second ridge. At about 2.5 miles is a small spring.

At four miles, there is a dry campsite at the junction of the Windy Creek Trail. Turn right (north); at about 4.8 miles, there is a beautiful campsite in larch in a delightful meadow. There is a splendid grassy ridge northeast of this campsite. The trail disappears here, and no tread can be seen for 200 yards. Follow cairns up and northeast through the meadow, picking up the trail again by the Pasayten Wilderness Area sign on a large larch tree. The trail is difficult to locate over the next mile beyond this sign; if in doubt, look for cairns. The footpath goes up through a boulder field and krummholz trees, reaching a flat at about 5.6 miles. This would be an ideal campsite but for the lack of water.

Going north from the flat is a high trail that follows the old phone poles and leads to the summit of Windy Peak. A lower, more apparent trail bypasses the summit to the west. The last 200′ to the summit is trailless, on Class 2 rock. There is a scrabble trail up from the hikers' trail to the summit on the west.

The view from Windy Peak at 8334′ is one of the most splendid in the North Cascades. To the northwest is a spire of Cathedral Peak. To the north are Arnold Peak and Goodenough Peak; to the west is the vast expanse of the Pasayten Wilderness. The broad meadow of Horseshoe Basin is to the northeast.

Windy Peak Loop

From Windy Peak one can retrace steps or continue north on what this author calls the Windy Peak Loop. After picking up the hikers' trail west of the summit of Windy Peak, continue north, drop and turn left at the first rock knoll, contour underneath it, and go through the next notch to the northwest (right looks correct at this point, but is not). Dropping further, 0.2 mile cross country leads to shallow, Windy Lake.

There are good campsites in the meadow near the lake and at elevated areas around the lake. The lake seems to have no fish. A half hour further on, roughly 9 miles from the trailhead, the trail crosses a stream in meadow where there are campsites; this is the low point. The trail then rises moderately and eventually connects with an old road about a mile from Sunny Pass; the turn-off from the road to the trail is marked. From Sunny Pass, return to the trailhead via the Boundary Trail.

The loop distance is about 15 miles, with an altitude gain of about 4000'. A fast hiker with a light pack can make the loop in 6½ hours, but most would want to make it a two-day trip.

(August 1978)

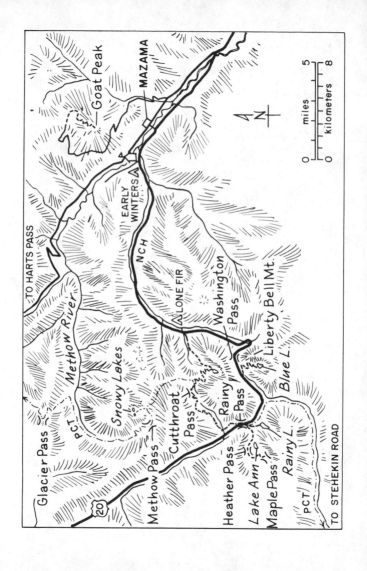

15

OKANOGAN NATIONAL FOREST

Trails:

BLUE LAKE (WASHINGTON PASS)

DESTINATION: Blue Lake, 6300'

TRAIL LENGTH: 2.3 miles

WALKING TIME (light pack): 1 hour in
45 minutes out

TRAILHEAD ELEVATION: 5200'

ALTITUDE GAIN, including ups and downs: 1400'

TOPOGRAPHIC SHEETS: USGS: Washington Pass 7.5'
Green Trails: Washington Pass

The trailhead is on the south side of the NCH 0.8 mile west of Washington Pass. The parking area is at Mile 161.5 alongside the highway, with the trailhead 0.1 mile east. The trail parallels the road east for about 150 yards, then turns south, ascending in a gentle series of switchbacks. At the 1.5-mile mark, where the trail crosses an avalanche meadow, the cross-country climbing route for the Early Winter Spires departs to the southeast. The trail crosses the outlet stream below Blue Lake before reaching the north end of the lake, which is surrounded by alpine larch.

Near the lake outlet is a deteriorating cabin, a relic of the Blue Whistler Mine. The lake, which has been stocked with trout, is not difficult to circumnavigate. Views from the south end of the lake, looking north to Cutthroat Peak, are quite spectacular. The area is most scenic in late September and early October, when the larch have turned golden yellow.

On the ridge to the west above the lake, there are two beautiful tarns; each offers the photographer nice reflection shots of the surrounding peaks. It is possible to climb higher for even better views; the photographer may want to shoot Blue Lake in the foreground with Liberty Bell and the Early Winter Spires in the background. A wide angle lens and color film are necessary to do justice to the area. Blue Lake is an intense blue; the color is like the saturated blue of Crater Lake in Oregon.

The area is restricted to day use; it is too fragile for overnight camping.

(September 1976)

LAKE ANN (RAINY PASS) AND MAPLE PASS

DESTINATION: Maple Pass, 6600'

TRAIL LENGTH: 4 miles

WALKING TIME (light pack): 2 hours in; 1½ hours out

TRAILHEAD ELEVATION: 4860'

ALTITUDE GAIN, including ups and downs: 1800'

FEATURES: Lake Ann, 5475'; Heather Pass, 6100'

TOPOGRAPHIC SHEETS: USGS: Washington Pass and Mt.
Arriva 7.5'
Green Trails: Washington Pass
and Mt. Logan

Turn south at the crest of Rainy Pass off the NCH, and park 0.2 mile further in the extensive parking area. Walk back on the access road 0.1 mile to the trailhead, which switchbacks up away from the lake at first but then moves southwest. The trail is muddy in places. At about 0.6 mile it breaks into an open area, crosses a talus slope (where there is considerable avalanche risk in snow conditions), and contours in a long half-circle to reach a ridge crest to the south. The trail meets the abandoned original trail to Lake Ann here; 0.2 mile further, the trail splits. The lower trail, to the left, crosses meadow and ends at Lake Ann in about 0.6 mile.

The Lake Ann basin is a day-use area only. Fishing is

often good in the lake. The area is scenic, particularly the tree-studded island in the lake. The distance to Lake Ann from the trailhead is about 1.8 miles, and the walking time up is a little over one hour; allow 50 minutes for the return trip.

Returning to the junction, the right (higher) trail gains altitude, crossing talus slopes and meadow. Above Lake Ann there are switchbacks. A short way trail to the right (north) brings the hiker to the Heather Pass area. This junction is not marked and is not obvious, so keep a sharp eye out when nearing the top of the ridge. At Heather Pass there is a broad meadow with campsites.

From the Heather Pass turnoff, the main trail switchbacks up through fairly steep meadow for slightly over a mile to the crest of Maple Pass. Scenery from this point is quite splendid. Corteo Peak is to the northwest. Mt. Benzarino is directly to the west; between the two peaks is Last Chance Pass. Below to the east is the Lake Ann valley with Whistler Mountain, Liberty Bell, and the Early Winters Spires in the distance. Below to the west is the Maple Creek valley, and further in the distance is the valley of Bridge Creek and the great peaks of the Stehekin. Glacier Peak looms in the far distance.

It is possible to follow trailless ridge crest south and east, gaining altitude, for better views. At one point, the wilderness traveler can look almost straight down into Lake Ann.

Camping is allowed at both Heather and Maple passes. There are level places for campsites. Late in the season, obtaining water can be a problem at both areas. Wildflowers and fall color are both splendid. Marmots and pika add their whistles and cheeps.

Wood is scarce to nonexistent at either pass, and both areas are too fragile to permit fire pits. Carry a stove and forego the pleasure of a campfire.

Lake Ann is a classic cirque lake, surrounded on three sides by meadows, mountains, and snowfields. The depression in which it lies was gouged out by a departed glacier.

At some time, a Pacific Crest Trail may be routed down Maple Creek to join Bridge Creek, making this trail part of the PCT, or an alternate route for the PCT.

(August 1976)

RAINY LAKE

DESTINATION: Rainy Lake, 4790'

TRAIL LENGTH: 0.9 mile

WALKING TIME (light pack): 20 minutes one way

TRAILHEAD ELEVATION 4860'

ALTITUDE GAIN, including ups and downs: 70'

TOPOGRAPHIC SHEETS: USGS: Washington Pass 7.5'
Green Trails: Washington Pass

The trailhead is on the west side of Rainy Pass, 50 yards on a side road from the North Cascade Highway. There is parking 0.1 mile north of the trailhead.

The trail to the lake is paved for its entire distance. Altitude gain is minimal; the trail can be traversed by people confined to wheelchairs. Deep, blue Rainy Lake is inviting, particularly in the late fall when framed by the golden colors of the mountain ash. A splendid waterfall descends from snow-clad peaks to the south. Scrabble trails continue along the west side of the lake, ending on a talus slope, where water is deep enough for fishing. Picnics are permitted at the lake, but overnight camping is prohibited in the area.

This trail offers almost everyone the opportunity to visit a high alpine cirque lake. Trail use is substantial; visitors should stay on the trail to avoid damaging the fragile meadows. It is particularly important in this area to avoid littering.

A steep ridge forms the south headwall of the lake; the ridge crest is about 7500′, and there is a glacier beneath the crest.

(September 1979)

CUTTHROAT PASS (EAST APPROACH)

DESTINATION: Cutthroat Pass, 6800′

TRAIL LENGTH: 5.4 miles

WALKING TIME (light pack): 3 hours in
2½ hours out

TRAILHEAD ELEVATION: 4500′

ALTITUDE GAIN, including ups and downs: 2350′

FEATURE: Cutthroat Lake, 4935′

TOPOGRAPHIC SHEETS: USGS: Washington Pass 7.5′
Green Trails: Washington Pass

Drive east from Winthrop on Highway 20, 1.5 miles beyond the Lone Fir Campground to the access road; coming from the west, the access road is 4.6 miles from Washington Pass. Turn west and proceed up a moderately steep one-way road with turnouts at about one mile. There is parking for about 10 cars to the right near the trailhead, and for about 20 cars in a large, undeveloped area on the south side of the loop. Camping in this area is restricted to one night only, for hikers planning to take the trail the next day. No camping is allowed at Cutthroat Lake.

The trail leaves from the western end of the loop. After 100 feet, turn right at the bulletin board, then cross the bridge to the north side of the creek. (From this point, it is 1.9 miles gaining 500′ to the lake, 5.4 miles to Cutthroat Pass, 10.5

miles to Rainy Pass, and 31.5 miles to Hart's Pass.) The trail enters the woods briefly, but breaks out after 0.3 mile. There are some fine views of the mountains to the south and west. There is a nice waterfall to the south at 0.5 mile. At one mile, a creek must be crossed. At 1.8 miles there is a junction, with the left trail going 0.1 mile to the outlet of Cutthroat Lake, and the right trail switchbacking up to Cutthroat Pass.

During spring runoff, it is difficult to reach the east side of Cutthroat Lake; in the summer and fall, water levels are lower, so the outlet can be crossed on rocks and timber. There are fish in the lake. In the summer and early fall the area is quite buggy; take insect repellant. The lake is beautiful in its cirque under high peaks.

At 0.1 and 0.3 mile past the junction the hiker must ford creeks on the way to Cutthroat Pass. Early in the year, the second ford particularly offers formidable difficulties; these two fords may be bypassed by going up cross-country from east of the two bridges on the lower trail to the lake: 0.1 mile through the woods, gaining 150', will put you on the trail to the pass without having to make the hip-deep ford.

There are no significant streams beyond this point. In the late summer and early fall, the trail is dry from here on; drink deeply and fill water bottles before proceeding.

The trail switchbacks up steadily but never steeply, gaining approximately 1900' from the junction to the pass. The time up from the junction is a bit over two hours. About 2 miles from the junction, where the trail passes through a level area before switchbacking higher, there are some campsites. Follow a faint way trail westward about 0.3 mile, losing 200', to a creek from which water should be obtainable all summer. There is no other place to camp until Cutthroat Pass.

As altitude is gained, views improve and trees (mostly larch) become more scattered. The trail crosses meadow to

Cutthroat Pass, where there are good camping areas; however, water here can be a real problem, unless there are still snowfields. There is classic krummholz, of whitebark pine, alpine larch, and mountain hemlock, just north of the pass. These trees resemble lowland shrubs. Views from the pass are very impressive, particularly in the fall when the needles of the larch have turned golden yellow and glow in the sun. Cutthroat Peak looms to the south. Cutthroat Lake nestles in the rocks far below. The surrounding rocks have an orange tinge; all mountains in this area were etched from the Golden Horn batholith. To the west, down the Porcupine Creek Valley, are the darker peaks sculpted from the Black Peak batholith.

This is a more scenic approach to Cutthroat Pass than the route from Rainy Pass to the west. The trail meets the Pacific Crest Trail at Cutthroat Pass. This trail goes down to Rainy Pass 5 miles to the south, or north about one mile to a viewpoint above Granite Pass. From here, Methow Pass, Azurite Peak, and some incredibly beautiful mountain country can be seen to the north.

(July 1980)

CUTTHROAT PASS (WEST APPROACH–PCT)

DESTINATION: Cutthroat Pass, 6800′

TRAIL LENGTH: 5 miles

WALKING TIME (light pack): 2½ hours in
2 hours out

TRAILHEAD ELEVATION: 4860′

ALTITUDE GAIN, including ups and downs: 2000′

TOPOGRAPHIC SHEETS: USGS: Washington Pass 7.5'
Green Trails: Washington Pass

To reach the trailhead, turn east off the NCH at Rainy Pass onto a side road; follow this road 0.2 mile to an extensive parking lot. The trail starts at the north end of the parking area, beyond the horse ramp. The trail switchbacks up to the north through timber. Brief views of the peaks and cirques to the west are at 0.8 and 1.3 miles, where the trail breaks out into open rocky knolls for a short distance. A variety of wildflowers and succulent rock plants grow here. The trail then turns northeast and reenters deep woods. It crosses Porcupine Creek on a bridge at 2 miles. The trail enters open meadow at about 3.2 miles; a waterfall descends from the north and crosses the trail nearby. This is a good place to fill water bottles, since in late summer and early fall water is scarce beyond this point. After brief stretch in forest, the trail remains in splendid alpine meadow. Scenery improves as altitude is gained. The only good campsite on the trail is at the 4-mile mark; look for a sign directing the hiker down via a way trail 0.1 mile west to a flat area. Small springs provide water. Beyond the camping area, the trail switchbacks up and south, then goes east; a few more switchbacks lead to the summit of Cutthroat Pass. Tread is faint to nonexistent for the last several hundred feet of trail.

In addition to the options of continuing north on the PCT or descending via the trail to the east, the hiker can walk cross-country on ridges to the south and northwest.

Please refer to Cutthroat Pass (east approach) for more about the Cutthroat Pass area. Do recall that this is an exposed location and wind can be fierce during storms. Wood supplies are very limited, and the area is ecologically fragile. Campfires should not be attempted at the pass.

(July 1980)

GOAT PEAK

DESTINATION: Lookout, 7000'

TRAIL LENGTH: 2.5 miles

WALKING TIME: 1½ hours in
1 hour out

TRAILHEAD ELEVATION: 5600'

ALTITUDE GAIN, including ups and downs: 1400'

TOPOGRAPHIC SHEETS: USGS: Mazama
Green Trails: Mazama

Take the north loop of the NCH; two miles east of Mazama (about 11 miles west of Winthrop), turn sharply north. From here it is 12 miles to the trailhead. At 2.7 miles, turn left. At 9 miles, turn right. The trailhead is marked, and there is parking for about 10 cars. A primitive road continues northeast past the trailhead (this is not the trail).

From the trailhead, a new trail runs to the lookout. Tread is difficult to locate but blazes and surveyor's tape flags may be helpful. The footpath goes up along a rocky ridge and makes a sharp turn right (west) at about 0.5 mile. A sign on a tree indicates this first junction. Another trail continues on here; be sure to make the right turn. The trail goes briefly through timber, then reaches a wide scenic ridge. In the late spring and early summer glacier lilies and other flowers bloom on the ridge crest. After the ridge, the trail switchbacks up the northeast side of a rather steep bluff to the north end of Goat Mountain Ridge; it follows the ridge crest roughly one-half mile south to the lookout.

The trail is botanically interesting. At the trailhead there are subalpine fir and even Douglas fir, but at the exposed summit, white bark pine, larch, and Englemann's spruce are the only trees that survive.

When the lookout station is manned, the fire watcher may well invite you in for a cup of coffee. You should take the opportunity to inspect the inside of the lookout.

Views from the summit are splendid in all directions. The NCH lies below. Sandy Butte and Gardiner Mountain rise in the south. The villages of Twisp and Winthrop can be seen to the east. To the southwest, Silver Star rears rocky spires into the sky. The road to Hart's Pass can be seen to the west and Lost River to the northwest. The great peaks of the Pasayten spread out to the north as far as the eye can see.

There are several places to camp along the trail. After the snow has melted, finding water would be a major problem. Day hikers should carry water.

(June 1980)

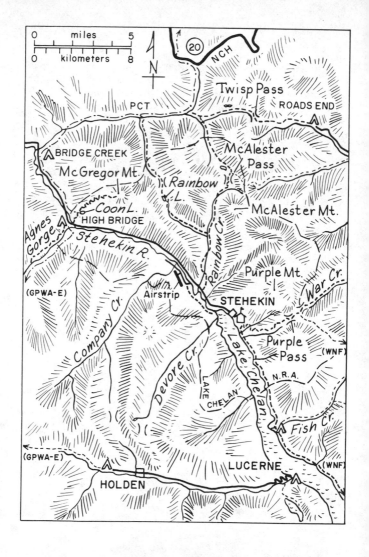

16

LAKE CHELAN NATIONAL RECREATION AREA

Trails:
Agnes Gorge (GPWA)
McGregor Mountain
Rainbow Creek and Lake
McAlester Pass and Lake
Purple Pass
Lake Shore Trail (WNF)
Stehekin River Trail
Twisp Pass (NCNP and WNF)

AGNES GORGE (GPWA)

DESTINATION: Agnes Gorge, 2000'
TRAIL LENGTH: 2.5 miles
WALKING TIME (light pack): 1 hour one way
TRAILHEAD ELEVATION: 1700'
ALTITUDE GAIN, including ups and downs: 350'
TOPOGRAPHIC SHEETS: USGS: McGregor Mt.; Mt. Lyall;
  Agnes Mt.
  Green Trails: McGregor Mt.

The trailhead is 0.2 mile above High Bridge and 0.1 mile beyond the Pacific Crest trailhead; it is marked. There are nice views of McGregor Peak to the east from the first portion of the trail, and a spectacular view of Agnes Mountain to the west at about 2 miles. There are wildflowers and dogwoods blooming in season. It is 2.5 miles to the gorge; it takes one hour to walk each way and elevation change is minimal.

The trail enters the Glacier Peak Wilderness from the National Park at 1.3 miles. Just beyond 2 miles, there is a very impressive view of the Agnes River running swiftly below. Just before the end of the trail, trilliums bloom in late May, and an occasional calypso orchid can be found. The main trail ends at the chasm of Agnes Gorge.

The hiker should follow the way trail that leaves the main trail a few feet before the gorge. One-tenth of a mile west and down, the head of the gorge is reached with reasonable safety, and with care you can climb a great pile of driftwood to the top of the precipice above the major falls within the gorge. The place is hypnotically beautiful. A waterfall is on the south side. There is a good campsite for two tents here. A footlog crosses the creek above the cataract, but be very careful: a fall into the torrent could be fatal.

This is a splendid trail for mountain views, wildflowers, views of the river and its impressive chasm and cataracts. There are reasonable amounts of water en route (at least in late May), but no other obvious campsites.

Along this trail, beware of the ticky thicket! Avoid contact with overhanging brush; apply repellant to the wrist, ankle, and neck areas before the hike. Check for ticks as soon as possible after coming off the trail.

(May 1978)

McGREGOR MOUNTAIN

DESTINATION: McGregor Mountain summit, 8100'

TRAIL LENGTH: 8 miles

WALKING TIME (full pack): 7 hours in
4½ hours out

TRAILHEAD ELEVATION 1700'

ALTITUDE GAIN, including ups and downs: 6500'

FEATURE: Heaton Camp, 6700'

TOPOGRAPHIC SHEETS: USGS: McGregor Mt. (trail not shown)
Green Trails: McGregor Mt.

This trail is without question strenuous, even to Heaton Camp. If pursued to the summit, it is also probably the most scenic and splendid trail in the Stehekin area. Watch for rattlesnakes on the lower portions of the trail. An early start helps to avoid the heat at low altitude. One quart of water is essential; an extra quart and several salt tablets are advisable.

The trail starts at the ranger cabin at High Bridge on the Stehekin Road 10.5 miles from Stehekin. Switchbacks start almost immediately. The old Stehekin Wagon Road joins the trail from the right at 0.4 mile. A 30-minute walk gaining 300' leads to Coon Lake, 1.2 miles from the trailhead. Agnes Mountain can be seen at two or three places along the trail to the lake. Coon Lake could be called a deep swamp or a shallow lake; it has no fish and is not scenic. Beaver frequent the area as do water fowl, particularly in the spring when several species of ducks mate.

The trail continues to the northwest end of the lake, where there is a marked junction. From here, the old Wagon Road continues 1 mile to its junction with the Stehekin Road above Tumwater Bridge, and then 3 miles, almost to the Bridge Creek Campground. The trail to McGregor Mountain turns east, drops slightly, and follows the north side of the lake; the trail begins its climb in seemingly unending switchbacks from the east side of the lake.

One mile from the Coon Lake junction the trail passes a waterfall on the right. Hikers can obtain water via a steep scrabble trail here. Drink deeply and fill canteens since the next water is several miles away. Just below this waterfall is a bluff with views of Coon Lake below and the Agnes Valley to the west.

From the waterfall the trail switchbacks upward continuously, in ponderosa pine forest at first. At about 3.5 miles there is another bluff; Coon Lake looks much smaller now. More mountains are visible, including Dome, Boston, Goode and Buckner. The trail then passes through the Canadian or Douglas fir zone. Between miles 4 and 5, scrabbles over difficult terrain allow access to water if desperate, but the first water easily available is at 5.5 miles, a few feet to the right of the trail. At 6 miles an unofficial campsite is below the trail, with water from a stream nearby. The first larch trees are seen at about this point; this marks the transition to the Hudsonian or alpine fir zone. At 6.3 miles the trail, which has been going up a fairly open valley for the past 2 miles, enters a talus bowl; there is one tent site at this point, without water.

After switchbacking up through the talus bowl, the trail reaches Heaton Camp 6.6 miles from the trailhead, located on the left (north) side of the talus bowl. This is the only designated camping area, at about 6700'. There is a 150-foot-long side trail to the left (west). There is a sign for this near the camp, but none at the junction.

Heaton Camp has 6 to 8 tent sites, two fire pits, a moderate wood supply, a toilet 300' to the north behind a granite outcrop, water from a small spring 100' below and northwest, and from a larger spring 0.1 mile down the trail. Water from the latter source can be sporadic. The area is almost bug-free. There is evidence of horses throughout the camp area. A faint trail up the ridge to the southeast was probably made by mountain goats.

A fairly steep 0.4-mile trail leads to the base of the talus slope beneath the summit. Here stand 2 timbers of the A-frame used to winch materials for the lookout to the summit. At the summit is the radio aerial of the Park Service repeater station.

From this point, the route to the summit looks formidable. If the proper route is followed, though, the ascent, though exposed, is not technical (Class 2). From the base of the talus slope, the best route is between two large rocks near the top of the rocky incline; both are marked with hard-to-spot red paint (a cairn was built on the left rock in 1980). Continue to the end of the highest left talus slope. Turn right here and follow a ledge approximately 200' to a gully on the right (look for red marker arrows). Just before the gully, turn left and return above a 20' rock block in the chute above the original talus slope. From here, the route is more obvious and better marked. It goes up the ridge to the left, and near the top cuts right and goes through a notch left of the first tor left of the summit. There are magnificent views of peaks to the north and east. Cross snow, or talus later in the year, on a faint trail east of this spire, and proceed upward on trail, snow, or talus 150 yards to the summit. Red arrows and dots mark the route, but they are not always easily seen.

There is no other safe route to the summit; do not go to the right at the base of the talus slope!

The flat 10' x 12' summit block was the site of the old McGregor Lookout. Today metal, fused glass, and other remnants of this structure can be found. Twenty feet below is the solar-powered Park Service repeater station and aerial.

From the summit is a panorama of practically every significant peak in the North Cascades, except Baker and Shuksan which are obscured by peaks to the northwest. Immediately below is the Sandalee Glacier. The whole Stehekin Valley is below, and Lake Chelan curves out of sight near Round and Domke mountains. The hiker is now in the arctic-alpine zone, where shrubs and flowers flourish briefly during the summer.

Descent, although easier on the lungs, is at best only a little faster since one missed step could have severe consequences.

On the way down, one can appreciate the creek flowers and the life zone changes. Only 35 minutes of walking separate the last larch (at about 5.5 miles) from the first ponderosa pine (at about 4 miles from High Bridge).

Allow 5½ hours up, fully packed, to Heaton Camp. Round trip from Heaton Camp to the summit takes 3 hours. It is 3 hours down to the trailhead from Heaton Camp.

Experienced climbers with appropriate equipment can continue cross-country over ice and rock from the summit to Rainbow Lake; this mountaineering traverse takes about 8 hours.

(August 1980)

RAINBOW CREEK AND LAKE

DESTINATION: Rainbow Lake, 5630'
SOUTH TRAILHEAD: Stehekin Road 1200'
TRAIL LENGTH: 10 miles
WALKING TIME (full pack): 6½ hours up
                               5 hours down
ALTITUDE GAIN, including ups and downs: 5000'
NORTH TRAILHEAD: South Fork Camp, Bridge Creek
                 (PCT), 3200'
TRAIL LENGTH: 6.2 miles
WALKING TIME (full pack): 5–6 hours in
                             3½ hours out
ALTITUDE GAIN, including ups and downs: 3100'
FEATURE: Pass under Bowan Mt., 6230' (high point)
TOPOGRAPHIC SHEETS: USGS: Stehekin; McAlester Mt.;
                       McGregor Mt.
              Green Trails: Stehekin; McGregor Mt.

This description will guide the hiker from the south trailhead at the Stehekin Road to Rainbow Lake, and thence to the north trailhead at the Bridge Creek section of the PCT.

The south trailhead is about 3 miles from Stehekin on the east side of the Stehekin-Cottonwood Camp Road. It is well marked. The trail goes up through typically dry east-side slopes. At 0.2 mile it passes a water reservoir for the orchards below; water bottles should be filled here since there is no water again until the Rainbow Creek Bridge, at 2.5 miles. (Get water from the creek below if the reservoir is not full.) Watch carefully for rattlesnakes.

From here, the trail switchbacks moderately steeply. At one mile, there is a fine view of Lake Chelan to the south, the Stehekin Valley below, and mountains to the west. Knolls off the trail provide many viewpoints and picnic spots.

The junction with the Boulder Creek Trail is at 2 miles. The Rainbow Creek Trail continues left for a few hundred yards (a scramble of 0.4 mile west from this point leads to the top of Rainbow Falls), and then drops into the valley to a bridge crossing Rainbow Creek. This is a very nice picnic spot, particularly in the spring when the entire valley is filled with blooming dogwood. Fill water bottles again, as this is the last water for a while.

The trail switchbacks up moderately onto the hill on the north side of the valley and follows the Rainbow Valley upward. (The Rainbow Loop Trail continues north 0.3 mile beyond the bridge.) At 3.2 miles, there is a view from a grassy knoll, particularly impressive when the yellow balsam is blooming in the late spring. It takes about 1¼ hours to get this far. From here there is a level traverse east for 1.4 miles, with many wildflowers in the spring.

Cross Rainbow Creek on a plank bridge. One mile above the crossing is Bench Camp, with 5 campsites. At this point the trail forks; the left path leads to Rainbow Lake 4.5 miles away; the right trail leads to McAlester Pass.

The Rainbow Lake Trail drops to reach Rainbow Creek again, which can be forded or crossed on a crude bridge. The elevation at the ford is 3600'; 2400' has been gained since the trailhead. Stock up on water as the next water is two miles, 1200' and 1½ hours up hot, steep, dusty, switchbacks.

After this steep segment the trail levels out, and water is available. Rainbow Meadow camp is 3.2 miles (2 hours) from the junction. This is a scenic camp. There are mosquitoes, however.

On this trail, the best is saved for last! There is 600' gained over the last 0.7 mile. Beautiful waterfalls nearby lessen the pain of trudging up again, and soon the path tops out and drops to Rainbow Lake, nestled under peaks and ridges at an altitude of 5630'.

Rainbow Lake is an emerald gem set in a horseshoe of crags and spires. There are fish in the lake. Four or five campsites are by the lake, but none of them are really comfortable. Firewood is available; mosquitoes are ubiquitous. Two lakes west of Rainbow Lake can be reached without much difficulty by traveling cross-country. These lakes retain ice much of the summer.

The trail north climbs 0.9 mile from the lake to a pass under Bowan Mt. at 6230'. The trail drops steeply from the pass through groves of larch trees, losing 1000' in the next mile. Difficult to locate in the meadow below the pass, the trail goes almost due north and can be found most easily by looking downhill when midway on the slope above the meadow, or by looking for cut ends of avalanche-felled trees in the meadow. A splendid waterfall comes from Bowan Mountain at this point.

The trail descends through forest for a few miles and then goes through avalanche slopes. The National Park boundary is three miles from the pass. Dan's Campsite is located midway between the pass and the Bridge Creek Trail. At five miles, cross Bridge Creek on a foot log. There is a 3000' loss from the pass to the junction with Bridge Creek/Pacific Crest Trail. It is 6.2 miles from Rainbow Lake to the PCT. There is a designated campsite (South Fork Camp, at 3200') on the north side of Bridge Creek 0.2 mile from the Bridge Creek Trail.

From Rainbow Lake it is a 6-hour walk to the North Cascades Highway (see Bridge Creek-PCT).

(September 1974)

McALESTER PASS AND LAKE

DESTINATION: McAlester Pass, 6017'

TRAIL LENGTH: 15.7 miles (10.1 miles from south
trailhead to McAlester Pass;
5.6 miles McAlester Pass to PCT)
add 3 miles to NCH

WALKING TIME: 6–7 hours south trailhead to McAlester
Pass;
3½ hours pass to PCT;
add 1½ hours to NCH

TRAILHEAD ELEVATION: 1200' (south trailhead on Stehekin Road);
3800' (Bench Creek Camp on
Rainbow Creek Trail);
3800' (north trailhead at
Fireweed Camp, PCT)

ALTITUDE GAIN, including ups and downs: 5000' from
south trailhead;
2300' from PCT

TOPOGRAPHIC SHEETS: USGS: McAlester Mt.
Green Trails: Stehekin

See the Rainbow Lake and Creek Trail for directions from
the Stehekin Road to Bench Creek Camp.

From Bench Creek Camp, continue up in forest 2.5 miles
and cross Rainbow Creek. Bowan Campsite is near this
crossing. McAlester Pass is another 2.5 miles; the last 0.5
mile is fairly steep. Although the trail is not too scenic, the
views from McAlester Pass are impressive. The pass is really
a meadow about a half mile long with a small tarn at the
southern end. A camping area, High Campsite, is at the pass
itself.

McAlester Pass is at 6017', 10 miles from the Stehekin
Road and 8.5 miles from the North Cascades Highway.

Near the center of the meadow is the trail junction to
South Pass. The trail switchbacks up moderately for about
0.3 mile, reaches a bench, and contours to the pass, which is
the boundary between the Recreation Area and the National
Forest. Views are spectacular and the meadow is superb
throughout this 1.2-mile stretch.

From South Pass, it is a 0.4-mile bushwhack over heather,

meadow, and talus to two lakes nestled under McAlester Mountain. There are camping areas at both lakes. Fish are in the larger lake. This faint scrabble trail is for experienced cross-country hikers only, since it is steep and particularly dangerous when wet and slippery.

(It is 7 miles from South Pass to a trailhead in the Okanogan National Forest. The altitude gain is 2200'. This trailhead is in the South Creek Campground, 22 miles up the Twisp River Road. The approximate hiking time up is 5½ hours; time down is 3 hours. Water and campsites are scarce along the South Creek Trail.)

It is one mile and about 500' down from the trail junction at McAlester Pass to McAlester Lake, the primary campsite in the area. Wood supplies were adequate at the lake in 1976. At the horse camp on the southeast side of the lake, there are several tent sites, a pit toilet, and a tether bar. The hikers' camp on the north side of the lake is preferred if available. It is drier, more scenic, and more private.

Below McAlester Lake, the trail to Fireweed Camp and the North Cascades Highway is in timber most of the way. It is 4 miles from the lake to the junction with the Twisp Pass Trail. Halfway Camp is midway between the lake and trail junction.

Turn left (west) on the Fireweed–Twisp Pass Trail. In 50 yards, turn right onto the Stiletto Spur trail; this is the shortest and quickest route north to the NCH. Or continue 0.3 mile west to Fireweed Camp and the Bridge Creek section of the PCT 0.1 mile further. At Fireweed Camp there are 6 or 8 campsites, tables, and adequate supplies of wood and water. From here it is 3.3 miles via the PCT to the NCH (see Bridge Creek trail).

The altitude loss from the lake to Fireweed Camp is 1900'; from Fireweed Camp to the highway, the altitude gain is 400'.

(1976)

PURPLE PASS

> DESTINATION: Purple Pass, 6884'
>
> TRAIL LENGTH: 7.8 miles
>
> WALKING TIME (light pack): 6 hours in (8½ hours with a
>   full pack)
>   3½ hours out
>
> TRAILHEAD ELEVATION 1150'
>
> ALTITUDE GAIN, including ups and downs: 5800'
>
> TOPOGRAPHIC SHEETS: USGS: Stehekin; Sun Mt.
>   Green Trails: Stehekin

The Purples were homesteaders in the Stehekin area. The creek, pass, and campground are named after them. There is nothing purple-colored in the area.

The trailhead is in back (east) of the Golden West Lodge; follow a poorly maintained road upward, past a concrete blockhouse, to the footpath. The trail switchbacks steeply and consistently up 7.8 miles to Purple Pass (6884'). The trail crosses Purple Creek at 1.8 miles; in the spring, this crossing can be difficult.

Drink and fill water bottles here; the next water is at Cougar Springs at 4.5 miles (unless the spring is dry) and at 4.7 miles via a scrabble trail going 200' to a creek. In the spring and early summer, water is available from melting snowfields near the summit, but later in the year this is a dry, hot trail. A minimum of two water bottles is suggested. Start early in the day in the summer to avoid overheating. It is a full day's walk for a strong hiker to Purple Pass and the additional 0.5 mile to the campsite near Juanita Lake. There is firewood here.

Beyond 2.2 miles, there are grassy knolls slightly off the trail where one can watch the clouds and peaks reflected in Lake Chelan. The 1500' gain to these areas is not too difficult, and will take about 2 hours. Views improve as one goes higher; at the pass, the spectacle of the North Cascades is stirring. Larch, the only deciduous conifer, appears at about 6.5 miles; a larch forest graces the area between Purple and War Creek passes.

Wildflowers are impressive in June. Deer are common on the trail; an occasional bear is seen. Carry an ice axe for ascents in May and June, since there is usually snow on the last one or two miles of the trail. (See Summit Trail description for more information about the Boulder Butte and Juanita Lake areas.)

(July 1979)

LAKE SHORE TRAIL (WNF)

DESTINATION: Stehekin, 1100'

TRAIL LENGTH: 17 miles

WALKING TIME (full pack): 9 10½ hours one way

TRAILHEAD ELEVATION 1100'

HIGH POINT: 2000'

ALTITUDE GAIN, including ups and downs: 3000'

TOPOGRAPHIC SHEETS: USGS: Stehekin; Sun Mt.;
                             Lucerne; Prince Creek
                    Green Trails: Stehekin; Lucerne;
                             Prince Creek

The boat disembarkation point on Lake Chelan is 0.2 mile north of the mouth of Prince Creek. The commercial boat, "Lady of the Lake," stops here. The Prince Creek trailhead is 0.1 mile to the southeast. From here it is 6 miles to Meadow Creek, 11 miles to Fish Creek, and 17 miles to Stehekin. To reach the Prince Creek Campground about half a mile south, cross Prince Creek on a narrow log bridge. There are also a number of satisfactory campsites near the Prince Creek trailhead.

Although called the Lakeshore Trail, the trail seldom runs along the lakeshore. Most of the time it is 200' to 500' above the lake, making it difficult to reach the lake for water or camping. The elevation gain in the entire 17 miles is just over 3000'. It appears easy on the map, but the trail is fatiguing. Water is available from creeks or at the lake. Good campsites are scarce. Perhaps 5 of the 17 miles are in the forest, without views, but the other 12 miles are relatively open and give panoramas over the lake. This hike is best in the spring and fall; it should be avoided during the heat of the summer.

High boots and long pants are recommended, since almost everyone walking this trail will see at least one rattlesnake. Check carefully for ticks.

In the first mile to the north, the trail gains 500', reaching a good viewpoint at the 16-mile marker. (The trailhead is at mile marker 17; Stehekin is at mile 0.) Another vantage point is a half mile further north. Just before the 14-mile marker there is a substantial altitude gain. Shortly thereafter, Rex Creek must be forded. Just beyond the creek there is a good trail shelter. At about the 11-mile mark, cross Cascade Creek. There is one poor campsite near the creek.

Near Meadow Creek, 10.4 miles from Stehekin, there is a well maintained trail shelter in an unattractive area. From the shelter, the only direct access to the lake crosses posted private property. The overnight camper should proceed 0.7 mile beyond the shelter, cut off the trail to the left, and cross country toward the lakeshore. After about 0.2 mile and the loss of 150', the hiker will find two splendid campsites beneath ponderosa pines on a bench above the lake. A short scramble over Class 2 rock gives access to the lake for bathing, drinking, and cooking water. There are great views. Lucerne is directly across the lake. There are no other good camping areas from here to Moore Point, 3 miles to the north.

At 9.8 miles from Prince Creek, the trail loses several

hundred feet as it switchbacks to a pasture east of Moore. The Fish Creek bridge is 0.4 mile further.

From the south end of the bridge, it is 0.5 mile downstream to the lakeshore and the campground at Moore Point. Remnants of the fire-destroyed Moore Hotel can be seen; indeed, lilacs and iris still bloom in the garden areas that surrounded the inn.

Several deteriorating roads join 0.2 mile beyond the bridge. The Fish Creek Trail leads east to the high meadows where it joins the Summit Trail. At the trailhead there is a shelter in excellent condition, with water available nearby; again, the location is not attractive.

The route now gains 1000' in the next 1.5 miles to reach the high point on Hunt's Bluff at the 5-mile marker. This is an excellent place to eat lunch. After descending the bluff, cross Hunt's Creek. In a mile, the trail reaches the boundary of the Lake Chelan National Recreation Area. Just north of this point is the Flick Creek Shelter, on the lakeshore with a delightful view south. This area probably could not handle more than five or six overnight campers, although it is the only designated campsite between the National Recreation Area boundary and Stehekin.

Cross pretty Flick Creek one mile north of the shelter; 0.9 mile beyond is Fourmile Creek and 1.3 miles after that is Hazard Creek. It is another 0.7 mile beyond Hazard Creek to the south end of Stehekin.

(May 1979)

STEHEKIN RIVER TRAIL

DESTINATION: Weaver Point, 1100'

TRAIL LENGTH: 4 miles

WALKING TIME (light pack): 1½ hours one way

TRAILHEAD ELEVATION 1200' (Harlequin Camp)

ALTITUDE GAIN, including ups and downs: 200'
SEASON FOR USE: late March to late November
TOPOGRAPHIC SHEETS: USGS: Stehekin
                     Green Trails: Stehekin

The trail starts at the Harlequin Campground, 4 miles from Stehekin village. Follow the Harlequin Campground road 0.2 mile from its junction with the Company Creek road. Turn right at the signed trailhead (the road continues beyond this point). (Horse access is via a road west of the Stehekin airstrip.)

The trail crosses streams, swamps, and ponds on interesting bridges, and passes through tranquil, grassy, open areas.

The hiker and horse trails join 0.7 mile from the trailhead. The trail enters the woods south of the Stehekin airstrip after crossing a creek on a foot log. The terrain is varied. The path at times traverses grassy savannas, and sometimes it passes through deep forest. In one location it follows a lazy, meandering side channel of the Stehekin River. This is a forest of substantial beauty.

At 1.6 miles a short scramble east of the trail onto a grassy bluff offers a fine view of the Stehekin River, with Rainbow Falls in the background. Harlequin ducks are often seen in this section of the river.

The junction with the Devore Creek Trail is 3.5 miles from the trailhead. The bridge across rocky Devore Creek is 0.1 mile further. The trail ends slightly northwest of the Weaver Point Campground. Any way through the woods that leads to the Weaver Point dock is a correct route.

By arrangement ahead of time with the concessionaire at the North Cascade Lodge, it is possible to obtain boat transportation from Weaver Point back to Stehekin. Occasionally, boaters departing down-lake are willing to drop the hiker off at the Stehekin Landing. Otherwise, steps must be retraced. From Weaver Point to the Harlequin Campground, there is about a 200' gain in altitude. There is ample time to make the round-trip walk between the morning and afternoon shuttlebus trips.

Watch out for yellow jackets!

(August 1979)

TWISP PASS (NCNP and WNF)

DESTINATION: Twisp Pass, 6066'
MAPS: USGS–Gilbert and McAlester Mt. 7.5'
        Green Trails—Stehekin

Twisp Pass may be approached from either east or west. The better approach, for beauty and ease of access, is from the east.

Twisp Pass itself is quite scenic. From the pass there are views of Stiletto Peak to the north, Gilbert Mountain to the east, Twisp Mountain to the south, Frisco Mountain to the west, and Dagger Lake below. Mountain goats are frequently seen in the area. Watch for rattlesnakes on the lower trail. At all camps, protect food from black bears, which are fairly common in the area.

East Approach

TRAIL LENGTH: 4.3 miles
WALKING TIME: 2 hours in
                1¾ hours out
TRAILHEAD ELEVATION 3700'
ALTITUDE GAIN, including ups and downs: 2400'

The eastern trailhead begins 0.2 mile before the end of the Twisp River road. There is parking for about 10 cars at the trailhead and for 10 cars at the road-end campground. The trail ascends moderately through brush and timber to the junction with Copper Pass Trail at about 1.7 miles. At 0.8 mile, there is a campsite on the left with water available 100 yards further down the trail. There is a reasonably good campsite at the trail junction; just beyond, the path crosses Copper Creek on a bridge. At 2 miles, there is a nice view down the valley to the east, and at 2.2 miles, a view to the south from just off of the trail to the left. At 2.5 miles, the trail breaks out into the open with splendid views to the south and west. From this point, the trail is quite scenic. A small creek provides water at 4 miles. The upper trail is brushy and not well maintained.

(September 1978)

West Approach

> TRAIL LENGTH: 7.2 miles from NCH (via Stiletto Spur)
> 4 miles from Fireweed Camp, 3700′
> (Bridge Creek, PCT)
> WALKING TIME: 3¾ hours in from NCH
> 2¾ hours out
> TRAILHEAD ELEVATION 4400′ (NCH)
> ALTITUDE GAIN, including ups and downs: 2400′

The western trailhead is 9 miles north from the Bridge Creek (PCT) trailhead on the Stehekin road, or 3.2 miles south from the Bridge Creek trailhead on the North Cascades Highway. There is parking for several cars on the south side of the highway and for 30 to 40 cars on the north side. The trailhead is at the lowest point between Rainy and

Washington Passes, where a short way trail joins the PCT. One mile south of the highway, there are two alternate routes, either following the PCT to Fireweed and going east, or taking the Stiletto Creek spur to the Twisp Pass trail. It is possible to enter one way and exit the other. The Stiletto Creek spur route is about 0.3 mile shorter. The National Park boundary is crossed about midway between the road and the Twisp Pass trail.

Water is easily available along the trail. Designated campsites are located at Fireweed Camp and Dagger Lake; neither are particularly recommended. The lake is shallow and muddy, with many mosquitos and flies. Views improve as altitude is gained beyond Dagger Lake, and Twisp Pass is quite enjoyable.

At the pass is the boundary between the National Forest on the east and the National Park on the west. No permit is needed for camping in the National Forest. There are several dry campsites next to the trail in the pass area. A scrabble trail north 0.25 mile leads to a shallow tarn, where there are superb campsites. There are also campsites south of the pass, but there is no obvious water source nearby after the snow has melted.

From the pass to the Stiletto Peak meadows, there is a cross-country trailless high route that is not difficult, but that should be attempted by experienced wilderness travelers only, since route finding may be a problem.

(July 1973)

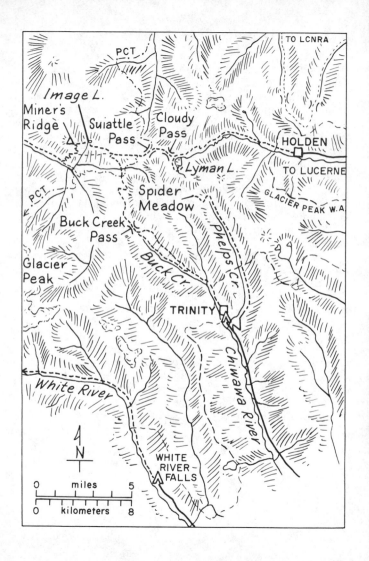

17

GLACIER PEAK WILDERNESS AREA
East Section

Trails:
White River
Phelps Creek—Spider Meadow
Agnes Creek (PCT)
Buck Creek Pass (Middle Ridge)
Lyman Lake (Railroad Creek)
Image Lake (Suiattle Pass)
(Pacific Crest Trail)

Of the four access routes to the Miner's Ridge, Suiattle Pass, and Lyman Lake areas, the most scenic are via Railroad Creek and Buck Creek Pass. The Agnes and Suiattle routes require long walks through deep woods; many people become somewhat bored with the long walking in deep forest before meadowland with its associated alpine scenery is reached. Hikers having access to two cars should give consideration to making a loop trip through this area; car keys can be exchanged at a pre-planned location and time. Cars can be left at 25 Mile Creek, or at Trinity, as well as at the end of the Suiattle River Road.

WHITE RIVER

DESTINATION: PCT junction near Reflection Pond, 5400′
TRAIL LENGTH: 14.2 miles
WALKING TIME (full pack): 9–11 hours in
7 hours out
TRAILHEAD ELEVATION 2300′
ALTITUDE GAIN, including ups and downs: 3800′
TOPOGRAPHIC SHEETS: USGS: Wenatchee Lake
Green Trails: Wenatchee Lake;
Holden; Glacier Peak

To reach the trailhead, turn north off U.S. 2, and drive to the north end of Wenatchee Lake. Continue 10.4 miles past the ranger station to the spacious parking lot at the end of the Wenatchee River Road. The trailhead is on the east side of the White River; there is a lovely waterfall at the trailhead. The trail enters the Glacier Peak Wilderness Area at about 2.5 miles. At 3.5 miles, there is a campsite near a bridge over a creek. At 4 miles there is an insect-infested camping area and a trail junction. The trail to the east leads to Boulder Pass in 7 miles, Napeequa in 10 miles, and the Chiwawa Road in 19 miles.

Between 4.1 and 6.1 miles the trail goes through the 4th of July meadow. Here there are lovely wildflowers and good views. Above and below the meadow, the trail is badly overgrown in places that can be wet, dank, and hot if the trail has not been brushed. At 6.2 miles the trail crosses Thunder Creek on a bridge; there is a pleasant campsite here. A less attractive camp is at 6.5 miles. There is another campsite at 9.5 miles; at 11 miles there is a fair campsite by a bridge over a creek. The trail is in forest from 6.1 to 12 miles. There are a number of unbridged crossings of minor creeks, and two bridge crossings of the White River. After 12 miles, views improve as the trail reaches subalpine meadow. The last 2.2 miles of trail ascends rather steeply as it traverses an enjoyable alpine meadow, ending high on the ridge where it joins the Pacific Crest Trail.

Water is available along the entire trail, even in late summer. Firewood is available at all campsites.

(See Pacific Crest Trail for information on the PCT north and south of the junction.)

(August 1974)

PHELPS CREEK—SPIDER MEADOW

DESTINATION: "Larch Knob," Spider Glacier Camp,
        6500'

TRAIL LENGTH: 7 miles

WALKING TIME (full pack): 6 hours in
        3½ hours out

TRAILHEAD ELEVATION 3450'

ALTITUDE GAIN, including ups and downs: 3000'

FEATURES: Phelps Creek Pass, 7050' (high point)
Spider Meadow, 5000'
TOPOGRAPHIC SHEETS: USGS: Holden
Green Trails: Holden

To reach the trailhead, follow the directions for Trinity as given for the Buck Creek Pass Trail. Turn right 11.2 miles from the end of the pavement, and 0.8 mile from Trinity. This side road, 2.4 miles long, goes uphill, makes two switchbacks, and ends at the trailhead where there is parking for about 15 cars.

The trail begins at the north end of the parking lot and follows an abandoned mining road. The Carne Mountain Trail junction is 0.2 mile from the trailhead. At about 2 miles, the trail forks just beyond a mining claim west of the trail; go right at this unmarked fork. The trail enters the Glacier Peak Wilderness Area after about 3 miles. There is a campsite at the boundary. At 3.5 miles there is a creek and a camp, and 100 yards beyond there is a camp with toilets. The road ends at Leroy Creek, which must be forded or crossed on a foot log. At 3.9 miles, the trail passes the Phelps Ridge Trail leading three miles west to the top of Phelps Ridge.

It is roughly 5.5 miles to Spider Meadow, taking about 3 hours and gaining about 1500'. There are several excellent campsites in the south portion of the meadow. The hiker must ford Phelps Creek, or find a foot log crossing, 0.8 mile into the meadow. Beyond this point, the trail steepens. In 0.3 mile is an abandoned mining cabin, and shortly after that is an important junction. The trail to the right (east) goes into Phelps Basin for about a half mile, to dead-end at about 5500'. The Spider Glacier–Lyman Lake Trail goes left, makes a sharp left turn about 100 yards beyond the junction, and thereafter climbs steeply. The tread deteriorates. The hiker will need to scramble up switchbacks, at first beneath the rock face to the southwest and then up the meadow, topping out about one mile further and 1000′ higher in a magnificent high camp on a larch-covered knob. This is one of the most splendid campsites in the North Cascades. There are great views down into Spider Meadow and the Phelps Creek Valley, from where the hiker has just come. Across the valley to the east are Seven Fingered Jack and Mount Maude, both rearing a shade over 9000′. To the southwest is Red Mountain. Behind the camp is the snow couloir leading to the pass, 0.8 mile away, between the Phelps Creek and Railroad Creek drainages.

Although there are campsites near the abandoned mining cabin, the campsite at "Larch Knob" is so superior that hikers should press on. There is space here for, at most, ten people. Water is easily available, but wood is very scarce; do carry a stove.

This is the turnaround point for the average hiker, who should spend the night at this campsite and then return to the trailhead. Those experienced in snow travel can proceed up the snow slope to reach the Spider–Lyman or Phelps Creek Pass, 35 minutes and 0.8 mile away. The alpine scenery is magnificent. Below to the north lie the Lyman Lakes and Lyman Glacier; beyond them are Cloudy Pass, Cloudy Peak, North Star Mountain, and Sitting Bull Mountain. Splendid alpine flowers grow in the rock crevasses near the pass. In their small way, they are as beautiful as the great vistas in the distance.

With regret, descend back into Phelps Creek Valley, or, if you have an ice axe and climbing experience, descend to the north on fairly steep snow, staying to the right of the ice of Lyman Glacier. If possible, cross below Lyman Glacier to the west of the upper Lyman Lakes. From the upper lakes, the hiker must descend along a long, beautiful waterfall; this is accomplished more easily on the west. If done on the east, the hiker must find a ford to the west side of Lyman Lake, since one cannot reach the Railroad Creek Trail from the east side of the lake. At splendid Lyman Lake there are a number of campsites. From here it is possible to return to Trinity, three miles via Cloudy Pass, Suiattle Pass, Miner's Ridge, and Buck Creek Pass. It is also possible to descend to Holden via Railroad Creek. (See trail descriptions of these options elsewhere in this book.)

(July 1975)

AGNES CREEK (PCT)

DESTINATION: Suiattle Pass, 5983'

TRAIL LENGTH: 17 miles

WALKING TIME (full pack): 11–12 hours in
7 hours out

TRAILHEAD ELEVATION 1700' (High Bridge)

ALTITUDE GAIN, including ups and downs: 4500'

SEASON FOR USE: lower portions: April to mid-November
high country: mid-July to mid-October

TOPOGRAPHIC SHEETS: USGS: McGregor Mt.; Mt. Lyall;
Agnes Mt.; Holden
Green Trails: McGregor Mt.;
Holden

The Agnes Creek trailhead is just beyond High Bridge on the Stehekin Road, 10.5 miles from Stehekin. The trailhead is a short walk from the High Bridge Guard Station.

After 0.1 mile the trail crosses Agnes Creek on a bridge and begins a gradual climb through deep woods to Suiattle Pass, 17 miles away. At 3 miles, the trail passes near the brink of the Agnes Gorge. Cross Trapper Creek at 3.8 miles. At 4.9 miles is the junction with the west fork of Agnes Creek Trail. There are good campsites at Fivemile Creek, 0.1 mile east of the junction, above Pass Creek. At 7.9 miles is the junction with the Swamp Creek Trail and Swamp Creek Camp at 2780'. Cedar Camp (also known as Spruce Creek Camp) is at 9.2 miles, and Hemlock Camp, with benches, table, and fire ring, is at 11.9 miles (3560').

Cross Glacier Creek at 12.1 miles. There is a campsite near the end of the forest at 13.5 miles. At 14.9 miles and 4400', the trail leaves the forest and enters a large, bushy meadow. At 16.6 miles there is a good campsite with table, firepit and toilet, and 0.1 mile beyond the campsite is the junction with the trail to Cloudy Pass. Railroad Creek Trail from Holden also joins Agnes Creek Trail here. Suiattle Pass (5983') is 0.4 mile beyond.

(The PCT from Hemlock Camp to Suiattle Pass will be rerouted higher and to the west by the time this book reaches print; the trail will also be longer. Check with the Wenatchee Forest Service for updated information.)

This long valley walk is probably the least enjoyable portion of the Pacific Crest Trail between Manning Park and Stevens Pass. There are few views until the last two miles of this trail. There is no shortage of wood or water en route. A fit hiker will require one long, hard day to go from the Stehekin Road to Suiattle Pass (17 miles and a 4500' gain); most hikers will take 1½ to 2 days to make the ascent, while the descent can be done in 8 hours.

(August 1981)

BUCK CREEK PASS (MIDDLE RIDGE)

DESTINATION: Buck Creek Pass, 5900'
TRAIL LENGTH: 10.5 miles
WALKING TIME (full pack): 7 hours in
                             5 hours out
TRAILHEAD ELEVATION 2772'

ALTITUDE GAIN, including ups and downs: 3550'
FEATURES: Flower Dome, 6300'; Liberty Cap, 6850';
           Helmet Butte, 7366';
           Middle Ridge, 6200'
TOPOGRAPHIC SHEETS: USGS: Holden
                    Green Trails: Holden

To reach the trailhead, turn north off U.S. 2 toward Lake Wenatchee. Turn right in 3.8 miles onto Highway 209 and continue to Plain, 4.9 miles away. From the east, Plain can be reached directly from Leavenworth. Turn left (north). Turn right 2.8 miles later. Seven miles from Plain, turn right onto the Chiwawa Road. Ten miles from this turnoff, the road narrows; 1.4 miles later, the pavement ends. After 11.2 miles the rough, dusty, one-lane road forks. (The right fork leads to the Phelps Creek trailhead.) Take the left fork 0.8 mile, where the road ends at the gate before the bridge over Phelps Creek. There is parking for about 40 cars in the Phelps Creek Campground west of the road. The total distance from U.S. 2 to the trailhead is 39.1 miles; from the village of Plain it is 31 miles.

The old mining town of Trinity is occupied private property. Passage along the trail is permitted, but areas in the immediate vicinity are off limits.

Follow the old county roadbed. Immediately past two large tanks on the left, take the left of the three roads. Take the right fork 0.2 mile further.

The trail crosses the boundary of the Glacier Peak Wilderness Area in 1.2 miles. Just beyond the boundary there is a campsite to the right of the trail. At 1.4 miles is the junction with the Red Mountain Trail; go left. The trail crosses the Chiwawa River on a bridge at 2.6 miles. A campsite is 0.1 mile up the trail, on a bluff above the river. There are plenty of campsites from 1.2 to 7.3 miles. A camping area with toilet is at about 6 miles within the deep forest.

In the forest is a profuse display of queen's cup bead lily. Open areas are often densely overgrown. Wildflowers are fabulous. In July the meadows are covered with glacier lilies and Western Pasque flower.

The trail is quite muddy in places; stretches may be bridged or puncheoned. At times the trail follows old sheep driveways. Years ago, sheep grazed on the high meadows; the driveways remain eroded and bare to this day.

At 7.1 miles the trail forks; the old trail drops to the left to ford Buck Creek immediately below. Early in the year this is a thigh-deep, hazardous ford, and the trail on the south side of the creek is often difficult to locate in snow. At 8 miles, below the switchbacks on the old trail, there is an excellent campsite. The old trail is maintained to this point, but not beyond.

At 7.3 miles, on the new trail, there is a campsite in the woods to the right of the trail. Those who are tired should stop here, for there are no more campsites until the campground at Buck Creek Pass or the junction of the Buck Creek Pass Trail with the Flower Dome Trail.

The route up to Buck Creek Pass offers views of Buck Mountain to the south, Liberty Cap, and Helmet Butte. Near the crest, Glacier Peak comes into view. In the last 3.2 miles to the pass the altitude gain is about 1500'. Early in the season the trail crosses one avalanche path (from Fortress Mountain) as well as four or five creeks; some are difficult to cross in the spring runoff or when filled with snow.

As the trail contours around the southwest shoulder of Helmet Butte, drop about 0.2 mile and 200' to the southwest to reach the campground. The horse camp is a quarter mile south of the hikers' camp. There are also 4 or 5 campsites at the beginning of the Flower Dome Trail. The rest of the Buck Creek Pass area is closed to camping and horse grazing.

Water is available from melting snow at the pass area until late in the season. Wood is scarce near the campground.

(There is more wood near the Flower Dome camping area.) Fire pits are rare; carry a stove.

Do spend a day in this area if at all possible. The views from Flower Dome, Helmet Butte, and Liberty Cap on a clear day are among the most spectacular in the North Cascades! Climb 400' in 0.7 mile west to the flat crest of Flower Dome, where you can see Glacier Peak to the west, Miners Ridge and Plummer Mountain to the north, Helmet Butte and Fortress Mountain to the northeast, and Liberty Cap to the south.

It's easy to follow the trail south from the campground up the north flank of Liberty Cap. The trail contours under the west and south sides; ascent on heather meadow and scree to the top is not difficult. Or continue on the High Pass Trail to a high rock promontory where you can see the great peaks in the area as well as the Buck Creek and Suiattle valleys.

Helmet Butte is not a technically difficult climb. Experienced climbers can cross High Pass and drop into the Napeequa Valley. For traversing the high trail, an ice axe is necessary until at least early August.

The Buck Creek Pass Trail continues north to Middle Ridge, dropping fairly steeply for about 1 mile; the descent begins just beyond the Flower Dome way trail. The trail crosses Small Creek (5125') then rises to about 6200' on Middle Ridge. It then drops about 1700' to cross Miners Creek on a foot log. A rather steep ascent leads to the Glacier Peak mines on the trail between Image Lake and Suiattle Pass. (See Image Lake Trail for information beyond this trail junction.)

To reach the Suiattle River take the Triad Trail, which descends on the south side of Flower Dome, 3 miles to the Suiattle River Trail.

(Trinity to Buck Creek Pass, High Pass Trail, and Flower Dome: July 1981. Buck Creek Pass to Glacier Peak Mines: August 1966.)

LYMAN LAKE (RAILROAD CREEK)

DESTINATION: Lyman Lake, 5600'

TRAIL LENGTH: 8.3 miles

WALKING TIME (full pack): 7 hours in
5 hours out

TRAILHEAD ELEVATION 3100'

ALTITUDE GAIN, including ups and downs: 2600'

FEATURES: Suiattle Pass, 6000'; Cloudy Pass, 6450' (high
point);
Phelps Creek (Spider) Pass, 7050'

TOPOGRAPHIC SHEETS: USGS: Holden
Green Trails: Holden

The trailhead is 0.75 mile west of Holden Village, just outside the Glacier Peak Wilderness Area. Holden can be reached by boat from Chelan to Lucerne, and by Holden Village bus from Lucerne.

Up the trail 0.9 mile is the junction with the Holden Lake Trail. About 3 miles further is Hart Lake, elevation 3956', where there is a good campsite. There is another campsite near a stream about a mile further. The trail then switchbacks up through brush, gaining over 800' before it levels out; from here the trail climbs gradually to reach the north end of Lyman Lake. The switchback section could be quite difficult if it has not been brushed by the trail crew.

The trail after Hart Lake offers views of magnificent waterfalls. A number of spectacular cascades coming off Bonanza Peak end in the Hart Lake area. Crown Point Falls, just below Lyman Lake, is gorgeous, and can be seen from the trail.

Lyman Lake is splendid. There is a way trail along the west side of the lake. An even less formal trail leads to the three smaller lakes higher in the basin to the southeast. Experienced back country travelers with ice axes can ascend to the Phelps Creek Pass area for better views. There are good campsites at the three lakes. Fishing is generally good in Lyman Lake. Water is not a problem, but wood is scarce. The area is buggy; bring insect repellant. Much of the area around Lyman Lake is marshy.

From the north side of the lake, the Railroad Creek Trail leads to Cloudy Pass. From here there is a wonderful view into the Lyman Lake basin and its backdrop of Chiwawa Mountain, the Lyman Glacier, Phelps Creek Pass, and Dumbbell Mountain. From the lake to the pass is about 2 miles and 1000' up. From Cloudy Pass there is a hiker's high route and a horseman's low route to Suiattle Pass, about a mile west. From this point, there are connections via the Pacific Crest Trail with the Stehekin Road to the northeast, and with various routes to the west (described under Image Lake). Lyman Lake can also be reached by the Phelps Creek Trail.

The country between Lyman Lake and Image Lake is among the most splendid in the North Cascades. In spite of difficult access, the area is fairly heavily used, and the lakeshore has been significantly affected. When obtaining a wilderness permit, check with the issuing office regarding camping restrictions in the Lyman Lake area.

A word of caution: the Lyman Glacier is crevassed. The area is dangerous and should be avoided by all except roped-up, experienced climbers.

Very strong hikers with day packs can make the round trip from the trailhead to Lyman Lake, or Cloudy Pass, in one long summer day. Two days is recommended, though. In spite of the bugs, the area is so pretty and enjoyable that departing back down the trail soon after arrival would be heartbreaking!

(1975)

IMAGE LAKE (SUIATTLE PASS)

DESTINATION: Image Lake, 6100'

TRAIL LENGTH: 15 miles

WALKING TIME (full pack): 10–12 hours in
                         7 hours out

TRAILHEAD ELEVATION 1550'

ALTITUDE GAIN, including ups and downs: 4600'

FEATURES: Miners Ridge Lookout, 6210';
         Suiattle Pass, 6000'

TOPOGRAPHIC SHEETS: USGS: Glacier Peak and Holden
                   Green Trails: Glacier Peak and
                   Holden

From either State Highway 20 or 530, drive to the beginning of the Suiattle River Road, midway between Darrington and Rockport, and continue 23 miles to the road end, where ample parking is available. There is a horse ramp in the parking area. The first mile beyond the parking lot follows the old road bed before leaving the road and becoming trail. (Trail mileages are from this point, not from the parking lot.)

The generally muddy trail winds through deep woods for the first five miles. Water is available. A few yards beyond the five-mile marker is the Canyon Creek Bridge and trail shelter. (In 1966 the structure was watertight, but without bunks.) Fishing in Canyon Creek is good. The trail continues 2.5 miles to a rough camp of tables and lean-to's. There is water just before this camp. A quarter mile past the camp the trail forks; take the left branch to Image Lake (the right continues to Middle Ridge).

Just before the 8-mile point the trail starts uphill and climbs for 5 miles, gaining approximately 4000'.

At 11 miles the Image Lake and Miner's Creek trails join.

Here there is another campsite with lean-to's and water a few hundred yards down the trail. The last 2 miles of the trail are steep, ending at the crest of Miner's Ridge about 0.2 mile east of the lookout at mile 13. A level walk over one mile leads to Image Lake.

Because of past abuse, camping at Image Lake is restricted to the designated camping area southeast of the lake. The lake basin and surrounding meadows fortunately are recovering from past abuse since the Image Lake area has been completely closed to overnight camping. The closest designated campsite is 0.75 mile past the lake at Lady Camp. Only very fast hikers can make the almost-16-mile walk from the parking area to Lady Camp in one day. The use of horses is restricted in the Image Lake basin. A guard is stationed in this area in summer, to assist visitors and to enforce regulations.

Miner's Ridge is one of the most beautiful places in the world. Glacier Peak reflected in Image Lake at sunrise is well worth getting up at 4:00 in the morning to see. From the Miner's Ridge lookout to Suiattle Pass, the hiker walks 5 miles hip-deep in wildflowers, surrounded by incredible beauty.

From Suiattle Pass, Glacier Peak dominates the skyline to the southwest. The hiker can also see Plummer Mountain to the north, North Star to the northeast, and Fortress Mountain to the southeast.

Just east of Image Lake, the Kennecott Copper Company has plans for a half-mile-wide open-pit mine. Few areas on Planet Earth are more beautiful than this area. A rise in the price of copper might well reopen Kennecott's desire to devastate the Glacier Peak Wilderness; this must be prevented.

From Suiattle Pass, the hiker has the option of descending the Pacific Crest Trail through the Agnes Creek valley.

Other options are to take the mile-long hikers' scrabble trail high, or to descend and take a longer trail with better tread, to reach Cloudy Pass. From here there is a fantastic view into the Lyman Lake basin (see Lyman Lake–Railroad Creek). Walking time from Image Lake to Suiattle Pass is about two hours; from Suiattle to Cloudy Pass it is another half hour.

Other campsites in the area are at the Glacier Peak Mines and below Suiattle Pass in the meadows of the upper Agnes Creek valley.

A three-day visit is a minimum in this area, and four or more days is preferable. The high country between Lyman Lake and the Miner's Ridge lookout offers perhaps the best scenery in the North Cascades.

(August 1966)

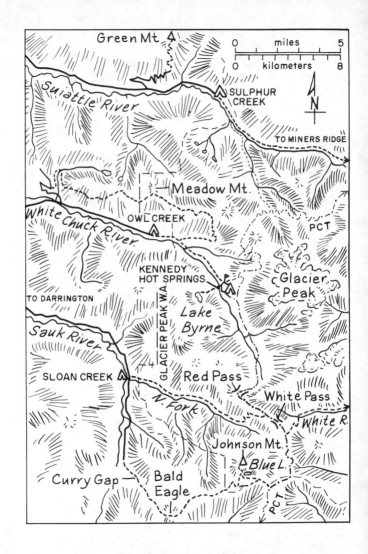

18

GLACIER PEAK
WILDERNESS AREA
West Section

Trails:
Meadow Mountain
Kennedy Hot Springs (Lake Byrne)
Blue Lake (Johnson Mountain)
White Pass and Red Pass (Sloan Creek)
Green Mountain
(Pacific Crest Trail)
(White River)

MEADOW MOUNTAIN

WEST TRAILHEAD: gate on Meadow Mt. Road, 2650'

EAST TRAILHEAD: end of White Chuck Road, 2300'

TRAIL LENGTH: 19.5 miles

WALKING TIME (full pack): 2 days

HIGH POINT: 5900'

ALTITUDE GAIN, including ups and downs: 4000' west to
                east; 4350' east to west

FEATURE: Meadow Lake, 4800'

TOPOGRAPHIC SHEETS: USGS: Glacier Peak 15'; Pugh Mt. 7.5'
                    Green Trails: Sloan Peak; Glacier Peak

This is one of the finest hikes in the North Cascades and
well worth the substantial effort involved to visit the area.

The nicest way to do this walk is to use two cars, leaving
one at the White Chuck trailhead and the other at the
Meadow Mountain trailhead. With the Forest Service gate in
place, Meadow Mountain for practical purposes is no longer
a day-hiking area: To make the loop requires a two-day trip
with an overnight camp in the high meadows.

The fall colors of the meadows are beautiful in late September and early October. Blueberries may be picked along
the route. Bear, deer, eagles, and grouse are often seen along
the high ridges.

To reach the west trailhead, drive the Mountain Loop
Highway either south from Darrington or north from Barlow
Pass. Take the White Chuck River Road east for 6 miles.
Turn left (north) on the Straight Creek Road and follow it for
2 miles to the Meadow Mountain Road.

The Forest Service has placed a gate across Meadow
Mountain Road at this location, to minimize damage from
overuse of the Meadow Mountain area. This has added 5
miles of road walking to the Meadow Mountain Trail loop.

The trailhead is now 0.1 mile south of the gate. A 0.2-mile way trail bypasses the gate. Just beyond the junction of the new trail with the road, the road forks; the left fork goes to Crystal Lake. Take the right fork and walk the road to the old trailhead.

The trail bends back sharply to the west from the road; do not bear east at this point. (The distances in the following descriptions are from this trailhead at the end of the Meadow Mountain Road; add five miles to take into account the road walk required to reach this point.)

The trail switchbacks up through dense woods for slightly over one mile, requiring about 35 minutes to reach the meadow. There is a small stream and a fairly good campsite at this point. The trail then angles east less steeply; at about 1.5 miles it forks. The poorly maintained left branch drops sharply to Meadow Lake at 1 mile and Crystal Lake at 2 miles. The well-maintained main trail continues to the right. It angles up a ridge at two miles and then runs east along the ridge through meadow and forest. At about 3.5 miles, climb the ridge and follow the trail 0.1 mile to the right to a fine view of Glacier Peak. Switchbacks go down to the left, dropping about 500' to a small valley with two streams and several nice but somewhat muddy campsites. Just past 4 miles the trail emerges from the forest and contours gradually upward across a meadow. A scramble directly up to the ridge top, several hundred feet above, and then down approximately 0.3 mile on the other side leads to Diamond Lake, an ideal campsite with a magnificent view. Access to Emerald Lake is not as easy.

The trail between the 6- and 8-mile marks is in poor condition and may well be difficult to locate through the meadow when the vegetation is high in midsummer. A tarn immediately to the south of the trail just before the high ridge, at about 6 miles, is another campsite.

The trail crosses at least two more meadows and ridges. At the remains of a shelter at about 8 miles, the trail descends rather steeply for several miles through open slopes, entering the woods near Fire Creek and remaining in deep forest back to White Chuck trailhead.

The lowland (deep woods) portion of the trail is muddy. From Fire Creek to the junction with the old Kennedy Hot Springs trail is about 3 miles, on the old Kennedy trail for almost 2 miles, and approximately 1.5 miles on the new Kennedy trail to the White Chuck trailhead. Total loop distance is about 14.5 miles. It can be hiked comfortably in 9 hours.

There is about 7 miles of high meadow walking which, after the initial gain of about 1000', is fairly level, with varying ups and downs. There are fairly good campsites at small creeks in various meadows. Spectacular views of Glacier Peak are available from the 4-mile mark on, in good weather. Water is available in several places, but wood is scarce in the meadows.

To summarize from the old Meadow Mountain trailhead: Mile 1, begin meadows; mile 2, near ridge; mile 3, along ridge; mile 3.5, Glacier Peak viewpoint; mile 4, just past valley campsite; mile 5, approach meadow south of Diamond Lake; mile 6, ridge top, elevation 6376' with spectacular views on both sides a couple of hundred feet off the trail to the north; mile 7, meadow; mile 8, remains of shelter, begin journey down; miles 9 and 10, switchbacks down; mile 10.5, cross Fire Creek on foot log; mile 11, junction with old Kennedy Hot Springs trail; mile 13, junction with new Kennedy Hot Springs trail; mile 14.5, White Chuck trailhead.

(September 1969)

KENNEDY HOT SPRINGS (LAKE BYRNE)

DESTINATION: Kennedy Hot Springs camp, 3300'
TRAIL LENGTH: 5.2 miles

WALKING TIME (light pack): 3 hours in
                                 2¼ hours out
TRAILHEAD ELEVATION 2300'
ALTITUDE GAIN, including ups and downs: 1000'
SEASON FOR USE: late April through November
FEATURE: Lake Byrne, 5600'
TOPOGRAPHIC SHEETS: USGS: Glacier Peak 15'; Pugh Mt. 7.5'
                             Green Trails: Sloan Peak; Glacier Peak

Kennedy Hot Springs has become very crowded! On summer weekends and holidays, the camping area is usually full early in the day. Camping at Kennedy is restricted to designated locations; users are asked to limit their stay to one night.

Take State Highway 530 to Darrington; drive 0.5 mile northeast to the Mountain Loop Highway just past the bridge over the Sauk River, and follow it south slightly over 10 miles. About 150 yards after the bridge over the White Chuck River, turn left and drive 11 miles east to the end of White Chuck Road, where there is a nice forest camp. Take the new trail to Kennedy Hot Springs; it is shorter and less muddy than the old trail. The junction with the east portion of the Meadow Mountain trail is about 1.5 miles, roughly 150 yards past a bridge over a beautiful, moss-lined stream (Fire Creek) with a spectacular waterfall 75 yards upstream. The trail winds leisurely, occasionally upward, above and along the White Chuck River, offering ample opportunity to descend to the stream for fishing. The trail intersects the old Kennedy trail at about 4.5 miles, and in another 0.75 mile is Kennedy Hot Springs.

At Kennedy, there is one shelter in fair condition. Firewood is extremely scarce; chemical stoves should be used. The hot springs and bath house are 100 yards up the White Chuck River from the guard station. The springs are about five feet deep and are excellent for tired muscles. Bathing suits and towels should be brought.

There are many campsites with water at Kennedy, and several areas en route where camp may be made in the deep woods or on gravel bars beside the White Chuck River.

The route to Kennedy has remarkable ground cover, large cedar and Douglas fir trees, quartz dikes twisted by geologic pressures, two rockfalls from the cliffs, pumice slides, and the vivid fall color of vine maples. At about the 1.5-mile mark, there is a hanging garden of thick green moss with maidenhair fern. Those who enjoy stream fishing should take rod and reel and probably hip boots. This hike is recommended as a one-day conditioning walk early or late in the season. When the meadows are open, nearby Meadow Mountain is far more scenic.

Lake Byrne and Other Side Trips

Many side trips are possible from Kennedy camp. (1) The hiker can ascend Glacier Ridge, connecting with Mica Lake (9.5 miles) and the Milk Creek trail. (2) Just before the Hot Springs you can pick up the Kennedy Ridge trail. A hike of about 2 miles, up fairly steeply at first, leads to the Cascade Crest Trail, with access to Glacier Peak. (3) The hiker can make connections to the south with Red Pass and White Pass, the latter about 10 miles from Kennedy Hot Springs. (4) From Kennedy you can switchback steeply, gaining about 2300' in 2 miles, to reach Lake Byrne. Camp Lake is one mile further to the west. Several other lakes (Hardtack, Sun Up, and Round) lie along the ridge crest to the west. Although there is no trail between Hardtack and Sun Up lakes, experienced hikers can run the ridge without great difficulty, leaving by the trail from Bingley Gap to the Sauk River road 3 miles from the Mountain Loop Highway.

To reach Lake Byrne, take the Lost Creek Ridge trail, which begins at the bridge across the White Chuck River from the Kennedy Guard Station. The left fork leads to the Hot Springs; the right fork proceeds up 2.5 miles to Lake Byrne, gaining 2350'. The time up with a full pack is 2 hours; the time down is 1 hour.

After about 1.5 miles, the trail reaches a ridge crest and contours southwest for about 0.2 mile. At this point, it turns sharply to the right (north); in snow, the route may not be apparent here. Beyond the turn, switchbacks resume and continue to the lake.

From Lake Byrne, the trail goes around the north end of the lake, gaining about 500', crosses near a tarn and descends to Camp Lake to the southwest from the highest knoll of the ridge crest. The walking time between the lakes is about 45 minutes.

Experienced wilderness travelers can walk the ridges around the circumference of Lake Byrne. The view from the high knob south of the lake is one of the best in the North Cascades. Below lies azure Lake Byrne, and the Sauk and Kennedy valleys. Great peaks of the range are visible, including Mt. Baker, Mt. Shuksan and, closer, Glacier Peak.

Insects are annoying in the Lake Byrne area. There are two good campsites north of the lake outlet. The lake can be almost iced in. A 30-minute walk directly west, there is a rocky ridge, with views to the west and east.

Although there is some wood in the area, the high meadow is fragile, and it is best to use a backpacker's stove.

Snow remains late in the Lake Byrne area; it is best visited after mid-August. The lake can be reached in a one-day trip from the Kennedy Hot Springs area. For hikers coming in from the trailhead, an overnight camp is best. The area is beautiful and still relatively isolated. Those hikers who really want isolation can camp at lakes further west.

(August 1972)

BLUE LAKE (JOHNSON MOUNTAIN)

DESTINATION: Blue Lake, 5500'

TRAIL LENGTH: 9.7 miles

WALKING TIME (full pack): 7 hours in to Blue Lake; 8
                          hours to PCT
                          6½ hours out from Blue Lake

TRAILHEAD ELEVATION 3300'

ALTITUDE GAIN, including ups and downs: 3000'

FEATURES: Curry Gap, 3900'; Johnson Mt. 6721';
          junction with PCT (Dishpan Gap), 5600'

TOPOGRAPHIC SHEETS: USGS: Sloan Peak; Blanca Lake;
                    Benchmark Mt.; Glacier Peak
                    Green Trails: Sloan Peak; Monte
                    Cristo; Benchmark Mt.; Glacier
                    Peak

The access road leaves the Mountain Loop Highway
about 0.5 mile north of the bridge over the north fork of the
Sauk and about 0.2 mile north of the guard station.
Trailheads passed on the access road include North Falls at
1.2 miles, Sloan Peak Trail at 4.6 miles, and Sloan Creek
Camp and White Pass trailhead at 6.8 miles (keep right at this
intersection). At 9.3 miles, the road forks; again keep right.
The Bald Eagle trailhead is at 12.1 miles, with the last 0.2
mile over rough road. There is parking for about two cars at
this point. In 1970, only four-wheel-drive vehicles (or cars
with high clearance) could drive the additional 0.25 mile on
the logging road and park at the trailhead; this quarter mile
may have been improved since the Forest Service put a trail
sign at this location in 1980.

According to the Forest Service, the Bald Eagle Trail is
lightly used. It is one of the best trails in the North Cascades
for solitude. Fall color along the trail is extraordinary. In the
late fall, be careful of sheet ice on the tread under Bald Eagle

Peak. Look for pikas in the talus slope beneath Bald Eagle
Peak. Grouse, hawks, ground squirrels, deer, and an occasional black bear can be seen in the area.

The footpath begins in the middle of a patch cut, switchbacks northwest, then contours to the southeast. The path
enters woods about 0.25 mile from where the trail leaves the
logging road. After entering the woods, it is about 1.1 miles
to Curry Gap. There is a nice meadow with a gurgling creek,
and lovely fall color in season. At Curry Gap is a good
campsite with water available 0.1 mile up the Bald Eagle
Trail. The trail forks at this point; the Quartz Creek Trail
goes down 4 miles to reach the Skykomish Road.

The walking time up to Curry Gap is about 45 minutes (30
minutes down). From Curry Gap, it is approximately 4 miles
to Spring Camp, 7 miles to the Blue Lake Trail junction, and
9 miles to Blue Lake.

From Curry Gap, the Bald Eagle Trail switchbacks fairly
steeply up, gaining approximately 1500' over 1.5 miles. It
then levels off along the southwest side of the ridge. Two
breaks in the forest cover permit extraordinary views to the
west and south of the peaks around Monte Cristo and of
Mount Rainier. About 2 miles from the gap, the trail contours under Bald Eagle Peak on the north and then drops to a
saddle between Bald Eagle Peak and Long John Mountain.
About 2.7 miles from the gap is a beautiful tarn and lovely
campsite in an exquisite meadow. About 4 miles from the
gap, or 5.5 miles from the trailhead, is Spring Camp. The
main camp is under several trees just beneath the steep
meadow of Long John Mountain.

From Spring Camp, the climb of Long John Mountain is
easy. From the summit there is a spectacular view of Glacier
Peak to the north, the ridge to the east (along which the trail
proceeds), Mount Rainier to the south, and the Monte Cristo
Peaks to the west. Walking time from the gap to Spring
Camp is 2½ hours up and 2 hours down. There is adequate
wood and water at all campsites.

From Spring Camp, the trail drops to the south. It winds through forest for about 0.3 mile, then goes across a long meadow marked by vertical posts. From here it runs an additional 0.6 mile, then switchbacks up rather steeply in meadow, gaining about 750' in 0.7 mile, to the boundary of the Glacier Peak Wilderness Area on the ridge crest. There is a spectacular view down to the Blue Lakes, and up to Johnson Mountain to the right and Glacier Peak to the left. The trail then goes up along the ridge crest, then drops into a notch after another half mile. (If the hiker follows the Bald Eagle Trail east, rather than detouring to Blue Lake and Johnson Mountain, it is about 2.6 miles further to the junction with the Pacific Crest Trail.)

The Blue Lake Trail turns north at the notch, loses approximately 750' rapidly, and then regains 200' in the last half mile to Blue Lake. It is about 1.5 miles from the ridge crest to Little Blue Lake. From Little Blue Lake a scrabble trail leads up to Blue Lake. A spectacular waterfall connects the two lakes. There are campsites at both lakes; however, snow-free campsites may not appear until about Labor Day.

By all means, if in the area, climb gentle Johnson Mountain for the 360-degree panorama from the top. From Blue Lake, continue north, gaining altitude, along the east end of the Pilot Ridge Trail. One and a half miles from the lake is the junction with the abandoned Johnson Mountain Trail. The walking time for the one mile to the top of Johnson Mountain is about 35 minutes, and the time down is 20 minutes. The view from the top is superb, with Glacier Peak to the north, the whole Cascade crest to the east, Little Blue Lake and Blue Lake to the south, and the Sloan Peak and Monte Cristo group of mountains to the west.

From Blue Lake, it is possible to climb east, regaining the Bald Eagle Trail about 0.7 mile from its junction with the Pacific Crest Trail.

If two cars are available, one can be left at the Sloan Creek camp. Leave the area on the Pilot Ridge Trail after climbing Johnson Mountain. This trail continues west on Pilot Ridge, and then drops sharply in switchbacks to join the trail going up the north fork of the Sauk River to White Pass. (August 1972)

WHITE PASS AND RED PASS (SLOAN CREEK)

DESTINATION: White Pass, 5904'

TRAIL LENGTH: 10 miles

WALKING TIME (full pack): 7 hours in
4½ hours out

TRAILHEAD ELEVATION 2100'

ALTITUDE GAIN, including ups and downs: 4000'

FEATURES: PCT junction between Red and White passes, 6000' (high point); Red Pass, 6500'; Sauk shelter, 3000'

TOPOGRAPHIC SHEETS: USGS: Sloan Peak 7.5'; Glacier Peak 15'
Green Trails: Sloan Peak; Glacier Peak

Take the Mountain Loop Highway, preferably from Granite Falls, to Barlow Pass and turn north about 7 miles to the north fork of the Sauk River. Alternatively, drive the loop from Darrington about 17 miles to the same point. Drive 6.8 miles to the Sloan Creek Campground. The trail starts on the east side of the camp, and climbs gradually through one of the most magnificent cedar forests in the northwest.

There are places to camp roughly 3.5 and 4.5 miles from the Sloan Creek Campground, in the deep woods. After 5 miles of walking and a gain of 900′, the hiker reaches the Mackinaw shelter next to the Sauk River. There are opportunities for excellent stream fishing. The shelter is watertight and sleeps four people. Deerflies are prevalent in warm weather.

Beyond the shelter, the trail steepens substantially; switchbacks seem unending. Scenic vistas begin a mile or so beyond the shelter, and improve thereafter as altitude is gained. This ascent should be avoided on warm afternoons, because of the heat and because the deerflies can be almost intolerable.

The footpath tops out about 9.5 miles from the trailhead, where it joins the Pacific Crest Trail. Via the left fork, it is 1.5 miles to Red Pass; via the right fork, it is 0.5 mile to White Pass.

This is spectacular meadow country! For better views, cross country up to the ridge crest immediately above the trail between White and Red Passes. From here the hiker can see Glacier Peak and the White Chuck Valley, with its volcanic cinder cone.

Very fit hikers can reach the ridge crest or White Pass in one day, but two days is more realistic, and three days really should be planned, with a full day in the White Pass area to explore the meadows. (See Pacific Crest Trail for more about the area.) The Forest Service asks hikers camping in the White Pass area to camp on the bench west of the pass, rather than in the pass itself.

The footpath from the campground to the Mackinaw shelter should be open from May through November in average snow years. Firewood is available in the shelter area, but is scarce higher, and campers should carry stoves. Water is available along the trail. Between the shelter and White Pass

there are no camping spaces because of the steepness of the terrain.
(August 1974)

GREEN MOUNTAIN

DESTINATION: Green Mountain lookout, 6500'
TRAIL LENGTH: 4 miles
WALKING TIME (light pack): 3 hours in
                          2 hours out
TRAILHEAD ELEVATION 3500'
ALTITUDE GAIN, including ups and downs: 3200'
TOPOGRAPHIC SHEETS: USGS: Downey Mt. 7.5'
                    Green Trails: Cascade Pass

Take either State Road 530 from Arlington or the NCH from Burlington; drive to the Suiattle River Road midway between Rockport and Darrington. Turn east; the Green Mountain Road is 19.1 miles from the turnoff. Turn left (north), and drive 6.2 miles to the trailhead. The road ends 0.1 mile further, where there is a turnaround area. There are no formal parking spaces, but the road is wide enough for parking on one side. Do not park in the turnaround.

The trailhead has a sign: "Meadow 1 mile; Lookout 4 miles." Water is available from a creek 0.2 mile from the trailhead. At one mile, there is a campsite in the woods 50' to the right of the trail. At 1.1 miles, the trail breaks in and out of meadow and woods, and after 1.3 miles is in open meadow. Old Man's Beard hangs from the trees just before the meadow. The trail goes west about a hundred yards and then turns up and east to cut around Green Mountain at about the 1.8-mile mark. This portion of the meadow is over-grown and at least three feet high; rain pants are strongly recommended during, or within 24 hours after, rain.

After another half mile, the trail drops, losing about 200', and passes a large alpine tarn. There are excellent campsites with water, wood, and a toilet in this area. From here the trail goes north. The last mile is steep switchbacks up the green meadow to the lookout. (On July 13, 1980, the trail was 95% snow-free.) There are two campsites on the high ridge, 0.2 and 0.1 mile from the lookout, both exposed but level enough for one 2-man tent.

Green Mountain is aptly named. From the time the footpath breaks out of the woods, the hiker traverses a fantastically green, thick meadow ablaze with wildflowers. This is one of the loveliest meadows in the North Cascades. Marmots live on the high grassy slopes between the tarn and the lookout. Hikers will hear their alarm whistles. This is one of the few places where marmots live in meadow without the protection of a talus slope. Grouse and bald eagles may also be seen from the trail. In late evening and early morning, deer frequent the meadows. There are copses of Alaska cedar in the upper meadows.

From the lookout, located almost on the boundary of the Glacier Peak Wilderness area, the hiker can look north into the pristine North Cascades. To the north are Buckindy Ridge and Snowking Mountain. Glacier Peak dominates the southeast skyline. Other peaks visible are Downey, Sulphur, Pugh, and Whitehorse. Views down into the Downey, Sui-attle, and Milk Creek valleys are impressive.

The old lookout house is one of the few remaining such structures in the North Cascades; it is still used when forest fire risk is high. Part of the balcony has departed downslope, and the building shows its years of exposure.

One precaution: During midsummer, it is easy to lose the trail in the overgrown meadow, particularly during or after rain when the vegetation collapses over the footpath. Also, the hiker will be soaked from the waist down if the lush meadow plants are wet. In good weather, however, this is one of the best one-day hikes in the entire Wilderness Alps. Expect company, particularly on weekends and holidays.

(July 1980)

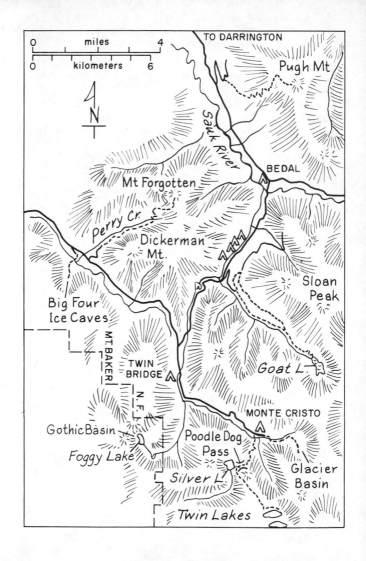

19

MOUNT BAKER–SNOQUALMIE NATIONAL FOREST
Central Section

Trails:
Mount Pugh
Big Four Ice Caves
Perry Creek (Mt. Forgotten)
Glacier Basin
Goat Lake
Poodle Dog Pass

A note on road access: In 1981 sections of the Mountain Loop Highway were closed because of washed-out sections. It is not scheduled to be opened in 1982. Check on the highway's condition with the Monte Cristo (Verlot) Ranger Station (see Resources at the back of this book).

MOUNT PUGH

DESTINATIONS: Stujack Pass, 5750'; Lookout site on summit of Mt. Pugh, 7201'

TRAIL LENGTH: Stujack Pass, 3.8 miles; Summit 5.5 miles

WALKING TIME: (light pack) 6 hours in to summit
4 hours out

TRAILHEAD ELEVATION 1900'

ALTITUDE GAIN, including ups and downs: 5500'

FEATURE: Metan Lake, 3250'

TOPOGRAPHIC SHEETS: USGS: Whitechuck Mt.; Mt. Pugh
Green Trails: Sloan Peak

The access road to the trailhead is the Mountain Loop Road. About two miles south of the White Chuck Bridge, take Pugh Mountain Road and drive one mile to the marked trailhead. The parking area is small. The trail ascends through deep forest. At about 1.5 miles, the trail passes Metan Lake, which covers about an acre surrounded by dense woods. There is a fine view of Pugh Mountain from here. The lake probably has no fish. The trail turns left at the lake and ascends in gradual, long switchbacks for about another 2 miles. (Look out for yellow jacket nests in this area.) At 3.5 miles the footpath enters meadow. Mountain goats frequent this area. From here, the trail steepens; switch-backs top out at Stujack Pass, where there are good views.

Hikers without climbing experience should turn back here. The footpath now threads over the top of a razorback ridge to Pugh Mountain. From here, the trail in places has been blasted out of rock. There is one 40-foot Class 3 rock climb. The ascents in the next 300 to 400 yards are more benign, but do require the use of hands. After these scrambles, the trail goes up steeply through heather and rock slopes to the knifelike summit ridge. Views from the summit are magnificent; all of the Cascades can be seen. The three great volcanoes—Rainier, Glacier Peak, and Mt. Baker—are quite visible on clear days. Patch cuts along the White Chuck River mar the view a bit. Other peaks in view are White Chuck Mountain, Meadow Mountain, Bedal Peak, and Mt. Forgotten.

From Metan Lake up, water is very scarce and supplies should be carried. There are few really good places for camping anywhere en route; since this is a long, arduous one-day trip, an early start is essential to reach the summit.

(September 1961)

BIG FOUR ICE CAVES

DESTINATION: Ice caves, 1900′

TRAIL LENGTH: 1.1 miles

WALKING TIME: 30 minutes one way

TRAILHEAD ELEVATION   1700′

ALTITUDE GAIN, including ups and downs: 200′

TOPOGRAPHIC SHEETS: USGS: Silverton 15′
  Green Trails: Silverton

Driving east from Granite Falls on the Mountain Loop Highway, continue 14.3 miles past the Verlot Ranger Station; turn right (south) and drive about 0.1 mile to the site of the fire-destroyed Big Four Inn and the Big Four Picnic Area. The trail at first follows the same concrete walks used when the Big Four Inn was a prominent, active hotel. There is plenty of parking. Elevated boardwalks and crushed rock convey the hiker across a marshy area 0.3 mile to the South Fork of the Stillaguamish River. After crossing the stream, the hiker enters a dense forest of western hemlock, western red cedar, and Pacific silver fir. It is 0.8 mile from the bridge to the trail end at a stream bed about 0.1 mile from the Big Four Ice Caves. Towering over the caves is the four-notched summit of 6135′ Big Four Mountain.

Over the years, avalanches have formed a small glacier at the base of the mountain. In the spring, melt water trickles down the rocks, gradually creating small channels within the ice. Large tunnels are eroded by warm air. Two or three ice caves are opened between August and October each year.

It is not really safe to enter the caves, particularly in hot weather when ice is likely to fall. Truck-sized chunks of ice may come crashing down at any time. In winter and early spring, avalanches are a constant threat to the hiker or skier. If you elect to take the risk, be aware that a constant ice-water drip from the ceiling makes it necessary to wear raingear in the caves. A flashlight is also needed in the far reaches of the caverns.

The trail is well maintained, although slightly muddy in places. No overnight camping is permitted in the area. The trail is snow-free from mid-May to December 1st; the caves emerge late in the season.

At the base of the snowfield is a small meadow, an area of unusual botanical interest. The microclimate in the area has stunted the vegetation. A bare area marks the zone of growth

and retreat of the ice and snow. In the summer, subalpine wildflowers grow here; many of these flowers are rare at this low elevation. For obvious reasons, the picking of wildflowers is strongly discouraged.
   (1975)

PERRY CREEK (MT. FORGOTTEN)

DESTINATION: 5000'
TRAIL LENGTH: 4 miles
WALKING TIME (light pack): 2½ hours in
                           1½ hours out
TRAILHEAD ELEVATION 2100'
ALTITUDE GAIN, including ups and downs: 3000'
FEATURE: Perry Creek Falls, 3200'
TOPOGRAPHIC SHEETS: USGS: Bedal 7.5'
                    Green Trails: Sloan Peak

   The trailhead is 15.2 miles east of the Verlot Ranger Station on Highway 92 (Mountain Loop). Turn left (north) about 0.1 mile east of the Perry Creek bridge, and drive up the logging road 1.1 miles to its end. There is cramped parking space for 4 or 5 cars here. The trail goes up moderately through talus slopes for about 1.9 miles. At about 1.0 mile a spectacular waterfall is on the left. At 1.9 miles is Perry Creek Falls, a beautiful mossy waterfall. There is a fair campsite at the pool just above the falls, and there are campsites in the timber for the next 0.1 mile. The time up to Perry Creek Falls is one hour; this alone is a fine hike since there are lovely views down the valley, and the altitude gain to this point is only 1100'.

From here, the trail switchbacks up through deep timber, gaining 2000' in 1.5 miles, until it breaks out in meadow at approximately 3.5 miles. The time up to this meadow is approximately 2 hours, and the altitude gain about 3000'. Here the trail forks, with the left fork forking again almost immediately.

The left fork of the left fork continues along the ridge approximately 0.3 mile and again divides, with the lower fork dropping and contouring to the southwest to a plateau and meadow. The right fork leads to a rocky ridge that can be traversed with moderate difficulty by experienced climbers. A Class 2 to Class 3 rock scramble also leads southwest to the plateau meadow.

The right fork of the left fork leads to a campsite overlooking a deep valley with impressive views of White Chuck, Shuksan and Baker. From here one can go north and rejoin the right fork of the original trail, which goes moderately steeply up an additional 0.5 mile to a saddle beneath Mount Forgotten.

A short scramble immediately to the south gains about 200' and a magificent 360-degree view. A fine campsite by a tarn is located at about the 3.9-mile mark.

Water is available at about 1.5 and 1.9 miles, once or twice on the switchbacks, and at the tarn. Wood is adequate anywhere. The climb of Mount Forgotten requires an uncomfortable scramble, dropping several hundred feet and then traversing scree and talus over quite difficult terrain to the skyline ridge on the right. It is not recommended for anyone but experienced climbers. Mountain goats are often seen on Mount Forgotten. Gray jays frequent the meadows.

(October 1969)

GLACIER BASIN

DESTINATION: Glacier Basin, 4500'
TRAIL LENGTH: 2.5 miles
WALKING TIME (light pack): 2¼ hours in
1¾ hours out
TRAILHEAD ELEVATION 2800'
ALTITUDE GAIN, including ups and downs: 1750'
TOPOGRAPIC SHEETS: USGS: Monte Cristo; Blanca Lake
Green Trails: Monte Cristo

To reach the trailhead, drive east from Granite Falls to the pavement's end at Barlow Pass; turn right and drive 4 miles to the end of the county road just before the commercial ghost town of Monte Cristo. (This 4-mile stretch was closed as of 1981.) There is limited parking. The footpath follows the bed of a mine-to-market road east for one mile. The trail starts at the road end.

The first several hundred yards goes up moderately steeply. The next mile is a very rough scrabble trail, going almost directly up the slope to the right of the waterfall. The footing is often insecure or slippery; the trail is not recommended for novice hikers. After the scramble, 0.3 mile of fairly level walking leads into the Glacier Basin cirque surrounded by Cadet, Monte Cristo, and Wilman peaks. Just below the main basin, the trail peters out. Scramble up 50' at this point to a scrabble trail in talus marked by an abandoned pipeline. Yellow and violaceous monkey flowers highlight the area. Excellent campsites are available; wood is scarce, and backpacker's stoves are necessary. The walk up should be avoided on a hot day because of overheating and deerflies. Once in the basin, alpine roamers can climb Ray's

Knoll or work their way higher for better views; do carry an ice axe if scrambling up steep snowslopes.

The area is heavily visited. Campfires are strongly discouraged in the meadow, and campers should consider the campsites, with excellent views, on Mystery Ridge to the south of the trail, rather than camping in Glacier Basin itself. Tread gently everywhere; the area may be in the process of being loved to destruction.

(August 1969)

GOAT LAKE

DESTINATION: Goat Lake, 3161'

TRAIL LENGTH: 4.7 miles by trail
5.5 miles by road

WALKING TIME: 3½ hours in
2½ hours out

TRAILHEAD ELEVATION   1900'

ALTITUDE GAIN, including ups and downs: 1500'

SEASON FOR USE: June–early November

TOPOGRAPHIC SHEETS: USGS: Bedal and Sloan Peak 7.5
Green Trails: Sloan Peak

Take the Mountain Loop Highway east from Granite Falls to Barlow Pass (2349'), and turn left (north) 3.5 miles then turn right (east) on the Elliott Creek Logging Road. (Sections of the access roads may be closed.) There is a locked gate 0.8 mile from the turnoff. Parking is limited at the road end, particularly on summer weekends. There is a turnaround area at 0.6 mile.

The trailhead is to the right of the gate. The trail enters

dense forest and drops to Elliott Creek. Unfortunately, even in mid-summer, the first two miles is a quagmire; ankle- and occasionally knee-deep mud is the rule! (See the logging-road alternative below.)

The trail follows the creek upstream. At 0.9 mile it reaches part of the seven-mile-long Puncheon Wagon Road built in 1896 for the mining claims at Goat Lake. There is a foot bridge at one mile. The trail ascends through the forest. There are some campsites available at 2 miles. At 2.4 miles, the trail breaks into an area that was clear-cut in 1960, and joins the logging road at three miles. It continues on the logging road for 0.3 mile, then plunges back into the forest, again following Puncheon Wagon Road. The trail steepens at 3.9 miles, and the last half mile to the lake is vigorously up in switchbacks. A faint path to the right descends to Elliott Creek and the site of the 1896 Penn mining camp. Near its end the main trail passes a waterfall, and at 4.7 miles it arrives at Goat Lake.

This deep, fairly large lake is quite scenic, with the northwest face of Cadet Peak rising to 7197′ at its east end.

Camping is prohibited within 100′ of the lake shore, but there is designated camping on the knoll at the northeast side of the lake outlet. In 1964, there were remnants of buildings on this knoll (these buildings included the headquarters of the Penn Mining Company, Coffin's Cabin and a rustic hotel).

A way trail continues around the northeast side of the lake. Views of Cadet Peak improve along this trail, but trail quality deteriorates, and the trail peters out at the northeast end of the lake. To climb Cadet or Foggy peaks, or traverse Ida Pass into the Monte Cristo area, go early in the year when you can pass on snow rather than attempting to penetrate the brush after the snow has melted.

A good alternative route to the lake is the old logging road. This road has collapsed in several places, and traversing the slide areas may be a bit difficult, but it presents no major problem as of July 1980. From the gate, go up the logging road a mile or so; take the right fork when the road branches. Continue up the logging road to the 3.3-mile mark on the trail. This alternative is less tiring, takes less time, and offers better views, although it is slightly longer. Only if the weather has been dry for several weeks should the boggy trail be considered. A loop trip, road one way and trail the other, is an alternative after a spell of good weather.

Although fast hikers can make the round trip in a day, most visitors will prefer an overnight backpack. This hike is particularly good in June before the rest of the high country is snow-free.

Check at the Verlot Ranger Station on the Granite Falls Highway about the condition of both road and trail approaches before making this trip. Drainage work on the trail planned "in the next few years" may improve the quagmire.

(1980)

POODLE DOG PASS

DESTINATION: Poodle Dog Pass, 4400'
TRAIL LENGTH: 1.8 miles
WALKING TIME (light pack): 1½ hours in
                            1 hour out
TRAILHEAD ELEVATION 2800'
ALTITUDE GAIN, including ups and downs: 1600'
FEATURES: Ridge to Twin Lakes, 5400' (high point); Twin
           Lakes, 4700'; Silver Lake, 4400'

TOPOGRAPHIC SHEETS: USGS: Monte Cristo and Blanca
Lake 7.5'
Green Trails: Monte Cristo

Drive to Monte Cristo via Darrington or Granite Falls. There is parking at the end of the county road just before the Monte Cristo resort, or park, for a fee, in the Monte Cristo parking lot. (The road to Monte Cristo may be closed.) The trailhead begins about 75 yards past the bridge, 150 yards from the gate, and has a sign for Silver Lake. Take the old logging road west of the ghost town and proceed south. (From Monte Cristo, a 0.1-mile way trail from the parking lot connects with the main trail going west.) After about 0.4 mile, turn right (west) onto the Silver Lake Trail and proceed rather steeply on badly eroded trail; this rough trail is inter-mixed with roadbed all the way to the pass. The trail is not well marked in places, but it is not too difficult to follow. The footpath can be steep, eroded, and rocky, but in spite of this the Forest Service reports it is heavily used.

The right (west) trail at Poodle Dog Pass drops gently about 0.25 mile, passing three beautiful tarns, to Silver Lake with its backdrop of Silver Tip Peak. There are excellent campsites at the lake and at the tarns. For better views of the surrounding areas cross the exit creek and ascend the ridge to the south of the lake, following a mountaineer's scramble trail. This is also the climbing route to the summit of Silver Tip Peak. The lake is deep, fed by a permanent snowfield, and may contain fish. From the lake's south side, the trail descends to Mineral City, a ghost town, some 3.5 miles further. This trail is not easy to locate.

From Poodle Dog Pass, the left fork turns east, goes up rather steeply to the ridge top, drops about 150', then pro-ceeds across the southwest face of a ridge through mountain ash and slide alder on a poorly maintained fisherman's scrabble trail. The trail is for experienced wilderness travelers only; it can be dangerous until the snow melts in midsummer. The tread is nonexistent in places, and it is easy to get lost.

After about 1.8 miles, the trail approaches the ridge top; a small tarn immediately above provides water. The trail then climbs relatively steeply, following the ridge crest most of the time. Watch for blazes or fluorescent flagging tape if tread cannot be found. Hands must be used at times to climb rocky areas; the trail is not suitable for horses. After gaining about 1500′ (including ups and downs) from Poodle Dog Pass, the trail reaches the ridge crest above Twin Lakes, drops about 150′ along the crest, and then drops steeply following talus and heather slopes to the lakes approximately 600′–700′ below. Two-thirds of the way down, there is an excellent campsite. There are a number of fine campsites by the lake and in the surrounding meadow. Way trails reach the lower lake by traversing the meadow on the southeast side of the upper lake.

The 3.5 miles from Poodle Dog Pass to the shore of the upper (north) lake takes about two hours (with a light pack). Many will stop at the 3-mile mark and gaze down on the lakes, but not attempt to descend and reascend. Other than the tarn, there is no water between Silver Lake and a small stream 0.1 mile from Twin Lakes. Since this is a warm, sunny slope, water bottles should be filled at Silver Lake.

There are no good camp sites except those at Silver and Twin lakes. Overnight campers should carry stoves; the Forest Service requests that fires not be built near the lakes. Wood is scarce at Silver Lake, but is not in short supply at Twin Lakes. These lakes are lovely, probably still isolated, and contain trout. Fall color is spectacular. Stout boots are essential, and the use of a staff or ice axe is suggested. Pikas are plentiful. The view of the Wilmon Peaks to the east is a feature of this hike. From this trail you can see the south face of Columbia Peak, a sheer rock scarp which by itself is well worth the walk.

(October 1970)

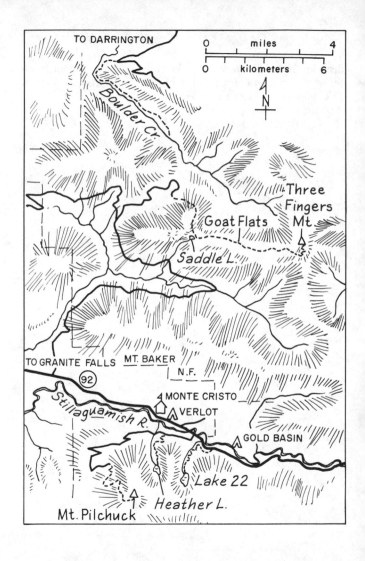

TO DARRINGTON

0   miles   4

0   kilometers   6

N

Boulder Cr.

Three
Fingers
Mt.

Goat Flats

Saddle L.

TO GRANITE FALLS   MT. BAKER

N.F.

92

MONTE CRISTO

Stillaguamish R.

VERLOT

GOLD BASIN

Lake 22

Heather L.

Mt. Pilchuck

20

MOUNT BAKER–SNOQUALMIE NATIONAL FOREST
Southwest Section

Trails:
Boulder Creek
Goat Flats (Three Fingers Mountain)
Mount Pilchuck
Heather Lake
Lake 22

BOULDER CREEK

DESTINATION: Boulder Ford, 1400′
TRAIL LENGTH: 4.2 miles
WALKING TIME (light pack): 2¼ hours in
2 hours out
TRAILHEAD ELEVATION 950′
ALTITUDE GAIN, including ups and downs: 900′
SEASON FOR USE: March through November
TOPOGRAPHIC SHEETS: USGS: Granite Falls and Oso
Green Trails: Granite Falls and Oso

(This trail should not be confused with the path beginning on the east side of the Boulder Creek Bridge on the Baker Lake Road, which deteriorates a short distance from the road. Also, do not confuse it with the Boulder Ridge Trail on the east side of Mt. Baker.)

To reach the trailhead, take State Highway 530 east from Arlington; drive 19.5 miles from the Arlington bridge toward Darrington. Watch for signs on the south side of the road for French Creek Campground. Take the side road a few feet east of milepost 41, to the south. Pass the campground on the left. At 1 mile, take the right fork in the road. The main road makes a sharp left turn 3.7 miles from the highway; an abandoned road continues straight ahead. The junction is marked. There is parking for 6–8 cars within 150 feet of the trailhead in either direction. The footpath is closed to horses, trail machines, and snowmobiles.

Walk up the soggy road bed. Just beyond a small bridge is a trailside register. At a sharp left curve on the road at 0.9 mile, a way trail leads southwest; 50′ below the main trail are several tent sites and a way trail to the Boulder River below.

One hundred yards beyond this curve, the road ends and

the footpath continues. From the road end to Boulder ford, the trail is rough, slippery, and quite muddy. A number of creeks must be crossed; none offer any major problems. Be very cautious on wet puncheon; it can be very slippery!

The trail enters a dense, magnificent stand of virgin timber, a true climax forest. (Boulder Valley is one of the few remaining lowland areas of primal forest in western Washington; it is being considered for wilderness designation.) At 1.2 miles, there is a moss and fern bank on the left; 100 yards further, a gentle lacy waterfall cascades from the cliff on the right into the chasm below. A way trail leads to the base of the falls, where there is a splendid tent site. The Boulder River is compressed between cliff and rock; water flow is tumultuous.

An elegant waterfall is 0.1 mile upstream; the water cascades 150′ or more down to the Boulder River. (At high water, the cascades are most impressive.)

Hikers may wish to stop here; the round trip is about 2.8 miles with perhaps 250′ of altitude gain.

At 2.4 miles, a third waterfall drops about 75′ into the Boulder River. The trail then ascends the side wall of the canyon, and the river is seldom seen until the trail descends to Boulder ford, 4.2 miles from the trailhead.

When the lookout on Three Fingers Mountain was first constructed, this was the access trail. Now that logging roads have intersected the trail to Goat Flats and Three Fingers at Tupso Pass, the trail between the ford and the pass is no longer maintained. Particularly at times of high water, this is the end of the trail for practical purposes. There are four possible creekside campsites. These, as well as a Forest Service toilet, can be reached by a way trail downstream. Two campsites were flooded in December, 1980 and are extensively silted, and a third has been partially occupied by the remains of a large recently fallen Douglas fir.

At the ford, the hiker can glimpse the summits of Three Fingers upstream. The forest is otherwise so dense that surrounding peaks cannot be seen along the trail.

The trail is accessible during thaws throughout the winter months. Under normal conditions, neither wood nor water are problems at any of the camping areas. With very high water, Boulder River is highly sedimented, and drinking water should be obtained from side creeks.

(December 1980)

GOAT FLATS (THREE FINGERS MOUNTAIN)

DESTINATION: Goat Flats, 5000'

TRAIL LENGTH: 5.3 miles

WALKING TIME (light pack): 2½ hours in
2¼ hours out

TRAILHEAD ELEVATION 3000'

ALTITUDE GAIN, including ups and downs: 2250'

FEATURES: Saddle Lake, 3800'; Three Fingers Lookout, 6854' (high point); Camp Pass, 5600'

TOPOGRAPHIC SHEETS: USGS: Granite Falls; Silverton
Green Trails: Granite Falls; Silverton

Take the Mountain Loop Highway east from Granite Falls 7.2 miles from the stop light in the center of town. Turn left on the Canyon Creek Road. Take left turns at 1.9, 8.0, and 8.9 miles. (At 11 miles, the Meadow Mountain Trail departs to the right; from here, it is 4 miles to the summit, 5 miles to Saddle Lake, and 8 miles to Goat Flats. The Forest

Service advises that this trail may be upgraded and become the main trail to Goat Flats and Three Fingers.) Turn right at 13.4 miles, and right again at 16.8 miles. The poorly marked trailhead is 17.5 miles from the Mountain Loop Highway, on the left side of the road just past large twin cedars.

The first three miles of the trail is difficult walking, since the trail is muddy, slick, and uneven, with large tree roots. After it reaches meadow, the trail's quality improves.

The trail climbs moderately through deep forest. After about one mile (30 minutes) it turns south, and from this point on there are views of Three Fingers to the east. At about 2 miles, the trail loses about 100' in altitude, crosses the floor of a rocky amphitheater and regains the altitude on the other side. Emergency camps could be made here. At about 2.3 miles, the trail passes the east side of Saddle Lake. From here, Saddle Lake Camp is 0.25 miles west, Goat Flats 3 miles east; the Three Fingers lookout on the south peak is a long two miles past the flats. Altitude gain to this point is 720'; walking time is 1 hour and 15 minutes.

About a mile past the lake, the trail breaks into subalpine meadow. There is a stream at 3.3 miles; tarns and campsites are at roughly 3.5 and 3.7 miles.

Goat Flats is an excellent camping area with tarns, many good campsites, and a splendid view of the Sisters, Baker, and Shuksan to the north, and of Three Fingers to the east. Day hikers may consider this their destination. No wood is available; campers should carry stoves. Goat Flats is the base camp for ascents of the peaks of Three Fingers Mountain. In mid-summer, the area is quite buggy; bring insect repellant. The Goat Flats shelter provides little if any protection from rain.

About a half mile below the flats to the south is a solitary magnificent specimen of mountain hemlock, perhaps the most splendid tree of this species ever observed by this author.

There are further options for the adventurous. From the shelter, the trail goes up about 0.2 mile along a grassy knoll, then turns into the forest to the right (south) of a rock knob. This turnoff may not be obvious in snow; the route to the left is exposed and hazardous, and should not be attempted.

The trail goes through timber for perhaps 0.1 mile and then, losing 100' or so, goes east through a meadow with fine views. Turning a corner, the footpath ascends considerably more steeply, crossing talus and scree slopes to Camp Pass about 1.4 miles from Goat Flats shelter. Views from this pass (5600') are quite nice, and there are level areas for tents. Water is obtained from snow fields. There are no campsites beyond this point!

For the experienced and equipped mountaineer, a scrabble trail continues from Camp Pass to the Three Fingers Fire Lookout, maintained by the Everett Mountaineers, about a mile away and 1250' higher. Permanent snow fields must be crossed to reach this airy aerie; an ice axe is essential. The final pitch to the lookout requires an exposed Class 2 rock climb. Hikers without the requisite skills and equipment should turn back at Camp Pass, but the experienced will enjoy the challenge of reaching the scenic lookout location. (October 1980)

MT. PILCHUCK

DESTINATION: Summit, 5300'

TRAIL LENGTH: 3 miles

WALKING TIME: 2 hours up
              1½ hours down

TRAILHEAD ELEVATION 3100'

ALTITUDE GAIN, including ups and downs: 2400'

SEASON FOR USE: mid-July–early November

TOPOGRAPHIC SHEETS: USGS: Granite Falls
Green Trails: Granite Falls

Boulder climbing is required for this trail, and it is recommended only for hikers with experience. Because of its accessibility, the trail is heavily used; the drive from Everett or Seattle and the hike to the summit are fairly easily accomplished in five to six hours.

Follow State Highway 92 east from Granite Falls. Turn south immediately east of the bridge one mile east of the Verlot Ranger Station. Drive 6.8 miles and park about 0.1 mile west of the chalet. There is parking for about 100 cars at the marked trailhead. The first 0.25 mile of trail is on a gravelled road bed. After the road ends the trail follows puncheon, then crosses a creek. The trail is muddy and difficult to walk for the first 0.5 mile; it takes about 15 minutes to reach the junction with the old trail. The next mile of trail remains difficult; muddy, rocky, and slippery with many tree roots. Brush overhangs the path in many places.

(The Pilchuck Road is closed to motor vehicles from beyond the Heather Lake trailhead to the old ski area parking lot, from early November until early April. The access road is no longer plowed in the winter.)

After about one mile (altitude gain 700'), the trail turns east and climbs gradually for 0.7 mile. It then ascends moderately steep slopes of granite and heather east of the lift. Yellow paint on the rocks marks the route from under the chairlift to the summit. Another 0.3 mile brings the hiker to the summit ridge, and about 0.3 mile beyond this, the trail forks. The left fork goes about 0.1 mile over granite boulders to a junction; here, a drop of 0.1 mile brings you to Frozen Lake. From the junction, the hiker can ascend directly to the summit via a Class 2 boulder scramble (recommended only for those with rock climbing experience). The right fork goes along the south face of Mt. Pilchuck, gradually ascending to near the summit, where a 40' to 50' boulder scramble leads to the renovated lookout. About 200' below the summit, a short walk of about 50' to the right leads to a ridge with superb views to the east. The entire boulder scrabble, and the last ascent on the trail route, are marked with patches of yellow paint.

There are one or two limited camping areas on the summit, with no water and little wood. Other camping areas are limited; one or two tarns might serve as campsites.

The Everett Mountaineers have refurbished the old lookout. It is now open on two sides, but closed to the south and west, whence come the storms. It is sufficiently tight to sleep in, even in a storm.

Views from the summit, particularly of Glacier Peak to the east, are nice; however, the extensive logging detracts from the scenery. The city lights of Everett can be seen at dusk from the summit.

The Forest Service advises that the entire trail will be reconstructed or relocated in the next few years, when funds become available.

(1976)

HEATHER LAKE

DESTINATION: Heather Lake, 2500'

TRAIL LENGTH: 2 miles

WALKING TIME (light pack): 1 hour in
50 minutes out

TRAILHEAD ELEVATION   1400'

ALTITUDE GAIN, including ups and downs: 1100'

SEASON FOR USE: late May–mid-November

TOPOGRAPHIC SHEETS: USGS: Granite Falls
                     Green Trails: Granite Falls

To reach the marked trailhead, turn south just east of the bridge over the Stillaguamish River, one mile east of the Verlot Ranger Station. Drive 1.4 miles up the Mt. Pilchuck road to the trailhead on the left (south) side of the road. There is no parking at the trailhead, but there is adequate parking on the right 0.2 mile below and on the left 0.2 mile above the trailhead.

The trail is a logging road for about a half mile; footing is uncertain on scree ballast on the old road. The footpath starts at the left a few feet before the road ends, and switchbacks up moderately through a patch cut. The trail enters beautiful climax forest of cedar and hemlock at about 0.9 mile. The footpath continues up through deep forest for another 0.6 mile, then levels out; the last half mile to the lake is level through forest.

The lake nestles under the high cliffs of Mt. Pilchuck. There are good campsites at the lake, and water is no problem. Since the trail is heavily used, wood for campfires is diminishing. Unfortunately, views to the north include extensive clear-cutting on Green Mountain Ridge across the valley.

(1969)

LAKE 22

DESTINATION: Lake 22, 2460′
TRAIL LENGTH: 2.7 miles
WALKING TIME: 1¾ hours in
               1¼ hours out

TRAILHEAD ELEVATION 1040'
ALTITUDE GAIN, including ups and downs: 1500'
SEASON FOR USE: early June–late November
TOPOGRAPHIC SHEETS: USGS: Granite Falls
Green Trails: Granite Falls

Drive east from Granite Falls on Highway 92; 1.4 miles east of the bridge over the south fork of the Stillaguamish River, turn south on an inapparent side road. There is parking for about 20 cars on a loop 0.1 mile off the highway. The trailhead is on the turnaround. This new connecting trail, 0.4 mile long, joins the old Lake 22 Trail roughly 0.1 mile from the highway. The new trail runs through verdant, deep forest. The trail was partially graveled and partially muddy in July 1980; probably the entire new link is graveled by now.

This trail stays in good condition, even after recent rains. From 0.4 to 1.7 miles, it switchbacks up moderately through deep forest. It crosses Twenty-Two Creek on a bridge at about 0.8 mile. Magnificent western red cedar and western hemlock dominate the lowland forest.

From about 1.6 to 2.1 miles, the trail switchbacks through a talus slope with vine and big-leaf maple. Fall color in October on this half-mile segment of trail is fabulous. From here there are pleasant views into the valley, partially marred by clear-cutting on the opposite hillside. This half-mile section in the autumn makes the hike well worthwhile.

The trail tops out at about 2.4 miles, after an altitude gain of about 1300', and runs fairly level for 0.3 mile to Lake 22, following the course of 22 Creek. A spectacular cliff to the south, with a large snowfield fed by avalanches, dominates the lake. One can walk partially around the lake on scrabble trails, particularly on the west. No camping or fires are allowed in the 790-acre Lake 22 Natural Area: this is a day-use area only. The trail is heavily used. The Forest Service reports a substantial problem with hikers cutting switchbacks; this makes trail maintenance difficult.

This is a nice hike for families. The trail is particularly fine in late September or early October for the brilliant fall color. Rock climbers find a challenge on the cliff south of the lake.

(1973)

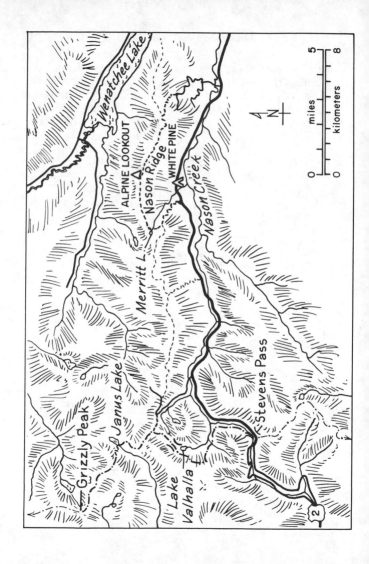

21

STEVENS PASS AREA
(U.S. Highway 2)

Trails:
Lake Valhalla (PCT)
Janus Lake–Grizzly Peak (PCT)
Alpine Lookout (Nason Ridge)
(Pacific Crest Trail)

LAKE VALHALLA (PCT)

DESTINATION: Lake Valhalla, 4800'
TRAIL LENGTH: 5.5 miles
WALKING TIME (light pack): 2½ hours in
                            2 hours out
TRAILHEAD ELEVATION 4000' (Stevens Pass)
ALTITUDE GAIN, including ups and downs: 1500'
FEATURE: Ridge above lake, 5100' (high point)
TOPOGRAPHIC SHEETS: USGS: Stevens Pass; Labyrinth Mt.
                     Green Trails: Benchmark Mt.

The trail begins by the Chelan County Power substation about 0.2 mile east of Stevens Pass. The first mile or so follows the old Great Northern Railroad grade, losing about 400'. This portion of the trail simply parallels the highway west of the canyon. (As an option, drive 1.7 miles east of Stevens Pass summit and park by the chalets on the west. Bushwack up and west, gaining about 200', to eliminate 1.7 miles of low-quality trail to Lake Valhalla.) At about 1.5 miles, the trail turns west and enters deep forest. Between 1 and 2 miles, the trail winds through underbrush and downed timber. At about 2.2 miles, it crosses a stream; there is a campsite here. At about 3.2 miles, it crosses a larger stream. There is a campsite here, and several campsites in the basin 0.1 mile west. Walking time to this point is 1 hour and 25 minutes.

At 3.8 miles, after a meadow with nice wildflowers, the trail meets the Johnson Ridge Trail which leads off to the ridge to the west. At the 5-mile mark there is a nice view down the valley, with U.S. 2 far below. At 5.2 miles is the Lake Valhalla overlook (5000'). A nice campsite is 0.3 mile further by a small stream in a meadow. Lake Valhalla is a stone's throw away from this camp.

One or two campsites are near a pleasant sandy beach at the lakeshore. A steep rock cliff to the east is a backdrop for the lake. The trail next goes up to the pass (5100′) above the lake at about 5.9 miles (3 hours) from the trailhead. Just before the pass, you can sit and look at the sparkling lake below and the peaks to the south. From here, it is about 1.7 miles to Union Gap (4850′). The first mile is on open ridge and the last 0.7 mile is in timber. At Union Gap the Smith Brook Trail comes up from the logging road about 0.8 mile below. (See Janus Lake–Grizzly Peak Trail.)

A good side trip is by the scrabble trail about 50′ north of the pass above the lake, gaining 750′ to the summit of a dome-like ridge. The views from here are magnificent, particularly in late September and early October when the fall color is at its height. Blueberries and huckleberries grow in this ridge. Follow a not-too-easily found track north, dip a few feet near the ridge end, and contour onto the west side of the ridge and then north 50 feet. At this point, look north to a fine view of Janus Lake, Glacier Peak and White Pass to the north. The view from the south part of the ridge directly down to Lake Valhalla and the face of Mt. Lichtenberg is grand. Allow at least an hour for this side trip.

Wood is scarce at Lake Valhalla, but adequate at the other campsites. Water is found all along the route. Lake Valhalla and surrounding streams are probably contaminated by heavy horse and human use; water decontamination is suggested.

(1971)

JANUS LAKE—GRIZZLY PEAK (PCT)

DESTINATION: Grizzly Peak, 5600′
TRAIL LENGTH: 7.5 miles

WALKING TIME (light pack): 4½ hours in
3⅓ hours out
TRAILHEAD ELEVATION 4200'
ALTITUDE GAIN, including ups and downs: 2700'
FEATURES: Union Gap, 4700'; Janus Lake, 4146'
TOPOGRAPHIC SHEETS: USGS: Labyrinth Mt. and Captain
Point, 7.5'
Green Trails: Benchmark Mt.

Drive 4.2 miles east of the crest of Stevens Pass; turn left (north) onto the Smith Brook Road. Drive 3.3 miles to the marked trailhead, about 0.3 mile beyond a hairpin curve. At the curve, there is parking space for about 10 cars, and space for parking 0.1 mile above and below the trailhead.

The trail goes up steeply 20' through the road cut. It then contours above the road for about 0.3 mile in open meadow; there are good views of Mt. Lichtenberg to the south. From 0.3 to 0.5 mile, the trail switchbacks up steeply through deep woods. The grade then lessens, and a nice meadow and campsite are on the left about 0.2 mile before Union Gap. Walking time for the 0.8 mile to Union Gap is 20 minutes. (All trail mileage hereafter starts at Union Gap on the Pacific Crest Trail, rather than at the Smith Brook trailhead.)

From Union Gap, the trail goes down moderately for about 1 mile. The trail is quite muddy. At about 0.3 mile, the trail passes a nice meadow for camping. It then turns north. At about 1.7 miles, there is a very pleasant waterfall. It is about 2 miles to Janus Lake, taking about 45 minutes, and losing around 1000' and regaining 250' in the two miles between Union Gap and the lake. The trail is in timber almost the entire way. There are forks in the trail about 0.1 mile before the lake. The Pacific Crest Trail bears left (west) but any of the trails will lead to the lake. At the southwest end of the lake is the Mountain Memorial Shelter. The roof was reasonably watertight in 1971; there is room to sleep seven people within. There are campsites at the south end of the lake if the shelter is occupied.

Janus Lake is about half a mile long. The forest comes down on the west shore of the lake, but there is meadow on the east. Fall color is quite spectacular. The lake is fairly shallow at the south end, with lily pads. The area around the lake is boggy; there are mosquitoes even in late fall.

The PCT crosses a creek directly west of the shelter, enters the forest, and switchbacks up through deep timber. There are no views of Janus Lake after entering the woods. At 1.5 miles past the shelter, an unmarked trail goes west into a small meadow where there is a small stream and campsite. A walk of 0.1 mile south leads to a very nice view from the top of a burn area. At about 3.8 miles the trail goes through a pass, and from this point on the views are magnificent and well worth the effort of reaching the ridge crest. Glacier Peak is to the north. From 3.8 to 4.2 miles, the trail runs on the east side of the crest, then passes through a notch to the west side. At about 4.5 miles, the trail makes a turn around a beautiful tarn and campsite. At 4.7 miles, a sign on a tree indicates the route to Margaret Lake (4800'), which can be seen through the trees about 500' below. At 4.8 miles, Glasses Lake, lying approximately 400' below and to the north, comes into view. Another 0.1 mile leads to a high camp where water is available. From here, a scrabble trail descends steeply to the lake. There are very nice campsites at the lake. Walking time to this point, from the road, is 3 hours; the estimated altitude gain from Janus Lake is about 1100'.

From the Glasses Lake overlook, the trail winds in and out and up and down following the ridge crest. Glacier Peak dominates the northern view. Grizzly Peak is to the northwest. At about 5.7 miles, the trail begins switchbacks upward, gaining 500' to the ridge crest, about 6.2 miles from Union Gap. Along this crest are rifts where part of the mountain appears to have slid away to the south. From 6.2 to 6.7 miles, the trail meanders along one of the loveliest ridges in the North Cascades, the Grizzly Meadows. In this magnificent meadow (particularly early October when the fall color is incredible), there is a 360-degree view that defies description. Mount Rainier can be seen to the south. High meadows, glaciated peaks, green forest, and deep valleys are spread out seemingly to infinity. The ridge ends at Grizzly Peak (5593').

Although there is no water unless there are snowfields in Grizzly Meadows, this is a magnificent place to spend time. Walking time from the Smith Brook trailhead to Grizzly Peak is 4½ hours. The time out is about 3½ hours.

Except for the area around the Janus Lake Shelter, there is no problem with wood at any of the campsites. Water is very hard to find on the ridge top in the fall, so the hiker should carry a supply after leaving Janus Lake.

On Grizzly Peak in places there was fresh snow about four inches deep in October. The red blueberry leaves projecting above the gleaming white new snow were indescribably lovely.

Although it is strenuous if walked in one day, and although the first 4.6 miles of trail is relatively "blah," the high ridge more than makes up for the difficulty of getting there. This is truly one of the spectacular walks in the High Cascades!

(October 1971)

ALPINE LOOKOUT (NASON RIDGE)

DESTINATION: Alpine Lookout, 6200'

TRAIL LENGTH: 5.3 miles

WALKING TIME (light pack): 3 hours in
2⅓ hours out

TRAILHEAD ELEVATION 3900'

ALTITUDE GAIN, including ups and downs: 2800'

FEATURES: Merritt Lake, 5000'
Junction with U.S. 2, 2600'

TOPOGRAPHIC SHEETS: USGS: Wenatchee Lake
Green Trails: Wenatchee Lake

The best route to the Round Mountain trailhead is via
Butcher Creek Road. This road, vaguely marked, is a few
hundred yards east of the rest area on Highway 2, roughly 18
miles east of Stevens Pass. The road crosses Nason Creek,
goes under power lines, then gains altitude. At 3.2 miles is a
junction; take the left fork. The trailhead is 4.5 miles from
Highway 2 on the north side of Butcher Creek Road and has
a sign: Round Mountain Trail. There is parking for 2 or 3 cars
at the trailhead, and a turnaround about 200 feet west with
parking for several cars.

Some 10 minutes, 0.4 mile, up the trail is Spring Camp,
with water and enough room for one tent site. This is the last
water until Merritt Lake, at least in the fall. Forty-five minutes of brisk uphill walking (1.5 miles), mostly through
forest but with an occasional view, leads to the junction with
the Nason Ridge Trail. From here it is 4 miles west to Alpine
Lookout and 7 miles to Merritt Lake; 6 miles east is the
south shore of Lake Wenatchee.

Just west of this junction, there are splendid views of the

valley below with Glacier Peak at the head; Lake Wenatchee is slightly to the east. Twenty-five minutes further on the Nason Ridge Trail is a grassy ridge with a good view to the south. In another 10 minutes the trail drops into a saddle; at about 1¾ hours the trail reaches the 8-mile mark and for the first time Alpine Lookout comes into view. After another half hour, the trail drops into a second saddle; there are clusters of yellow larch in the hollow to the north. In 2½ hours is the junction to the lookout (roughly 0.4 mile further), and the hiker reaches the lookout after almost 3 hours over a total distance of roughly 5.3 miles.

From the lookout there are views in all directions; the views of Glacier Peak are badly marred by extensive patch cutting. Salt licks at the lookout attract deer and mountain goats.

From the junction below the lookout, Merritt Lake is 3 miles, Rock Lake is 9 miles, and Rock Mountain is 10 miles. The Nason Ridge Trail is open to cycles, but the trail west of Alpine Lookout is not. The Nason Ridge Trail is scenic from Round Mountain to Merritt Lake. There are a number of level campsites on the ridge, but all are dry on the ridge east of the lookout. West of the lookout, there is no really good place to camp until Merritt Lake. There are several small streams in the first mile below Merritt Lake, but the trail for the first 2.5 miles coming up from the highway is also dry.

Continuing the loop, the trail loses several hundred vertical feet on the south side of Nason Ridge under Alpine Lookout and contours along the ridge for about 2 miles. It then approaches the ridge crest again. Roughly 50 feet past the 12-mile sign is a junction above Merritt Lake, where a sign indicates the Alpine Lookout is 4 miles east. Neither the trail to the west nor the trail down is marked. Approximately 0.3 mile (10 minutes) of downhill walking leads to Merritt Lake, where there are good campsites. The lake is pretty, but not spectacular. From the lake, it is about 3.5 miles to

Highway 2. There are not many views, and the trail is rough. About 2.9 miles from the highway, 0.5 mile from the lake, is the junction with Nason Ridge Trail. (Rock Lake is 4 miles from here.) The trail switchbacks down to Highway 2. The trailhead there is marked, and there is parking for 5 cars, 75 to 100 feet from Highway 2. Trail distance, for the loop, is about 12 miles including the 0.4 mile up and down from Alpine Lookout.

The Merritt Lake trailhead on U.S. 2 is about 12.5 miles east of Stevens Pass. From the highway, the altitude gain for the loop is between 4000' and 4500', figuring ups and downs.

Including lunch and stops for photos, the loop trip takes about 7 hours. Going to Alpine Lookout, the Round Mountain access is strongly recommended over the Merritt Lake access. The view just above the junction of the White River valley with Glacier Peak in the distance really is very impressive, and the walk is worthwhile just for that. Take a telephoto lens for shooting Glacier Peak from Alpine Lookout, since with a standard lens, the patch cuts in the foreground are most distracting. Carry lots of water. This is a better hike in the fall than in mid-summer. The area becomes snow-free usually in late June.

(October 1978)

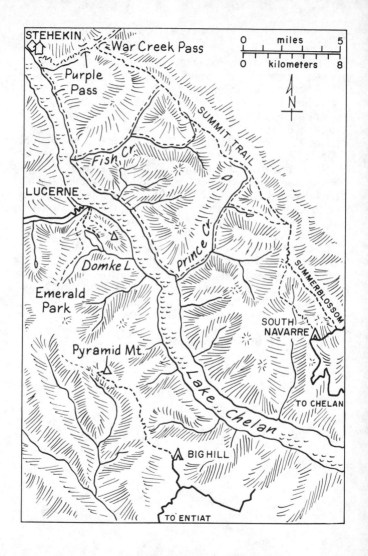

22

WENATCHEE
NATIONAL FOREST

Trails:
Domke Lake
Summit Trail
Pyramid Mountain Viewpoint

DOMKE LAKE

DESTINATION: Domke Lake, 2200'

TRAIL LENGTH: 2.5 miles

WALKING TIME (light pack): 1 hour in
45 minutes out

TRAILHEAD ELEVATION 1125'

ALTITUDE GAIN including ups and downs: 1100'

TOPOGRAPHIC SHEETS: USGS: Lucerne 15'
Green Trails: Lucerne

The trailhead is a block or so from the Railroad Creek Bridge and from the Lucerne Resort. The trail goes up a rocky draw for about 200 yards, and then starts switchbacking up. At 0.4, and again at 1.3 miles, the forest cover breaks, allowing good views of Lake Chelan to the northwest. The trail climbs steadily to the 1.7-mile point, where it intersects the Emerald Park Trail; from here, Emerald Park is 6 miles and Milham Pass is 8 miles. From the junction, it is a half mile to the resort at Domke Lake (where boats are available for rent), and another quarter mile to the campground, where there are campsites, a high rock, and a swimming beach. (The walking times given above are to and from this campground.) Fishing is good at the lake. Between Lucerne and the lake, there are no campsites, and only one partially reliable water source. Almost all the altitude gain is in the first 1.9 miles.

Domke Lake is quite beautiful, nestled in a setting of mountain splendor. Wood is plentiful at the campsite. Lake water should be boiled or treated with iodine for drinking.

The trail to Domke Mountain is no longer maintained. The junction with it is at about 1600', just under a mile from the trailhead. It is 2.8 miles from the junction to the summit

(4000'), where the Forest Service used to maintain a lookout. Views from here down to Lake Chelan are impressive. Route finding is a problem, and only experienced wilderness travelers should hike this trail.

(July 1975)

SUMMIT TRAIL

NORTH TRAILHEAD: Purple Pass, 6884'

SOUTH TRAILHEAD: Forest Service road near Falls Creek
                 (Summerblossom), 6400'

HIGH POINT: 7400' (pass near Star Peak)

TRAIL LENGTH: 30 miles

WALKING TIME: 3–4 days

ALTITUDE GAIN, including ups and downs: 8750'

TOPOGRAPHIC SHEETS: USGS: Sun Mt.; Oval Peak 7.5' or
                    Buttermilk Butte 15'; Prince
                    Creek; Martin Peak
                    Green Trails: Prince Creek; But-
                    termilk Butte; Stehekin

From Purple Pass (see Chapter 16), the trail drops 0.7 mile to Juanita Camp. At 0.2 mile is the junction with Boulder Butte Trail. This half-mile-long side trail up to the site of an old lookout (7372') must not be missed. There is an incredible 360-degree panorama. This is one of the most beautiful places in the North Cascades. Ideally, one should visit in late afternoon, at sunset, and in the morning in order to appreciate the views under different lighting.

Juanita Camp is pleasant, except for the mosquitoes, and has camping areas scattered over 0.3 mile. Juanita Lake is shallow and does not contain fish. Walk above Juanita Lake to the junction with the Summit Trail and, above that, to War Creek Pass.

From this junction, the Summit Trail proceeds southeast, losing 500′ in the first mile. Then it switchbacks up to a high, flat ridge at about the 3-mile point. This ridge is the boundary between the Wenatchee National Forest and the Lake Chelan National Recreation Area. It is very scenic, with many good campsites. In July, there usually is snow as a water source, but it would be a dry camp later in the year.

The path runs along the ridge for about 0.3 mile and then descends. In 0.5 mile, the 26-mile marker is passed. Less than 1 mile further is Camp Comfort, a pleasant campsite with good access to water, but no views. Continue down. Near the low point between the 23- and 24-mile markers is the junction with the north fork of the Fish Creek Trail. This junction was neither marked nor obvious in 1979. Uphill 1.5 miles is the junction with Eagle Pass Trail. It is one mile to the pass, and another 7.5 miles from the pass to the head of Eagle Creek Trail.

From this junction, the Summit Trail goes up to a scenic pass at the 21-mile marker (miles are measured from the south, not from Purple Pass). The tread then descends one mile into enjoyable meadow; there is a splendid campsite 150′ beyond the 20-mile marker. At the campsite is the junction with the no longer maintained Horseshoe Spur Trail, which descends to the west, joining the East Fish Creek Trail in 1.5 miles, and reaching Lake Chelan 10 miles away.

There is also a way trail east here, with no tread in places. Go northeast from the campsite, passing the lower edge of a talus slope. To the left (north) of the small creek is obvious tread which switchbacks up to the bench above. Continue up the valley, turning near the headwall to reach isolated splendid Tuckaway Lake. This way route to the lake is 0.6 mile long and gains 500′. There is an ideal campsite with a log table on the east side of the lake. Rising trout will tempt the fisherman and the hiker whose palate has tired of dehydrated trail food. You can follow the scrabble trail on the south side of the valley up to Oval Pass. Enjoy the views; you can proceed to one of the Oval Lakes east of the crest.

At the campsite on Summit Trail, water is next to the camping area. There are many places to wander in the open meadow around the camp.

Immediately past the camp, the trail ascends sharply and gains 200'. From here, it contours gradually up to the 18-mile marker, where there is a junction. From here, Fish Creek Pass is 0.5 mile east on the West Fork Buttermilk Trail. There are campsites north and south of the 18-mile marker. South of the junction, there is no tread in the meadow for about 150 yards; contour south through the meadow to pick it up. From here, the trail climbs steeply and crosses a high pass beneath Star Peak; there are good views in all directions.

The trail again goes down. In one mile, it reaches the junction with Surprise Lake Trail. The trail is difficult to locate for 200' at the junction; be careful to take the right path. The Summit Trail continues down from the junction to the North Fork Shelter near the 15-mile marker; the shelter is in good condition with water close by.

Surprise Lake, Indianhead Basin, Horton Butte, and the Fish Creek Trails can be reached by turning right (southwest) at the junction. It is 1.5 miles gaining 800' to the start of the Surprise Lake way trail; from here, it is 1.1 miles to the lake. The last 0.5 mile is steep and rocky. There is a campsite, primarily for trail bikers, just before the descent. Hikers and horsemen will prefer the campsites at the lake. Continuing through Indianhead Basin, it is 2.8 miles to the junction with Horton Butte Trail; from here, it is 2.5 miles to the lookout site, and about 2 miles to Fish Creek Trail.

On the Summit Trail 0.5 mile beyond the North Fork Shelter, the trail reaches the junction with the north fork of Prince Creek Trail. From here, the main Prince Creek Trail is 2 miles, and Lake Chelan is 9 miles, to the west.

The trail goes up from this point, reaching a scenic pass with great views at about the 12-mile marker. Along the ridge 0.5 mile further is a splendid view down Prince Creek. In another 0.9 mile is the junction with the trail to HooDoo Pass, one mile to the east. South 0.2 mile is the junction with the Boiling Lake Trail to the east and the middle fork of Prince Creek Trail to the southwest.

There is a good campsite 100' north of this junction. There are even nicer campsites at Boiling Lake, which is 0.5 mile further and 500' higher. From Boiling Lake, Horsehead Pass is 0.5 mile east; beyond lie the Eagle Lakes. Via the middle fork of Prince Creek Trail, Cub Lake is 2.5 miles west, and Lake Chelan is 11 miles away. A new trail connecting Boiling and Cub lakes was scheduled for construction in 1980.

One can continue southeast from Boiling Lake to the primitive road near South Navarre Mountain, or take the Summerblossom cutoff (for hikers only) to the primitive road near Falls Creek. The latter option is better because it avoids trail machines and because the access road is of better quality, although still a difficult drive.

From the Boiling Lake/Summit Trail junction, it is 1.2 miles south to water and a campsite. South 1.6 miles further is the junction with the east fork of Prince Creek Trail. From this point, it is 3 miles to Prince Creek and 8 miles to Uno Peak. In 1979 this way trail was difficult to locate, but marked "closed to cycles."

Just south of the junction, the trail switchbacks up a ridge. The junction with the Summerblossom Trail is 6.7 miles from the South Navarre Campground. This trail is marked only by a diagram prohibiting cycle use. The Summerblossom Trail turns left at the ridge; the more obvious

Summit Trail continues to the right, dropping somewhat into forest.

Summerblossom Trail

From the junction, the Summerblossom Trail goes southeast, passing a way trail in 0.5 mile. From here the trail drops, losing about 400', to a campsite with water in the meadow below the ridge. The trail then goes up and, about 3 miles from the Summerblossom trailhead, reaches a crest with impressive views. Then it descends, somewhat less steeply, to the road at 6.0 miles. There is no water from the campsite to 0.5 mile from the road. There is parking for several cars across the road from the trailhead, and water is available from Falls Creek 50 yards away.

To reach the Summerblossom trailhead by car, drive north from Chelan on U.S. 97 and turn left at Pateros, 19 miles from the bridge in Chelan. Continue on State Highway 153 for 16.8 miles and turn left immediately before a bridge over the Methow River. Turn left 0.8 mile beyond onto the Gold Creek Road. After a mile, turn left and drive 5.5 miles. Turn right at a junction, and follow the road 8.3 miles to the crest between the Okanogan and Chelan drainages. Turn right and follow the one-lane primitive road north 8.4 miles to the trailhead, where there is parking for several cars. The road is difficult, exposed, rough, and dusty, and for experienced backcountry drivers only.

(July 1979)

PYRAMID MOUNTAIN VIEWPOINT

DESTINATION: Pyramid Mt., 8247'
TRAIL LENGTH: 9.2 miles

WALKING TIME: 5½ hours in
4½ hours out

TRAILHEAD ELEVATION 6600'

ALTITUDE GAIN including ups and downs: 3250'

FEATURE: Longview Camp, 6350'

TOPOGRAPHIC SHEETS: USGS: Lucerne
Green Trails: Lucerne

Starting at Ardenvoir on the Entiat Canyon Road, drive about 20 miles up the canyon. After passing the Lake Creek Campground sign, be on the alert for Forest Road #298, with a sign for Shady Pass, which angles back sharply from the paved road. Turn right on this road; at 1.6 miles, pass Halfway Spring. Turn left (north) at Shady Pass and Camp at 8.5 miles.

Although the road is marked "Limited maintenance— Unsuitable for Passenger Cars," it is drivable in a passenger car (it's good to check at the Entiat Ranger Station anyway). Continue left at 10.5 miles. (The road to the right goes to the Big Hill Campsite.) This left fork ends 0.3 mile further, in a spacious parking lot. The trail is open to both horses and trail machines.

The high ridges may be cold, even in midsummer. Do be prepared with appropriate clothing and a good tent for cold nights and inclement weather. There is plenty of wood at all of the campsites. Aside from those described here, there are no other campsites with water nearby.

The trail slopes down 25 feet, on the west side of the parking lot. After 0.1 mile the trail drops, losing perhaps 200' over the next 0.2 mile, then turns left off the fire road. There is a post here, but no sign. (In 1980, the fire road was a more direct, although steeper, route up; it is probably the better route down.) At 1.0 mile, the trail rejoins the fire road and follows it for 0.2 mile. At 1.5 miles, the trail passes Poodle

Camp in a pleasant larch forest; there is no water. The altitude gain from the parking lot to this point is about 600'.

The trail passes over a saddle 0.1 mile past Poodle Camp, then contours along the west side of Crow Mountain for half a mile. It then begins a descent to a ridge below. At 3.1 miles is the junction with the Butte Creek Trail with a sign: "Pyramid Creek Trail 2 miles, Closed to Motor Vehicles." There is a dry campsite at this point. At 3.2 miles the trail passes Butte Camp 100' to the left and 75' below the trail; there is no water here. The trail is now in forest; 0.6 mile further is the first water on the trail, in a spring 25' to the right of the trail. Keep a sharp eye out or you'll miss it. Twenty-five feet to the left of the trail, across from the spring, is a campsite with a fire pit and room for two tents. At 4.1 miles is a better campsite in a meadow, 200' to the right of the trail. The trail crosses a creek at 4.2 miles, where Longview Camp is on the left.

The walking time from Longview Camp with a full pack is about 2 hours in either direction. The walking time from Longview Camp to the summit of Pyramid Mountain with a light pack is approximately 3½ hours; from the summit back to Longview Camp takes 3 hours.

The trail passes a second creek 0.1 mile further, and there is a campsite on the left. From here, the trail climbs on rough tread, in switchbacks, gaining about 650' over the next half mile; mountains to the west and northwest come into view. The high point of the trail as it contours around the west side of Graham Mountain is at 5 miles. From here, the trail descends 650' to a saddle at 5.5 miles. There is a splendid view of Lake Chelan to the east from a rock knob 100' right of the trail. Another 0.4 mile, losing 150' more, leads to a small spring just left of the trail. Another 0.1 mile across the meadow is a campsite a few feet left of the trail.

The trail climbs from another meadow, gaining 400', to the junction with Pyramid Viewpoint Trail at roughly 6.6

miles. The summit of Pyramid Mountain is about 3 miles away. It is about 6.8 miles to this point from the trailhead (although the signs say 6 miles). From this junction, the Viewpoint Trail runs level for about 0.3 mile and then drops, losing 200′, to a meadow where there is water from a small spring and a good campsite 150′ left of the trail. There is a second spring 0.2 mile further and another good campsite with a fire pit 50′ left of the trail.

Beyond this point, the trail steepens. At 7.5 miles it crosses an avalanche path; the awesome power of the winter avalanche is apparent from the shattered larch trees. The last water is crossed at 7.6 miles. From here, it is 2 miles up via switchbacks to the summit of Pyramid Mountain and the site of Pyramid Lookout. The trail first switchbacks up the southwest side of the peak, then goes up west of the peak to the north side, then switchbacks back to the south side, and finally reaches the summit from the south. Before reaching the top, the trail passes a storage cave, primitive bathroom, and horse hitch area. The foundations of the destroyed lookout are clearly apparent.

The view is fantastic. A bit over 7000′ below are Lake Chelan and the mouth of the Prince Creek alluvial fan. Both forks of Prince Creek are apparent. To the east are the cliffs of Big and Little Goat mountains. To the northeast is Cardinal Peak, and beyond it, Pinnacle Mountain and Borealis Ridge. To the west below is the north fork of the Entiat River, with Fern Lake directly west. To the southwest is Duncan Ridge and Duncan Hill. Looking to the south are Graham Mountain, Crow Hill, and Big Hill. Castle Peak near Stehekin can be seen far to the northwest.

Perhaps a third of the walk is in timber, and two-thirds in meadow, with wildflowers and scenic panoramas. There is larch forest along the entire trail; in the fall the larch needles glow yellow in the sun. Tree succession and the krummholz phenomenon are obvious past timberline at about 8000′ on Pyramid Mountain. Wildflowers bloom on the summit.

For those with more time and energy, there are a number of other loop trails further up the valleys and ridges, shown on a Wenatchee National Forest map.

(August–September, 1980)

"Sea of Peaks" effect. Only the airborne and the mountaineer are privileged to see the rocky "waves" of the North Cascades, seemingly stretching to infinity. (Photo by Austin Post—USGS.)

23

PACIFIC CREST TRAIL

PACIFIC CREST TRAIL

TRAIL LENGTH: 182–185 miles (Stevens Pass, U.S. 2 to
Manning Park, Canadian Highway 3)

WALKING TIME: 2–3 weeks

SOUTH TRAILHEAD: Stevens Pass, 4061'

NORTH TRAILHEAD: Manning Park, 4200'

HIGH POINT: 7100' (near Hopkins Lake)

LOW POINT: 1700' (High Bridge, Stehekin)

TOPOGRAPHIC SHEETS: USGS: Stevens Pass; Labyrinth
Mt.; Benchmark Mt.; Poe Mt.;
Glacier Peak 15'; Holden 15';
Agnes Mt.; Stehekin;
McGregor Mt.; Washington
Pass; Mt. Arriva; Azurite Peak;
Slate Peak; Pasayten Peak;
Castle Peak
Green Trails: Stevens Pass; Bench-
mark Mt.; Glacier Peak;
Holden; McGregor Mt.; Stehe-
kin; Washington Pass; Mt. Lo-
gan; Pasayten Peak; Jack Mt.
Canadian maps: Manning Park

Portions of the Pacific Crest Trail between Stevens Pass and Canadian Highway 3 in Manning Park have been described as separate trails. These include: Stevens Pass to Lake Valhalla; Smithbrook Road to Janus Lake and Grizzly Peak; Agnes Creek from the Stehekin Road to Suiattle Pass; Bridge Creek from the Stehekin Road to the North Cascade Highway; NCH to Cutthroat Pass; and Manning Park to Castle Pass.

The following sections of the PCT will be described in this chapter:

Grizzly Peak to Suiattle Pass
Harts Pass to Cutthroat Pass
Harts Pass to Castle Pass.

GRIZZLY PEAK TO SUIATTLE PASS

See Janus Lake Trail in Chapter 21 for the route to Grizzly Peak.

Leave flat-topped Grizzly Peak reluctantly. It is a splendid place for wildflowers in the summer and for the reds and yellows of autumn. Descend one switchback into the saddle south of Grizzly Peak. Contour north beneath the summit, gradually losing altitude. Half a mile north of the summit, the trail crosses from the west to the east side of the ridge crest, then drops until it crosses Wenatchee Pass. From here, there is a gradual ascent to reach Pear Lake. The walking time from Grizzly Peak to Pear Lake is about 1¾ hours; in the reverse direction, about 2½ hours (with a light pack). One-and-one-half miles south of Pear Lake is the half-mile-long way trail to Top Lake to the east. Top Lake is ice-free earlier in the year than Pear Lake is. There are very nice campsites on the southeast and north sides of Top Lake, and at the northeast end of Pear Lake. Snow remains late along this section of the PCT.

Leaving Pear Lake, the trail switchbacks up and west to Frozen Finger Gap. Well into midsummer there is a steep snow slope to traverse in this area; an ice axe is essential.

Steps must be cut early in the day or kicked later when the snow has softened. The trail then descends in switchbacks by a tarn, crosses a creek, and goes up across a magnificent flowered meadow. Three miles further, there is one campsite by a stream in the meadow. The trail tops out on a ridge crest, descends into a forested area, and then climbs to Saddle Gap 3¾ hours from Pear Lake. The trail then contours north and slightly west about half a mile, passing the West Cady Ridge Trail junction, then descends in switchbacks to Pass Creek, where the way trail to the west (North Fork of the Skykomish) joins it. One-third mile further is Cady Pass, with its eastern way trail to the Wenatchee River Road. From Saddle Gap, Pass Creek is 1 hour and Cady Pass 1¼ hours.

The trail then gains about 1100′. Foggy Camp is passed 1½ hours from Cady Pass; it could better have been called Soggy Camp since the runoff from melting snow was running through the middle of the camp area. Ten minutes further, there is another single campsite. Lake Sally Ann is 4 hours from Saddle Gap. In August, 1974 it was necessary to cut steps over fairly steep snow slopes for the last 2 miles to Lake Sally Ann. There are at least 8 nice campsites around this almost continuously frozen little lake. The area is quite scenic, and is recommended for camping.

Cady Ridge, which requires a descent, is 0.4 mile north. There are good camping spots on the ridge, with splendid views of Glacier Peak and Kodak Peak to the north. It is easy to wander cross-country east on Cady Ridge for a substantial distance. The tread of the Cady Ridge Trail may not be obvious.

From Cady Ridge, the trail turns northeast and goes up over Ward's Pass. This portion of the trail can be solid snow, requiring step kicking upward, crossing the crest north of the summit knob from west to east, and glissading down the snow slopes to Dishpan Gap, where the Bald Eagle Trail can be seen contouring beneath June Mountain to the northwest toward its junction with the PCT.

Considering the ascents and descents from Pear Lake to Lake Sally Ann, the estimated altitude gain for the 11 miles is 3500', approximately 40% of which was done on snow in August 1974. Route finding was a problem at times. Topographic maps and a reliable description of the trail are invaluable under snow conditions.

Indian Pass and White Pass

After leaving Dishpan Gap, the trail goes northeast to the side of Kodak Peak. It then passes through a lovely meadow to a ridge crest to enter the Glacier Peak Wilderness Area. Almost half of the trail from the gap to the Wilderness Area boundary was snow covered in August, 1974. From here, the trail goes northwest to Indian Pass, a large pretty meadow in which camping is prohibited. From Indian Pass, the trail gains several hundred feet while traversing forest for half a mile, then breaks into the meadowed west flank of Indian Head Peak, where there is a magnificent view down the Sauk Valley all the way to lower White Pass.

Way trails from the east reach the PCT at both Indian Pass and lower White Pass. From Lake Sally Ann to lower White Pass is about 6.8 miles.

Reflection Pond can often barely be discerned through the deep snow. There are several nice campsites in the ridge above the pond that, in August, were snow-free. Glacier lilies bloom in profusion between lower and upper White passes, as the snow melts from the meadows. The PCT goes north and a bit west to reach upper White Pass. Campers are asked to camp at a bench west of the pass, rather than in the pass itself. There is a lot of splendid meadow walking to be done in this area, although considerable portions of the meadow are boggy, and the camping areas tend to be damp.

Red Pass

Half a mile from upper White Pass to the northwest is the junction with the trail coming up from the North Fork of the Sauk River. Red Pass is 1.5 miles further northwest. In snow conditions, experienced wilderness travelers can cross country up to the top of the meadowed ridge a half mile or so before reaching Red Pass, and glissade down the snow slopes on the other side, saving over a mile of walking; an ice axe is mandatory. Even in mid-August in 1974, an ice axe was necessary on the solid, steep snow on the north side of Red Pass.

There is a good campsite near trees a hundred yards east of the cinder cone, but no water close by. The PCT descends east of this campsite. Half a mile north is a stand of silvered tree trunks. The trail goes west of campsites near these trees. Locating the trail under snow conditions is quite difficult: go west cross-country to pick it up in meadow a half mile from the large creek below the campsites; this is the headwaters of the White Chuck River. The trail descends, crosses the White Chuck River on a bridge, then enters forest. There is a meadow about 2.5 miles beyond the bridge.

It is three hours from the cinder cone to the Sitkum Creek crossing. Fill water bottles at Sitkum Creek. From this point, it is two miles to Kennedy Hot Springs, nine miles on to Fire Creek Pass and eight miles back to Red Pass.

Fire Creek Pass and Mica Lake

It takes another hour to reach the Kennedy Ridge Trail junction about 0.4 mile after crossing Kennedy Creek. (Kennedy Creek is not a satisfactory source of water.) From this point it is a steep, dry, 1.9 miles up to Glacier Creek; full-packed, the ascent to Glacier Creek takes 1½ hours. There are several campsites below the crossing of Glacier Creek, with good water available. A half hour beyond the Glacier Creek crossing is the Glacier Ridge Trail junction. It is another half hour to Pumice Creek. Another 1½ hours brings the hiker to a nice campsite just below the switchbacks leading up to Fire Creek Pass. Just west of this camp is an enjoyable view down the White Chuck Valley.

From this campsite, a constant upward walk brings one to Fire Creek Pass in an hour. This is the most technically difficult pass on the PCT, since in most years snow persists in the pass area well into September. In cloud and rain conditions, with unbroken snow underfoot, it is exceedingly difficult and potentially hazardous to find the route down.

Under snow conditions, descend about thirty degrees west of north, down moderately steep snow, then continue down, losing about 600', to a flat area where occasional patches of rock and heather are visible. Two or three short sections of trail may be apparent on the way down along the ridge to the left of Fire Creek Pass. From the flat area there are two potential routes: to the right (east), and to the left (west); the latter is the correct one. A level 100 yards brings the hiker to a rock from which Mica Lake can be seen below. Descend moderately steep snow to the east side of Mica Lake, and contour just above the lake to its outlet on the north. Climb up a 20' snowbank. The PCT can be seen in places to the west of the outlet, but under snow conditions it is best to stay east of the outlet and glissade moderately steep snow 0.2 mile (losing 400') almost due north to where the footpath enters from the east the relatively flat valley below.

Of course, if the snow has melted and the trail is visible, simply follow the tread. However, until Labor Day, do carry an ice axe for Fire Creek Pass.

Suiattle Pass

From north of Mica Lake, seemingly unending gentle switchbacks, broken only by an avalanche valley where there is a campsite (the only one between Fire Creek Pass and the Milk Creek Bridge), leads the hiker to the junction with the Milk Creek Trail between 3.5 and 4 miles beyond Mica Lake.

After the junction with the Milk Creek Trail, the trail switchbacks up the east wall of the canyon. Heavy alpine vegetation overhangs the trail. If the trail has not been brushed, when the plants are wet they will saturate the hiker. Rain pants help.

After gaining about 2000′ over 2.5 miles, the trail reaches a ridge crest; near a small pond, there is a campsite in open meadow. To the south is Kennedy Peak, a spire on the north ridge of Glacier Peak.

The footpath now contours east, slowly gaining altitude. One and a half miles further, there is a campsite 100 yards below a small knoll. After the trail crosses a boulder field and a ridge at about 6100′, there is another campsite below and to the north of the trail. Shortly thereafter, the switchbacks down to Vista Creek begin. After a few of these is the Dolly Creek Campsite, nestled among mountain hemlocks. Water is 100 yards down slope. There is another campsite half a mile further on Vista Ridge. A little over 2½ miles further, at 3650′, is a campsite beside Vista Creek. The stream is crossed on a log about 2 miles further and 750′ lower. There is a good campsite at the crossing.

The footpath now contours east across a gentle slope to cross Gamma Creek 0.8 mile further. The junction with the Suiattle River Trail is 0.7 mile beyond the creek. There are campsites upstream from here. The trail then turns north and after about a mile crosses the Suiattle River on a 50-yard-long horse bridge. Just after the river there is a junction: the Suiattle River Trail goes to the northwest at this point. There are campsites near the junction.

The PCT continues up to the east. This recently added segment of the PCT makes long easy switchbacks as it ascends Middle Ridge. Four and a half miles from the river, the trail between Buck Creek Pass and the Glacier Peak Mines is intersected. Another new section of the PCT climbs gradually up, crosses Miners' Creek, and reaches the trail between Suiattle Pass and the Glacier Peak Mines 2.3 miles from the junction. From here, it is one mile further east to Suiattle Pass.

The total distance between Milk Creek and Suiattle Pass is roughly 23 miles. The altitude gain from the Suiattle River crossing to Suiattle Pass is slightly over 3000'.

HARTS PASS TO CUTTHROAT PASS

This is an excellent day hike. To reach the trailhead, drive to Mazama, which is 74.4 miles east of Marblemount and 13.5 miles west of Winthrop, on the NCH. If on the southern loop, take the half-mile road connection to the north. On the northern loop, the road passes the grocery store–post office–gas station at Mazama. From Mazama, drive west.

The road, fairly good at first, becomes tortuous, narrow, and exposed. It is 19.4 miles from Mazama to the guard station at Harts Pass. Slightly east of the summit, turn south and drive about 2 miles to the road end. There is parking for 6 or 7 cars at the trailhead itself and a substantial parking area at the campground 0.7 mile from the trailhead.

The PCT for the first half mile goes up moderately through larch and alpine fir forest to a ridge crest with good views. The footpath then contours gradually up to the west, reaching another crest at about 2 miles, after an altitude gain of another 500'. From this ridge, there is an excellent view from north of the Slate Peak lookout. The trail descends gradually over the next 2 miles. At four miles is 99 Basin

Campsite immediately beneath Tatie Peak. The first water source since beginning the trail is at this excellent camping area.

Over the next 1.5 miles, the PCT gains about 500′ to reach a ridge crest from which there is a splendid view of Azurite Peak to the west. The round trip from Harts Pass to this viewpoint is 11 miles.

Although not on the map, this high point is often called Grasshopper Pass. This segment of high trail is lovely in late September and early October, when the larch forests glow golden in the autumn sun.

Glacier Pass and Methow Pass

From here, the footpath switchbacks down, losing about 1300′ over the next 2 miles. Forested Glacier Pass is 8 miles from the trailhead. South of Glacier Pass, the trail drops gradually into Brush Creek (so named because of the slide alder). At 9.3 miles (a 5-hour walk, full packed), the trail reaches the first campsite since 99 Basin. The altitude loss from Grasshopper Pass to the campsite is about 2000′. Wood for campfires is adequate, and water can be obtained from Brush Creek 100 yards to the west. Bear are common here; be sure to hang food supplies.

Beyond this camp, the PCT drops gradually, losing 800′ until, 10 miles from the trailhead, it intersects the way trail ascending from the east along the Methow River. A few feet beyond the junction, the trail crosses Brush Creek on a bridge. This is the low point of the PCT between Harts Pass and Cutthroat Pass. Immediately east of the bridge is a campsite that can accommodate only 4 people.

After the creek crossing, the trail climbs gradually near the Methow River. Twelve miles from the trailhead there is a good campsite, known as Horse Heaven Camp, about 200′

south of the trail in a meadow adjacent to Jet Creek. One tenth of a mile further, the way trail to 3-mile-distant McBee Pass comes in from the west. At 12.8 miles the footpath crosses the Methow River on a bridge. Nearby is a rudimentary campsite, good water, and probably good stream fishing. Willis Camp is at 13.5 miles.

The trail is now substantially steeper. At 17 miles there is a fair campsite in a meadow north of Methow Pass. Methow Pass (6600') is 18 miles from the Harts Pass trailhead. There are good campsites at the pass, but water is obtainable only from snowfields. Just under one mile beyond the pass there is an excellent campsite with good water. From this campsite, there is a scrabble trail to upper (6839') and lower (6735') Snowy lakes, roughly 0.5 and 0.7 mile away. There are splendid camping areas around both Snowy lakes. The upper lake is especially scenic, with Mt. Hardy reflected in its waters. Above the lake rises the orange granite of Tower Mountain and Golden Horn, both well above 8000'.

From the upper Snowy lakes, a ridge between the lakes and Methow Pass is easy to climb for better views.

Cutthroat Pass

Continuing south, the trail makes a high traverse to reach Granite Pass (6300') 2.5 miles southeast. From here, the trail switchbacks up steeply, gaining 600' over the next half mile. The PCT then contours the east side of a ridge at around 6900' to Cutthroat Pass, about 23 miles from the Harts Pass trailhead.

It is substantially easier to do this segment of the PCT from the north to the south, rather than south to north, since altitude gain is considerably less. With full packs, walking time is about 15 hours.

(August 1971)

HARTS PASS TO CASTLE PASS

To reach the trailhead, turn right at the crest of Harts Pass and drive just over a mile toward the Slate Peak lookout. The trailhead is located on a sharp curve. Parking in the area is very limited; overnight parking is not permitted at the Slate Peak parking area.

For an introduction to the area, hikers should visit the Slate Peak lookout (7440'). From here, the route of the trail can be seen for a number of miles.

From the trailhead, the PCT contours north beneath Slate Peak, gradually losing altitude and passing a good campsite with access to water at about 2 miles. The elevation at the trailhead is 6800'. Windy Pass, 4 miles from the trailhead, is at 6257'.

From the trailhead to Windy Pass, views to the west are marred by scars of mining activity around the ghost town of Barron. Jeep trails still reach almost to Windy Pass; miners' cabins are located in Indiana Basin below the pass. The views of Mt. Baker, Crater Mountain, and Jack Mountain compensate to a degree for the intrusions into the wilderness made by the gold seekers.

Pasayten Wilderness—Oregon Basin

Evidence of mining is left behind after entering the Pasayten Wilderness 100' north of Windy Pass. Half a mile beyond Windy Pass is Windy Basin, where there are good campsites and water. The trail switchbacks up after Windy Basin, reaching a ridge crest at about 5 miles, with an altitude gain of about 500'. The PCT then descends to reach Oregon Basin and its excellent campsite with water, at roughly 5.5 miles. Foggy Pass is at 6 miles. The footpath then gains altitude on the west side of the ridge, reaching a grassy knoll at about 6.5 miles. This is a good place for lunch or for the turn-around point for vigorous one-day hikers. There is a large campsite about 200' below the ridge. The trail then goes around the east side of the ridge, reaching another crest at about 8 miles, north and slightly east of the Devil's Backbone. Switchbacks go down thereafter, losing about 400'. At 8.7 miles is a good water supply. To the northeast there is an impressive avalanche slope. An immense amount of snow pulled off Jim Peak and the Devil's Backbone has deposited avalanche debris well down into the Shaw Creek Valley.

Holman Pass, Rock Pass, Woody Pass

For the next 4.3 miles north, hiking is mostly in forest. About 10 miles from the trailhead, the trail turns west and switchbacks down 2.1 miles to reach Holman Pass (5150'). The Holman Creek Trail leaves to the east, destination Pasayten Airstrip. There is an alternate route back to Harts Pass via the west fork of the Pasayten; it is less scenic, but does make a loop trip possible. At Holman Pass there are tent sites, but no water and no view. Also at Holman Pass is the junction with the Devil's Ridge Trail to the west.

From Holman Pass, the PCT gains altitude, gradually entering meadow. Goat Lake Basin is 2.3 miles north of the Pass, a truly lovely area although somewhat spoiled by horsemen during the High Cascade hunting season. There are many good campsites in this meadow, and 3 or 4 dependable water sources. A walk of 0.5 mile to the southeast leads to lower Goat Lake, where there is a secluded, sheltered campsite. Upper Goat Lake is a half hour walk above the lower lake. These are the best overnight camping areas since Oregon Basin.

The PCT continues north rising across the Goat Lake Meadow to reach Rock Pass (6491') about one mile from the center of the meadow. There is a tent site at this point, but no water; there are lots of marmots in the area.

The PCT splits at Rock Pass. There is a low trail which loses about 500' but is easy technically, and an upper trail which is covered with scree, talus, and in places steep snow without runouts. The average hiker should use the lower trail; the experienced wilderness traveler with an ice axe may use the upper, shorter trail reasonably safely. Both trails do lose some altitude. They join, after about one mile on the upper trail and two on the lower trail. The recombined trail then switchbacks up moderately to Woody Pass (6624'). About 200' south of Woody Pass is an excellent campsite with water from a snowfield. En route to Woody Pass, the trail intersects an east way trail leading into the Coney Basin and ultimately reaching the Middle Fork of the Pasayten.

There is no water from Woody Pass to Hopkins Lake, although there are several good dry camps. It is best to stay overnight below Woody Pass, or to continue to the campsite at Hopkins Lake or the campsites below Hopkins Pass.

Hopkins Pass and Lake

North of Woody Pass, the trail makes a long, high and level contour beneath Three Fools Peak. The views to the west are spectacular: Crater, Hozomeen, Baker, Shuksan, Spickard, Joker Mt., and Castle Peak can be seen easily.

Three Fools Peak can be climbed with relative ease. Views from the 7965' summit are among the best in the North Cascades. A beautiful, shallow, emerald green lake surrounded by larch is below to the north. Lake of the Pines can be seen to the east, as can other great peaks in the Pasayten Wilderness.

Returning to the Crest Trail, continue northward beneath Three Fools Peak. Another impressive avalanche path is below. About 2 miles north of Woody Pass, the PCT makes a sharp turn to the right (east). A scrabble way trail below drops several hundred feet to Mountain Home Camp; another way trail connects the camp with Lakeview Ridge. The PCT starts upward at this point, topping out on a knob slightly over 7000′ and 1.5 miles to the north. The trail then drops sharply, losing 300′; this segment is called the Devil's Stairway. The PCT contours on the level along the ridge crest, and then switchbacks down, losing about 600′, to Hopkins Pass (6122′) slightly over 22 miles from the trailhead. From Lakeview Ridge, there are splendid views of Hopkins Lake below.

One third of a mile south of Hopkins Pass is the way trail to Hopkins Lake, where there are excellent campsites, and a magnificent view of the mountains to the east, reflected in the waters of this delightful and uncrowded high alpine lake.

There are a number of excellent campsites in the vicinity of Hopkins Pass. The hiker can drop 0.1 to 0.2 mile to the headwaters of Chuckuwanteen Creek and find campsites by tarns or by a small stream. The Chuckuwanteen Trail leaves at this point to the east, leading to Monument 83 12 miles away, Big Hidden Lake at 20 miles, and the Billy Goat Corral at 38 miles.

It is 3 miles from Hopkins Pass to Castle Pass, losing about 650′. The walking time down is 1 hour; it is 1.5 hours coming up from the north.

See Monument 78 Trail for data on the PCT to the Canadian border, and from the border to Canada Highway #3 in Manning Park.

Strong, fast hikers can reach the Goat Lake Meadows in one day from the trailhead. Hopkins Lake or Castle Pass could be reached the second day, and Manning Park the third. The average hiker could walk the PCT from Harts Pass to Manning Park in four days.

(August–September 1974)

RESOURCES

LAND MANAGEMENT AGENCIES

National Park Service—
U.S. Forest Service
Joint Information Center
Room 110, 915 Second Ave.
Seattle, WA 98174
(206) 442-0170

National Forests
Pacific Northwest Regional
  Office
319 SW Pine St.
P.O. Box 3623
Portland, OR 97208
(503) 221-2877

· *Mount Baker—Snoqualmie*
  National Forest
Supervisor's Office
1022 First Ave.
Seattle, WA 98104
(206) 422-5400

Baker River Ranger Station
Concrete, WA 98237
(206) 853-2851 or 826-3118

Darrington Ranger Station
Darrington, WA 98241
(206) 436-1155

Glacier Ranger Station
Glacier, WA 98244
(206) 599-2714

Monte Cristo Ranger Station
  (Verlot)
Granite Falls, WA 98252
(206) 691-7791

Skykomish Ranger Station
P.O. Box 305
Skykomish, WA 98288
(206) 677-2414

· *Okanogan National Forest*
Supervisor's Office
P.O. Box 950, Okanogan, WA
  98840
(509) 422-2704

Conconully Ranger Station
P.O. Box 432 (Post Office
  Bldg.)
Okanogan, WA 98840

Tonasket Ranger Station
Tonasket, WA 98855
(509) 486-2186

Twisp Ranger Station
P.O. Box 188
Twisp, WA 98856
(509) 996-2266

Winthrop Ranger Station
Winthrop, WA 98862
(509) 996-2266

· *Wenatchee National Forest*
Supervisor's Office
301 Yakima St.
P.O. Box 811
Wenatchee, WA 98801
(509) 662-4335

Chelan Ranger Station
P.O. Box 189
Chelan, WA 98816
(509) 682-2576

Entiat Ranger Station
Entiat, WA 98822
(509) 784-1511

Lake Wenatchee Ranger
  Station
Star Rt. 109
Leavenworth, WA 98826
(509) 763-3103

National Parks
Pacific Northwest Regional
  Office
4th & Pike Bldg.
Seattle, WA 98101
(206) 442-4830

· *North Cascades National
  Park*
Superintendent's Office
800 State St.
Sedro Woolley, WA 98284
(206) 855-1331

for backcountry information,
  NCNP, call Skagit District
  (North unit NCNP) and Ross
  Lake National Recreation
  Area
Marblemount, WA 98267
(206) 873-4590

Stehekin District (South unit
  NCNP) and Lake Chelan
  National Recreation Area
Manson Rd. & Cedar
P.O. Box 549
Chelan, WA 98816
(509) 682-2549

Stehekin Ranger Station
Stehekin, WA 98852
No phone; contact by radio
  from district office:
(509) 682-2549

Canadian Provincial Parks

· *Manning Provincial Park*
District Superintendent, Parks
  Branch
Manning Park, B.C. Canada
  VOX IRO
(604) 840-8836

· *Cathedral Provincial Park*
District Superintendent, Parks
  Branch
Box 318, Summerland
B.C. Canada VOH IZO

When requesting information from land management agencies,
the hiker should be aware that the receptionist, particularly on
weekends, almost never has had any personal experience with ac-

cess roads and/or trails. For accurate information, advance contact by letter should be made, preferably with the ranger who patrols the area, or at least with a permanent staff person with knowledge of the mountains. Write early, as it may take a substantial amount of time to reach the appropriate person.

Knowledgeable individuals are rarely on duty during weekends. Request the information at the time of first contact, and ask that you be phoned or written, or advise when you will come to the local office, asking that the information be left at the reception desk for you. This usually is effective but it does require advance planning.

LAKE TRANSPORTATION

There is no scheduled public transportation on Ross Lake. Arrangements may be made with the Ross Lake Resort (M. Dameron, Rockport, WA 98283; phone via Mt. Vernon operator Newhalem 4735) for up-lake drop-off, and later down-lake pick-up. Canoes can be portaged from the highway, or more easily, taken between Diablo and Ross Lakes by boat and truck for a fee. All trailheads can be reached by land except Little Beaver.

Boat transportation from Chelan to Stehekin is available daily in the summer, four times a week in the spring and fall, and three times a week in the winter. Contact the Lake Chelan Boat Co., P.O. Box 186, Chelan, WA 98816; (509) 682-2224, for information. Charter air service is also available from Chelan; contact Chelan Airways, Chelan, WA 98816; (509) 682-5555, for information and reservations.

The round trip by boat takes all day. Flying time from Chelan to Stehekin is a half hour.

CONSERVATION ORGANIZATIONS

Sierra Club
National Office:
530 Bush St.
San Francisco, CA 94108

Sierra Club
Northwest Office:
4534½ University Way NE
Seattle, WA 98105

National Parks Association
1701 18th St. NW
Washington, D.C. 20009

The Wilderness Society
1901 Pennsylvania Ave. NW
Washington, D.C. 20006

Planned Parenthood–World
  Population
810 Seventh Ave. 7th floor
New York, NY 10019

Zero Population Growth
1346 Connecticut Ave. NW
Washington, D.C. 20036

Washington Wilderness
  Coalition
6541 17th Ave. NE
Seattle, WA 98115

North Cascades Conservation
  Council
214 Crestmont Place NW
Seattle, WA 98199

Friends of the Earth
4512 University Way NE
Seattle, WA 98105

Washington Environmental
  Council
119 South Main
Seattle, WA 98104

Federation of Western Outdoor
  Clubs, Northwest
    Conservation
    Representative
4534½ University Way
Seattle, WA 98105
    for information and for the
    outdoor club nearest you.

BIBLIOGRAPHY

Arno, Steven. *Northwest Trees*. Seattle: The Mountaineers, 1977.

Bake, W.A. *Stehekin—A Wilderness Journey Into The North Cascades*. National Park Service, 1977.

Beckey, Fred. *Cascade Alpine Guide: Climbing and High Routes—Rainy Pass to Fraser River*. Seattle: The Mountaineers, 1981.

Beckey, Fred. *Cascade Alpine Guide: Climbing and High Routes—Stevens Pass to Rainy Pass*. Seattle: The Mountaineers, 1977.

Beckey, Fred. *Climbers Guide to the Cascade and Olympic Mountains of Washington*. Boston: American Alpine Club, 1961.

Byrd, Robert. *Lake Chelan in the 1890's*. Wenatchee, WA: World Publishing Co., 1972.

Crowder, D.F. and R.W. Tabor. *Routes and Rocks*. Seattle: The Mountaineers, 1965.

Cyca, Robert and Andrew Harcombe. *Exploring Manning Park*. Vancouver: Gundy's and Bernie's Guide Books, 1970.

Darvill, Fred T. *Darvill's Guide to the North Cascades National Park and Associated Areas, Vol. I & II* 2nd. ed. Mt. Vernon, WA: Darvill Outdoor Publications, 1975.

Darvill, Fred T. *Mountaineering Medicine—A Wilderness Medical Guide*. 9th ed. Mt. Vernon, WA: Skagit Mountain Rescue Unit, 1980.

Darvill, Fred T. *North Cascades Highway Guide*. Mt. Vernon, WA: Darvill Outdoor Publications, 1973.

Darvill, Fred T. *Stehekin—The Enchanted Valley*. Edmonds, WA: Signpost Books, 1981.

Easterbrook, Don J. and David Rahm. *Landforms of Washington*. Bellingham, WA: Western Washington University, 1970.

Franklin, J. and C. Dryness. *Vegetation of Oregon and Washington*. Portland, OR: United States Department of Agriculture, 1969.

Fries, Mary and Ira Spring. *Wild Flowers of Mt. Rainier and the Cascades*. Seattle: The Mountaineers, 1970.

Furniss, R. and V. Carolin. *Western Forest Insects*. Washington, D.C.: United States Department of Agriculture, 1977.

Harris, Stephen L. *Fire and Ice*. 2nd edition. Seattle: Pacific Search, 1980.

Heller, Ramon. *Mount Baker Ski Area*. Bellingham, WA: Mt. Baker Recreation Co., 1980.

Holland, Andy. *Switchbacks*. Seattle: The Mountaineers, 1980.

Ittner, R. et al. *Recreational Impact on Wildlands*. U.S. Forest Service, Pacific Northwest Region, 1979.

Kozloff, Eugene N. *Plants and Animals of the Pacific Northwest*. Seattle: University of Washington Press, 1976.

Kritzman, Ellen B. *Little Mammals of the Pacific Northwest*. Seattle: Pacific Search Press, 1977.

Majors, Harry M. *The First Crossing of the North Cascades*. Seattle: Northwest Press, 1980.

Majors, Harry M. *Mt. Baker—A Chronicle of Its Historic Eruptions and First Ascent*. Seattle: Northwest Press, 1978.

Manning, Harvey. *The Wild Cascades: Forgotten Parkland*. San Francisco: Sierra Club Books, 1965.

Marshall, Louise B. *High Trails* 4th ed. Edmonds, WA: Signpost Books, 1973.

Marshall, Louise B. and Ira Spring. *Hundred Hikes in Western Washington*. Seattle: The Mountaineers, 1966.

May, Allen. *In and Around the North Cascades National Park*. NPS: Mount Rainier Natural History Association.

McDougall, Randy. *Snow Tours in Washington*. Edmonds, WA: Signpost Books, 1976.

McKee, Bates. *Cascadia*. New York: McGraw-Hill, 1972.

NPS: *Birds, Trees, Mammals, Amphibians, and Reptiles in the North Cascades National Park Service Complex*. 7 page brochure.

Pitzer, Paul C. *Building the Skagit*. Portland, OR: Galley Press, 1978.

Prater, Gene. *Snow Trails: Ski and Snowshoe Routes in the Cascades*. Seattle: The Mountaineers, 1976.

Roe, JoAnne. *The North Cascadians*. Seattle: Madrona Publishers, 1980.

Russell, F. *Snake Venom Poisoning*. New York: Lippincott and Crowell, 1980.

Schaffler, Jeff and Bev and Fred Hartline. *The Pacific Crest Trail, Volume 2: Oregon and Washington*. Seattle: Wilderness Press, 1974; 3rd edition 1979.

Spring, Ira and Byron Fish. *Fire Lookouts*. Seattle: The Mountaineers, 1982.

Spring, Ira and Harvey Manning. *High Worlds of the Mountain Climber*. Seattle: Superior Publishing, 1959.

Spring, Ira and Harvey Manning. *The North Cascades National Park*. Seattle: Superior Publishing, 1969.

Spring, Ira and Harvey Manning. *101 Hikes in the North Cascades*. Seattle: The Mountaineers, 1979. (2nd ed.)

Taylor, Ronald, George Douglas, and Lee Mann. *Mountain Wild Flowers of the Pacific Northwest*. Portland, OR: Binford and Mort, 1975.

Thompson, Erwin. *North Cascades National Park, Ross Lake National Recreation Area, and Lake Chelan National Recreation Area*. National Park Service, 1970.

Udvardy, Miklos. *The Audubon Society Field Guide to North American Birds—Western Region*. New York: Alfred A. Knopf, 1977.

U.S. Government Printing Office. *The North Cascades Study Report*, 1965.

Wilkerson, James A. et al. *Medicine for Mountaineering*. Seattle: The Mountaineers, 1976.

Woodhouse, P.R. *Monte Cristo*. Seattle: The Mountaineers, 1979.

TRAIL INDEX